A SECOND COLLECTION

BOOKS BY BERNARD J. F. LONERGAN, S.J.
PUBLISHED BY THE WESTMINSTER PRESS

A Second Collection

Philosophy of God, and Theology

A SECOND COLLECTION

BY

Bernard J. F. Lonergan, S.J.

EDITED BY

WILLIAM F. J. RYAN, S.J.

AND

BERNARD J. TYRRELL, S.J.

W

THE WESTMINSTER PRESS
PHILADELPHIA

COPYRIGHT © 1974 BERNARD J. F. LONERGAN, S.J.

PUBLISHED BY THE WESTMINSTER PRESS ®

PHILADELPHIA, PENNSYLVANIA

PRINTED IN THE UNITED STATES OF AMERICA

Library of Congress Cataloging in Publication Data

Lonergan, Bernard J. F.
  A second collection.

  1. Catholic Church—Collected works. 2. Theology—
Collected works—20th century. I. Title.
BX891.L644   1975   230'.2'08   74-14798
  ISBN 0-664-20721-9

CONTENTS

INTRODUCTION

THE TRANSITION FROM A CLASSICIST WORLD-VIEW
TO HISTORICAL-MINDEDNESS   I

THE DEHELLENIZATION OF DOGMA   11

THEORIES OF INQUIRY: RESPONSES TO A SYMPOSIUM   33

THE FUTURE OF THOMISM   43

THEOLOGY IN ITS NEW CONTEXT   55

THE SUBJECT   69

BELIEF: TODAY'S ISSUE   87

THE ABSENCE OF GOD IN MODERN CULTURE   101

NATURAL KNOWLEDGE OF GOD   117

THEOLOGY AND MAN'S FUTURE   135

THE FUTURE OF CHRISTIANITY   149

THE RESPONSE OF THE JESUIT AS PRIEST AND APOSTLE IN
THE MODERN WORLD   165

THE EXAMPLE OF GIBSON WINTER   189

PHILOSOPHY AND THEOLOGY   193

CONTENTS

AN INTERVIEW WITH FR. BERNARD LONERGAN, S. J.   209

REVOLUTION IN CATHOLIC THEOLOGY   231

THE ORIGINS OF CHRISTIAN REALISM   239

INSIGHT REVISITED   263

INDEX   279

INTRODUCTION

William F. J. Ryan, S. J.
Bernard J. Tyrrell, S. J.

The title of these assembled papers of Bernard Lonergan, *A Second Collection*, recalls the earlier publication of some of his other papers in the work, *Collection*.[1] That collection spans twenty-two years. It begins with a study on logic (first published in 1943, though written earlier) and proceeds to a final paper on the notion of meaning (1965). The papers not only take up widely diverse topics, but they also record a crucial shift in Lonergan's thinking. It is the last two papers, *"Existenz* and *Aggiornamento"* and "Dimensions of Meaning," which record this shift.

This shift, a watershed in Lonergan's thinking, can be dated: the years 1964–1965.[2] Frederick Crowe and David Tracy in their excellent writings have clarified Lonergan's development before and since that shift.[3] For our purposes we can point out that Lonergan's overall concern is intentionality analysis and then single out two major themes that run through all of these present papers: first, the clear emergence of the primacy of the fourth level of human consciousness, the existential level, the level of

[1] *Collection: Papers by Bernard Lonergan, S. J.*, F. E. Crowe, S. J., ed., London and New York, 1967.

[2] See F. E. Crowe, "Early Jottings on Bernard Lonergan's *Method in Theology*," in *Science et Esprit*, 25 (1973), 121–138.

[3] See, for example, the article of F. E. Crowe cited in the preceding text; David Tracy, *The Achievement of Bernard Lonergan*, New York, 1970.

evaluation and love; secondly, the significance of historical consciousness. These papers, then, besides the unity which they possess by appearing within the same seven year period, share a specific unity of theme not found in *Collection*.

Value, though it emerges in these papers as related to the unfolding of what Lonergan in *Insight* calls the notion of being, or the pure detached desire to know, is also clearly distinguished as a fourth level of consciousness. In *Insight* there is a discussion of the fourth level in terms of decision and ethics. There is also Lonergan's explicit remark in *Insight*[4] where, as he acknowledges the significance of the vast topic of personal relations, he gives the reasons why he believes that it requires a special study as detailed as that which *Insight* undertakes of the other three levels. These papers and the monumental *Method in Theology* represent part of Lonergan's effort to undertake this special study of the fourth level. And finally, it is enlightening to note that Lonergan's first important publication, *Grace and Freedom*,[5] his doctoral dissertation, is concerned with the fourth level of evaluation and Christian love. So the existential level is not entirely missing in Lonergan's earlier work. But because of *Insight's* goals, the three levels of experience, understanding, and reflection gained a special prominence.

To take up our two themes: there exists, first of all, the transcendental notion of value that is the same as the transcendental notion of being. It underpins all particular judgments of value, or evaluations. At an institute in Dublin in 1971 on method in theology, Lonergan was asked whether, just as he had spoken of a pure detached desire to know in *Insight*, he would now be willing to identify it with a pure detached desire for value. He answered yes.

[4] London and New York, 1957, p. 730, n.
[5] J. Patout Burns, S. J., ed., London and New York, 1970; originally published as "St. Thomas' Thought on *Gratia Operans*," in *Theological Studies*, 2 (1941), 289-324; 3 (1942), 69-88; 375-402; 533-578.

The transcendental notion of value is the single unfolding through four levels of the one intention of what is good, of what is worthwhile, that manifests itself in each individual evaluation. It is the universal principle of appraisal and criticism prior to any choosing. This single unfolding, in manifesting itself in different stages, determines the specific levels of human consciousness: experience, understanding, reflection, and evaluation. Evaluation is the keystone of the structure of intentionality. It constitutes the level of the existential subject who freely and responsibly makes himself what he is, whether good or evil.

Religious experience has emerged with its clear identity since the turn in Lonergan's thinking. Lonergan locates it on the fourth level of consciousness. But it is not man's achievement; it is God's gift. It is being-in-love with God. In traditional language, it is grace and charity. Throughout these papers, when he is speaking of religious experience, Lonergan constantly cites Paul: "God's love has flooded our inmost heart through the Holy Spirit he has given us" (Rom. 5: 5). Borrowing a phrase from Nietzsche and transvaluing it, he calls this religious experience the transvaluation of all values.

Lonergan likewise discusses religious experience in terms of conversion, a notion that he introduces in "Theology in Its New Context" (the fifth paper in the present work). There is religious conversion in which a person receives God's love and then transvalues his life's values. Lonergan quotes Paul: "When anyone is united to Christ, there is a new world; the old order has gone and a new order has begun" (2 Cor. 5: 17). At the time of these papers, Lonergan begins to speak of two other conversions: intellectual and moral. He treats all three conversions fully in *Method in Theology*. Intellectual conversion is the abandonment of the myth that human knowing is essentially a type of perception.[6] Moral conversion is the rejection of satisfaction and the

---

[6] See below pp. 75 ff.

acceptance of value as the motive for a person's actions.[7] What Lonergan is doing is once again to orientate in a striking manner his intentionality analysis in relation to the four levels of consciousness. Thus religious conversion is aligned with religious experience, moral conversion with evaluation, and intellectual conversion with reflection.

While working out the implications of intentionality analysis and the levels of consciousness, Lonergan makes a clean break with faculty psychology. He no longer speaks of intellect and will, but rather of the second, third, and fourth levels of conscious intending: intelligent grasp, critical reflection, and evaluation and love. His reason is that intellect and will are not given directly to consciousness but rather are reached through metaphysics. Then, since metaphysics follows intentionality analysis for Lonergan, he prefers to speak of the conscious, intending subject rather than of the soul.

So we are led to the second theme which we have singled out in these papers: historical consciousness. Historical consciousness is opposed to a normative conception of culture, the classicist, according to which there is but one culture, valid once and for all. Historical consciousness is rooted in the recognition of the four levels of consciousness. Upon them is based an empirical notion of culture. Then culture may be said to be any set of meanings and values that inform a common way of life. Diversity and development become a possibility in human institutions, and to be specific, in theology.

From theology as a product, one shifts his attention to the concrete subject who is doing theology. The subject can and

[7] See *Doctrinal Pluralism* (The 1971 Père Marquette Theology Lecture at Marquette University), Milwaukee, 1971, pp. 33-39 (the section entitled "Pluralism and Conversion"). This lecture—contemporaneous with these papers—with its main ideas, including those on conversion, is incorporated into *Method in Theology*. One sees that in 1971 Lonergan has clearly distinguished the three conversions.

does develop. So, then, does his theology. Lonergan drily observes in "The Subject" that truth is not so objective that it can get along without human minds. If Lonergan refuses to cast anchor on the immutable shores of classicist certainties, he is not drifting aimlessly. He fixes his course according to the dictates of the four intentional levels of the subject. For Lonergan what is invariant is not a series of theological formulations. What is invariant is the normative pattern of conscious intending. From it all formulations emerge.

These papers, like those in *Collection* before them, bear the cachet of Lonergan's work: the broad interests and erudition, the ability to consistently grasp the precise issue in question, undeviating clarity, a systematic avoidance of faddism. Tags like "traditional" and "radical," "conservative" and "liberal," make no sense here—if they do anywhere else either. Perhaps Lonergan best of all has already in the last two pages of *Insight* epitomized what his work is: a contribution to the immense programme, *vetera novis augere et perficere*, to enlarge and enrich the old with the new.

The last paper in this collection, "*Insight* Revisited," is a return from a far, advanced position that Lonergan has reached since *Insight*. Lonergan tells what he was doing in *Insight*, and then tells what he thinks he should have done. He speaks of intentionality analysis and where it led him. He speaks of the two themes we have picked out in this Introduction. "*Insight* Revisited" serves as a fitting close to these papers. They moved on from *Insight*. It returns to that masterpiece and paces off the distance that Lonergan has come since then. It is not journey's end. It is a revisit in order to move on again to new studies that a work like *Method in Theology* hints at. As these papers have done, they will come like new letters postmarked from the distant places he is visiting.

Finally we, too, must revisit this present collection, but in another way. We must thank several persons whose type of contribution is too often unfortunately minimized, worst of all by themselves. Our sincerest gratitude is due: to Father Charles Keenan, S. J., for his expert help in editing the text; to Denise Mark for her generous and careful work in drawing up the index of names; to the collaboration of Philip and Fiona McShane with Father Frederick Crowe, S. J., for their contribution of an index of subjects.

Gonzaga University
Spokane, Washington

THE TRANSITION FROM A CLASSICIST WORLD-VIEW TO HISTORICAL-MINDEDNESS[1]

I had best begin by quoting my terms of reference. In the mimeographed circular the ninth topic area was:

"The Church addresses the world. A theological perspective on how a community of love adapts and directs itself for effective mission and witness. Are the transition of forms and the principle of change theological requisites"?

More fully in a letter of July 22, 1966 from Fr. Coriden:[2]

"It seems to me that the transition of organizational and structural forms in the Church is a pattern that parallels the transcultural transmission and consequent development of dogma. The changing laws and forms and methods in the Church down the centuries, the borrowing from different cultures and civilizations and adaptation to altered circumstances in the world—all these seem to be more than mere facts of history, they seem to be a theological requisite. The pattern of adaptation and change appears to be a mandate based on the very nature and mission of the Church, just as growth and development are inherent in the nature of a living organism.

---

[1] An address delivered at a meeting of the Canon Law Society of America in 1966. Reprinted in *Law for Liberty: the Role of Law in the Church Today*, James E. Biechler, ed., Baltimore, 1967.

[2] Rev. James A. Coriden, S.T.L., J.C.D., of the Catholic University of America.

"This point seems to me to be much more than a nice theological observation. It seems to be central and synthetic. It is the motive for the whole effort toward renewal and relevancy. It sums up the basis for a fearless adaptation of forms and structures. The theological point should be made very clearly and forcefully right at this time."

State of the Question

I do not think any Catholic would exclude all change on *a priori* grounds. Even the most embattled conservative would grant that circumstances alter cases, that positive Church law has not the same immutability as divine law or natural law, that besides the substance of things there are the accidents; that, *salva substantia*, the accidents may at times be modified, provided, of course, that the change is made prudently and, above all, that one keeps ever in mind that human nature is always the same.

At the other extreme I am not certain it should be maintained that change in the Church's forms, structures, methods, etc., should be a continuous, irreversible, ongoing process. There are static periods in most cultures and civilizations and, while the rest of society is quiescent, it is not clear that the Church must keep on initiating change.

Between these extremes there are two positions. One may be named classicist, conservative, traditional; the other may be named modern, liberal, perhaps historicist (though that word unfortunately is very ambiguous). The differences between the two are enormous, for they differ in their apprehension of man, in their account of the good, and in the role they ascribe to the Church in the world. But these differences are not immediately theological. They are differences in horizon, in total mentality. For either side really to understand the other is a major achievement and, when such understanding is lacking, the interpretation of Scripture or of other theological sources is most likely to be at cross-purposes.

2

Accordingly, though I have been asked for a theological opinion, I must proceed in roundabout fashion. Only after the differences between classicist and historicist viewpoints have been indicated, can their respective merits in the eyes of the Christian be estimated.

Human Nature and Historicity

If one abstracts from all respects in which one man can differ from another, there is left a residue named human nature and the truism that human nature is always the same. One may fit out the eternal identity, human nature, with a natural law. One may complete it with the principles for the erection of positive law. One may hearken to divine revelation to acknowledge a supernatural order, a divine law, and a positive ecclesiastical law. So one may work methodically from the abstract and universal towards the more concrete and particular, and the more one does so, the more one is involved in the casuistry of applying a variety of universals to concrete singularity.

It seems most unlikely that in this fashion one will arrive at a law demanding the change of laws, forms, structures, methods. For universals do not change; they are just what they are defined to be; and to introduce a new definition is, not to change the old universal, but to place another new universal beside the old one. On the other hand, casuistry deals with the *casus*, with the way things chance to fall. But every good Aristotelian knows that there is no science of the accidental (Aristotle, *Metaphysics* VI [E], 2, 1027a 19 f.), and so from casuistry's cases one can hardly conclude to some law about changing laws.

Still, the foregoing is not the only possible approach. One can begin from people as they are. One can note that, apart from times of dreamless sleep, they are performing intentional acts. They are experiencing, imagining, desiring, fearing; they wonder, come to understand, conceive; they reflect, weigh the evidence, judge; they deliberate, decide, act. If dreamless sleep may be compared to

3

death, human living is being awake; it is a matter of performing intentional acts; in short, such acts informed by meaning are precisely what gives significance to human living and, conversely, to deny all meaning to human life is nihilism.

As meaningful performance is constitutive of human living, so common meaning is constitutive of community. A common field of experience makes for a potential community; and without that common field people get out of touch. Common and complementary ways of understanding make for a community of mind; and without it there are misunderstanding, suspicion, distrust, mutual incomprehension. Common judgments constitute a consensus; and without it an easy tolerance gives way to amazement, scorn, ridicule, division. Common commitments, finally, are the stuff of fidelity to one another, of loyalty to the group, of faith in divine providence and in the destiny of man; and without such commitments community has lost its heart and becomes just an aggregate.

Now the common meanings constitutive of community and of the lives of individuals in community are not some stock of ideal forms subsistent in some Platonic heaven. They are the hard-won fruit of man's advancing knowledge of nature, of the gradual evolution of his social forms and of his cultural achievements. There is such a thing as historical process, but it is to be known only by the difficult art of acquiring historical perspective, of coming to understand how the patterns of living, the institutions, the common meanings of one place and time differ from those of another.

It may be objected that substantially there are always the same things to be known and the same things to be done. But I am not sure that the word "substantially" means anything more than that things are the same in so far as you prescind from their differences. In contrast, the point I am endeavouring to make is not verbal. Modern man is fully aware that he has made his modern world. There are modern languages and modern literatures, consciously

4

developed by turning away from the Latin and Greek languages and literature. There are modern mathematics and modern science, and they differ not only in extent but also in their fundamental conceptions from the Greek achievement. There are modern technology and industry, modern commerce and finance, the modern city and the modern state, modern education and modern medicine, modern media and modern art, the modern idea of history and the modern idea of philosophy. In every case modernity means the desertion, if not the repudiation, of the old models and methods, and the exercise of freedom, initiative, creativity. So to modern man it seems self-evident that he has made his own modern world and, no less, that other peoples at other times either have done the same or else have made do with a world fashioned by bolder ancestors and inertly handed on.

I have been contrasting two different apprehensions of man. One can apprehend man abstractly through a definition that applies *omni et soli* and through properties verifiable in every man. In this fashion one knows man as such; and man as such, precisely because he is an abstraction, also is unchanging. It follows in the first place, that on this view one is never going to arrive at any exigence for changing forms, structures, methods, for all change occurs in the concrete, and on this view the concrete is always omitted. But it also follows in the second place, that this exclusion of changing forms, structures, methods, is not theological; it is grounded simply upon a certain conception of scientific or philosophic method; that conception is no longer the only conception or the commonly received conception; and I think our Scripture scholars would agree that its abstractness, and the omissions due to abstraction, have no foundation in the revealed word of God.

On the other hand, one can apprehend mankind as a concrete aggregate developing over time, where the locus of development and, so to speak, the synthetic bond is the emergence, expansion, differentiation, dialectic of meaning and of meaningful performance. On this view intentionality, meaning, is a constitutive component of human living; moreover, this component is not fixed, static, immutable, but shifting, developing, going astray, capable of redemption; on this view there is in the historicity, which results from human nature, an exigence for changing forms, structures, methods; and it is on this level and through this medium of changing meaning that divine revelation has entered the world and that the Church's witness is given to it.

Propositional Principles and Transcendental Method

In the article on *Naturrecht* in the *Lexikon für Theologie und Kirche* (7: 827) Father Karl Rahner observed that natural law should be approached through a transcendental method.

Any serious elaboration of this remark would take us too far afield, but three assertions may perhaps be permitted.

First, just as the abstract apprehension of man provides itself with abstract ontological and ethical foundations in primitive propositions from which its doctrines, criteria, norms, etc., are deduced or somehow proved, so the more concrete and historical apprehension of man provides itself with its appropriately concrete foundations in structural features of the conscious, operating subject, by a method that has come to be named transcendental.

Secondly, the stock objections that historical-mindedness involves one in relativism and situation ethics are to be met by adverting to the distinction just drawn. One cannot ground a concrete historical apprehension of man on abstract foundations: but this does not establish the inadequacy of the quite different foundations provided by a transcendental method.

Thirdly, what moves men is the good, and good in the concrete (*verum et falsum sunt in mente, bonum et malum sunt in rebus; bonum ex integra causa, malum ex quocumque defectu*). If at one time law was in the forefront of human development, as one might

6

infer from the language of the Deuteronomist, from the fervent praise of law in the Psalms, from the role of law in the history of the clarification of such concepts as justice, responsibility, guilt; still, at the present time it would seem that the immediate carrier of human aspiration is the more concrete apprehension of the human good effected through such theories of history as the liberal doctrine of progress, the Marxist doctrine of dialectical materialism and, most recently, Teilhard de Chardin's identification of cosmogenesis, anthropogenesis, and christogenesis.

The People of God in the World of Today

I have been asked for "a theological perspective on how a community of love adapts and directs itself for effective mission and witness." Presumably the reason for the request lies in points I have made elsewhere. There is in my book *Insight*[3] a general analysis of the dynamic structure of human history, and in my mimeographed text *De Verbo Incarnato*[4] a thesis on the *lex crucis* that provides its strictly theological complement.

The analysis distinguishes three components: progress, decline, and redemption.

Progress results from the natural development of human intelligence: ". . . concrete situations give rise to insights which issue into policies and courses of action. Action transforms the existing situation to give rise to further insights, better policies, more effective courses of action. It follows that if insight occurs, it keeps recurring; and at each recurrence knowledge develops, action increases its scope, and situations improve" (*Insight*, p. xiv).

Next, a flight from understanding results in a similarly cumulative process of decline.

For the flight from understanding blocks the insights that concrete situations demand. There follow unintelligent policies and inept courses of action. The situation deteriorates to demand

[3] London and New York, 1957.
[4] Rome, 1964.

still further insights and, as they are blocked, policies become more unintelligent and action more inept. What is worse, the deteriorating situation seems to provide the uncritical, biased mind with factual evidence in which the bias is claimed to be verified. So in ever increasing measure intelligence comes to be regarded as irrelevant to practical living. Human activity settles down to a decadent routine, and initiative becomes the privilege of violence (*Insight*, p. xiv).

If human historical process is such a compound of progress and decline, then its redemption would be effected by faith, hope, and charity. For the evils of the situation and the enmities they engender would only be perpetuated by an even-handed justice: charity alone can wipe the slate clean. The determinism and pressures of every kind, resulting from the cumulative surd of unintelligent policies and actions, can be withstood only through a hope that is transcendent and so does not depend on any human prop. Finally, only within the context of higher truths accepted on faith can human intelligence and reasonableness be liberated from the charge of irrelevance to the realities produced by human waywardness (*Insight*, chap. XX).

This analysis fits in with scriptural doctrine, which understands suffering and death as the result of sin yet inculcates the transforming power of Christ, who in himself and in us changes suffering and death into the means for attaining resurrection and glory.

Sin universal: Rom. 1: 18—3: 20; 7: 14-24; Eph. 2: 3.
Sin leads to death: Gen. 2: 15; 3: 19; Rom. 5: 12; 6: 22, 23.
The first and last Adam: 1 Cor. 15: 20-22; Rom. 5: 12-21.
Christ died to rise again: Jn. 10: 17; Phil. 2: 9 f.; Heb. 2: 9.
He died and rose for our salvation: Rom. 4: 25; 5: 10; 1 Cor. 15: 55; Phil. 1: 21; Eph. 1: 7; Col. 1: 14; Tit. 2: 15; Heb. 2: 14.

As Christ's death is a principle of salvation, so also are our own deaths, whether understood physically (Phil. 3: 20, 21), ascetically

(Rom. 8:13; 1 Cor. 9:27), morally (Rom. 6:11; Col. 3:1–4), sacramentally (Rom. 6:4; 1 Cor. 11:26; Col. 2:12).

So we have the law of the cross: Mk. 7:34, 35; Mt. 16:24, 25; Lk. 9:23, 24; Jn. 12:24, 25; Mt. 5:11, 12, 28–48. See *De Verbo Incarnato*, pp. 552 ff.

Concluding Questions

It was recommended that the papers conclude with a few salient questions. There occur the following:

Does law function in the same fashion in a dynamic society as in a static society? If there are differences, in what do they consist?

What contribution does law make to progress? Are there direct as well as indirect contributions? Could law impede growth, development, progress?

Is the proper Christian ethic the law of the cross, i.e., the transformation of evil into good? Does law "use good to defeat evil?" (Rom. 12:21).

THE DEHELLENIZATION OF DOGMA[1]

With considerable warmth Prof. Leslie Dewart appeals to Pope John's decision "to adopt a historical perspective: to 'look to the present, to new conditions and new forms of life . . . to dedicate ourselves with an earnest will and without fear to that work which our era demands of us' " (p. 172). This decision, he feels, and the unhesitating acclamation that greeted it reversed a policy that had been gaining strength for centuries. "This policy was, for the sake of protecting the truth and purity of the Christian faith, to resist the factual reality, and to deny the moral validity, of the development of man's self-consciousness, especially as revealed in cultural evolution" (p. 172).

His purpose, then, is "to sketch an approach to . . . the problem of integrating Christian theistic belief with the everyday experience of contemporary man" (p. 7). He aims at "the integration of Christian belief with the post-medieval stage of human development" (p. 15). He understands contemporary experience "as the mode of consciousness which mankind, if not as a whole at least in respect of our own civilization constituting man's cultural vanguard, has reached as a result of its historical and evolutionary development. And the integration in question must be a true organic process of coordination, interrelation and

[1] A review in *Theological Studies*, 28 (1967), 336–351, of *The Future of Belief: Theism in a World Come of Age*, by Leslie Dewart, New York, 1966. © 1967 by *Theological Studies*.

unification" (p. 9). What is at stake is the unity and coherence of Christian and, in particular, Catholic consciousness: ". . . the problem is, at its most basic level, whether one can, while complying with the demand that human personality, character and experience be inwardly integrated, at one and the same time profess the Christian religion *and* perceive human nature and everyday reality as contemporary man typically does" (p. 19).

So much for the problem. The suggested solution is "that the integration of theism with today's everyday experience requires not merely the *demythologization of Scripture* but the more comprehensive *dehellenization of dogma*, and specifically that of the Christian doctrine of God" (p. 49). Demythologization integrates no more than the Christian's *reading of Scripture* with his contemporary everyday experience; and it creates several dogmatic problems for each scriptural one it solves (p. 47). To go to the root of the matter, to become both coherent and contemporary, we have to transcend our Hellenic past and consciously to fashion the cultural form which Christianity requires now for the sake of its future. So "dehellenization means, in positive terms, the conscious creation of the future of belief" (p. 50). This future, he feels, is likely to depend on whether Christian theism "chooses to contribute to the heightening of man's self-understanding and to the perfection of his 'education to reality.' This would in turn imply that Christian theism should first become conscious that its traditional form has necessarily and logically been childish and infantile to the very degree that it corresponded to an earlier, relatively childish, infantile stage of human evolution. Theism in a world come of age must itself be a theism come of age" (p. 51).

I.

The principal means for dehellenizing dogma and obtaining a mature theism seems to be "the theory of knowledge assumed here" (p. 168 n.). While its precise nature is not disclosed in any detail, apparently it involves a rather strong repugnance to propositional truth in some at least of its aspects.

In the theory of knowledge suggested here human knowledge is not the bridging of an original isolation but, on the contrary, the self-differentiation of consciousness in and through its objectification (of the world and of itself); and conceptualization is the socio-historical mechanism through which the self-differentiation can take place. Concepts are not the *subjective* expression of an *objective* reality (nor, therefore, a means whereby we become reflectively conscious of a self which already existed prior to reflection). Concepts are the self-expression of consciousness and, therefore, the means by which we objectify (the world and the self), and the means by which we self-communicate with another self (*including God*), that is, the means by which we objectify ourselves for another self, and by which we objectify ourselves for ourselves (p. 116 n.; here and elsewhere italics in text).

Hence we are repeatedly warned against the view that truth involves an *adaequatio intellectus et rei*.

Truth is not the adequacy of our representative operations, but the adequacy of our conscious existence. More precisely, it is the fidelity of consciousness to being (p. 92).

It is the result of the mind coming-into-being through the self-differentiation of that-which-is into self and world (p. 93).

Now we have seen that . . . truth can be understood as an existential relation of self to being which must by definition develop in order to realize itself—and not as relation of conformity to an objective thing which must by definition be stable in order to be at all (p. 97).

Although truth is not the adequation of the *intellect* to *being* . . . truth might nevertheless be called an adequation of *man* to *reality*, in the sense that it is man's *self-achievement* within the requirements of a *given situation*. . . . In this context *adequation* would not connote *conformity*, *correspondence*, *likeness or similarity.* It would *connote adjustment, usefulness, expediency, proficiency, sufficiency* and *adaptation* (p. 110).

The truth of human experience is the result of consciousness' incessant tending towards being—a tendency which, far from satisfied by the achievement of its goal, is further intensified by whatever success it may meet. Hence, the only valid "criterion" of truth is that it create the possibility of more truth (p. 111).

. . . the concept is true *to the degree* that by its elevation of experience to consciousness it permits the truth of human experience to come into being (p. 113).

. . . the concepts in which Christian belief are cast are true, not in virtue of their representative adequacy, but in virtue of their efficacious adequacy as generative forms of the truth of religious experience (p. 113).

To conclude with a citation from Maurice Blondel's *Carnets intimes*: ". . . truth is no longer the *adaequatio rei et intellectus.* . . . But truth remains, and this truth that remains is living and active. It is the *adaequatio mentis et vitae*" (p. 118).

Prof. Dewart's grounds for his view on truth seem to be partly the flood of light he has derived from phenomenological and existential thought and partly the inadequacy of his interpretation of Scholasticism.

To the light I have no objection. I would not deny that the authenticity of one's living, the probity of one's intellectual endeavors, the strategy of one's priorities are highly relevant for the truth by which one is truly a man. I have no doubt that concepts and judgments (on judgments I find Dewart strangely silent) are the expression of one's accumulated experience, developed understanding, acquired wisdom; and I quite agree that such expression is an objectification of one's self and of one's world.

I would urge, however, that this objectification is intentional. It consists in acts of meaning. We objectify the self by meaning the self, and we objectify the world by meaning the world. Such meaning of its nature is related to a meant, and what is meant may or may not correspond to what in fact is so. If it corresponds, the meaning is true. If it does not correspond, the meaning is false. Such is the correspondence view of truth, and Dewart has managed to reject it without apparently adverting to it. So eager has he been to impugn what he considered the Thomist theory of knowledge that he overlooked the fact that he needed a correspondence view of truth to mean what he said.

Let me stress the point. Dewart has written a book on the future of belief. Does he mean the future of belief, or something else, or nothing at all? At least, when he asserts that God is not a being, he assures us that what his statement "means is literally what it says, that God is not a being at all" (p. 175). Again, he wants his proposals tried by the touchstone of public examination (p. 50). But what is that examination to be? What can the public do but consider what he means and try to ascertain how much of what he says is certainly or probably true or false?

Dewart urges that the correspondence view of truth supposes what is contrary to both logic and observation, "as if we could witness from a third, 'higher' viewpoint, the union of two lower things, object and subject" (p. 95). But such a statement is involved in a grave confusion. The witnessing from a higher viewpoint is the nonsense of naive realism, of the super-look that looks at both the looking and the looked-at. On the other hand, the union of object and subject is a metaphysical deduction from the fact of knowledge, and its premise is the possibility of consciousness objectifying not only itself but also its world.

Again, Dewart urges that a correspondence view of truth implies an immobility that precludes development (p. 95) and, in particular, the development of dogma (p. 109). Now I would not dispute that a wooden-headed interpretation of the correspondence view of truth can exclude and has excluded the possibility of development. But that is no reason for rejecting the correspondence view along with its misinterpretation. Least of all is that so at present, when "hermeneutics" has become a watchword and the existence of literary forms is generally acknowledged. For the root of hermeneutics and the significance of literary forms lie precisely in the fact that the correspondence between meaning and meant is itself part of the meaning and so will vary with variations in the meaning.

Just as he discusses truth without adverting to hermeneutics, so Dewart discusses the development of dogma without adverting to the history of dogma. But the development of dogma is a historical entity. Its existence and its nature are determined by research and interpretation. Moreover, on this approach there are found to be almost as many modes of development, almost as many varieties of implicit revelation, as there are different dogmas, so that a general discussion of the possibility of cultural development, such as Dewart offers, can provide no more than philosophic prolegomena.

Unfortunately, it seems of the essence of Dewart's prolegomena to exclude the correspondence view of truth. Such an exclusion is as destructive of the dogmas as it is of Dewart's own statements. To deny correspondence is to deny a relation between meaning and meant. To deny the correspondence view of truth is to deny that, when the meaning is true, the meant is what is so. Either denial is destructive of the dogmas.

If there is no correspondence between meaning and meant, then, in Prof. McLuhan's phrase, it would be a great mistake to read the dogmas as if they were saying something. If that is a great mistake, it would be another to investigate their historical origins, and a third to talk about their development.

If one denies that, when the meaning is true, then the meant is what is so, one rejects propositional truth. If the rejection is universal, then it is the self-destructive proposition that there are no true propositions. If the rejection is limited to the dogmas, then it is just a roundabout way of saying that all the dogmas are false.

II.

The same view of truth is applied not only to the dogmas but also to faith and revelation. We are told that "belief must bear directly upon the reality of God, not upon words or concepts" (p. 167). In a footnote we are warned against the doctrine of St. Thomas which has faith terminating at God himself through the mediation of the propositions of the Creed. Dewart holds that to believe in God by believing a proposition about God is to believe in a proposition and not to believe in God. But this follows only on Dewart's assumption that truth is not correspondence. On the contrary assumption, to assent to the truth of the proposition does not differ from assenting to what the proposition means. *Verum est medium in quo ens cognoscitur.*

With faith detached from assent to propositions (p. 167), it has to be ontic rather than ontological (p. 136 n.).

Faith is the existential response of the self to the openness of the transcendence disclosed by conscious experience. It is our decision to respect, to let be, the contingency of our being, and, therefore, to admit into our calculations a reality beyond the totality of being. It is a lived response, identical with our freely willing to exist in a certain self-conception and self-resolution. . . . It is no less a coming-into-being than the "act" of existence which is, likewise, a perpetual achieving of the unachieved. In real life we find not the act but the life of faith (pp. 64 f.).

Such faith seems to coincide with religious experience. This differs from ordinary knowledge inasmuch as it is an experience of a transcendent reality first adumbrated negatively in the empirical apprehension of the contingency of our own being. So it is a conscious experience of something inevident, something which unlike this desk and this chair is not seen to be there, even if it enters into the fabric of our personal relations to reality with at least as much force, relevance, and moment as things which are seen to be there. Further, in the traditional phrase, faith is due to God's initiative. Again, faith as Christian is faith as conceptualized under some or other cultural form of the Christian tradition. Its continuity in truth requires the continuity of God's self-communication to man, and the continuity of man's correlative religious experience in response to God's initiative. But this is not the continuity of sameness or the continuity of that which remains (substantially) unchanged in the midst of accidental change. Truth cannot remain the same. It would make as little sense as to say that existence remains the same, that one moment of consciousness is the same as another, or that life is the same thing over and over again (pp. 113–16).

Correlative to faith is revelation:

... although God does not reveal propositions or formulae or concepts about himself, he truly reveals himself.... He does it personally, by his own agency, through his personal presence to human history, in which he freely chooses to appear and to take part.... His revelation to man in the Judaeo-Christian tradition is unique and extraordinary: the Christian religion and the Catholic Church are, in this extraordinary and unique sense, the true religion and the true Church to which all men are called (p. 115 n.).

Dewart, however, does not seem to consider that the call to the true Church calls for some attention to the pronouncements of Vatican I and II on revelation and faith. Instead we have the caricature of a "popular faith" in which "revelation has indeed tended to become God's transmission of cryptic messages. Correlatively, the magisterium of the Church has tended to become the decoding of these messages, and faith the Christian's assent to the accuracy of the translation. ..." (p. 165 n.).

No doubt, Dewart's esotericism is inevitable, once the mediating role of propositions has been eliminated both from God's revelation to man and from man's faith in God. But if one is inclined to doubt the soundness of the "theory of knowledge assumed here" (p. 168 n.), if one's modernity includes a greater interest in exegesis and history than is exhibited in the opinion that "Christianity has a mission not a message" (p. 8), then one

18

will find abundant evidence from New Testament times right up to the present day that the Church has been explicitly aware not only of a mission but also of a message. Moreover, while it is true that the message can be and has been abused to the detriment both of living faith and of the transcendent Revealer, such an abuse does not show that a rejection of the message is not also a rejection of the mission.

III.

Prof. Dewart dislikes the Greeks. He deplores the "inability of hellenic metaphysical thinking to discern *reality* except in *ens*, that-which-is" (p. 80). He places at the sad root of both Greek and Scholastic thought Parmenides' postulate that "that which can be thought is identical with that which can be" (p. 153). He would get beyond "speculative-ideological metaphysics" (p. 163) and establish a metaphysics of presence (p. 109). Then we could get along without the training and education that only relatively few can afford. "Christian theology and philosophy would then cease to be 'academic' subjects, and theo-logical enquiry would once again take place predominantly within the public, everyday, real life of the whole Church" (p. 145 n.). In anticipation of this imminent utopia, he notes that "there is no need, if we discard Parmenides, to make God fit in the mould of being" (p. 176). Hence, he desires a philosophy concerned with the presence and reality of God, a God that is not even partially the God of Greek metaphysics (p. 170). Similarly, he suggests that Christian theology is not to assume any fundamental principle or essential part of that very mode of philosophizing on which was erected the concept of God which can no longer be integrated with contemporary experience (p. 41).

This hostility to Hellenism is of a piece with the already noted hostility to propositional truth; for not only do propositions mediate reality, but also the first-level propositions that do so may be themselves mediated by second-level propositions. So dictionaries speak of words, grammars of languages, logics of the clarity, coherence, and rigor of discourse, hermeneutics of the relation between meaning and meant, and, to come to the villain, metaphysics of what is meant. Such second-level mediation of the first-level mediator was the secret of the Greek miracle that effected the triumph of *logos* over *mythos*.

Obviously, then, if one does not want a first-level mediation of reality by propositions, much less will one tolerate the second-level mediation associated with Greek metaphysics. Moreover, if one does not care to be entirely cut off from reality, one will have to turn to some nonpropositional mode of access such as presence. So Dewart praises a metaphysics of presence but blames a Hellenic metaphysics.

Again, the Greek miracle had its price. It demanded a second differentiation of consciousness, a second withdrawal from the world of immediacy. In that world of immediacy the infant lives, but when the child learns to talk, he also learns to inhabit the far larger world mediated by meaning. For the student, however, there is the further learning that mediates the mediator, that reflects on articulate sounds to correlate them with an alphabet, that uses dictionaries, that studies grammars and logics, that introduces hermeneutics and even perhaps metaphysics. The basic purpose of this further learning is to control the mediation of reality by meaning, to hold in check the affect-laden images that even in the twentieth century have the power to make myth seem convincing and magic seem efficacious.

But however beneficial, the second differentiation of consciousness is onerous. It is all the more onerous, all the more resented, when compulsory, universal education attempts to extend to all what once had to be endured by but few. So the word "academic" acquires a pejorative sense that expresses disapproval of any cultural superstructure. Despite his devotion to the mode of consciousness reached by man's cultural vanguard (p. 9), Dewart feels free to appeal to that disapproval and to look forward to the day when Christian philosophy and theology will no longer be "academic" subjects (p. 145 n.).

A similar ambiguity appears in Dewart's attitude to science. On the one hand, he assures us that "modern man creates himself by means of science, that is, by means of his scientific mode of consciousness," and it "is *scientific culture* that defines *contemporary man*" (p. 18). On the other hand, he is all for discarding Parmenides' identification of the possible object of thought with possible being (pp. 153, 165, 168, 174, 176, 181, 184). But to attack this identification is also to attack a cardinal point in contemporary science; for what is defined by a hypothesis is a possible object of thought, and what is to be ascertained by verification is a real state of affairs. But modern science demands that every hypothesis be verifiable, and so it demands that its hypothetical objects of thought be possible beings. Not only is it thoroughly committed to the Parmenidean identity, but also it has so extended and developed the second differentiation of consciousness as to erect a cultural superstructure far more elaborate and far more abstruse than anything attempted by the Greeks or the Scholastics.

One begins to suspect that Dewart is not a reformer but just a revolutionary. He is dealing with a very real and very grave problem. He would have written an extremely important book, if he had distinguished between the achievements and the limitations of Hellenism, if he had listed the ways in which modern culture has corrected the errors and so transcended the limitations of its ancient heritage, if he had pointed out the precise bearing of each of these advances on each of the many levels on which Christians live and Christianity functions. He has not done so. He fails to discern the elements of Hellenism that still survive in the cultural vanguard, and so he plumps for vigor. Let's liquidate Hellenism. He does not distinguish between integrated consciousness and undifferentiated consciousness, and so he thinks and talks and prescribes his remedies as if prayer, dogma, systematic

A SECOND COLLECTION

theology, philosophy, and contemporary common sense were or should be a single homogeneous unity.

IV.

Prof. Dewart conceives the development of the Trinitarian and Christological dogmas to have been a matter of taking over Hellenic concepts for the expression of Christian doctrine; for he feels "it would be unhistorical to suppose that at the first moment of the development of Christian consciousness this consciousness could have created the concepts whereby to elaborate itself—it is not until our own day that such a possibility has begun to emerge" (p. 136). Further, he laments that the Church still retains such outworn tools, for today this results in a crypto-tritheism (p. 147) and in a crypto-docetism (p. 152).

It is, I should say, quite unhistorical to suppose that the development of Catholic dogma was an effort of Christian consciousness to elaborate, not the Christian message, but Christian consciousness. Further, it is unhistorical to suppose that Greek philosophy supplied all the principal elements in which we have for centuries conceptualized the basic Christian beliefs of the Trinity and the Incarnation (cf. *America*, Dec. 17, 1966, p. 801). My first contention needs no elaboration, and so I turn to the second.

It is true, then, that profound affinities may be discerned between Hellenic thinkers and some ecclesiastical writers. The Stoic notion that only bodies are real seems intrinsic to Tertullian's account of the divinity of the Son in his *Adversus Praxean*. Middle Platonism is prominent in Origen's account of the Son in his *De principiis* and *In Ioannem*. But the subordinationism of these two writers, along with Arianism, was rejected at Nicea. Moreover, the term enshrining that rejection was *homoousios*, and while one might speculate that here if anywhere one has a concept forged by deep Hellenic thought and simply taken over by the bishops at Nicea (see p. 136), it happens that historical research does not justify such a view. According to G. Prestige (*God in*

22

Patristic Thought [London, 1936], p. 209; cf. p. 197), down to the Council of Nicea *homoousios* was understood in one sense and in one sense only; it meant " of one stuff"; and as applied to the Divine Persons, it conveyed a metaphor drawn from material objects. The Fathers at Nicea, then, did not find ready to hand a sharply defined, immutable concept which they made into a vehicle for the Christian message; on the contrary, they found a word which they employed in a metaphorical sense.

It may be urged, however, that the metaphor meant something and that meaning must be some other Hellenic concept. It happens, however, that while the metaphor had a meaning, still the meaning was determined not by some Hellenic concept but by a Hellenic technique. What *homoousios* meant exactly, was formulated by Athanasius thus: *eadem de Filio quae de Patre dicuntur, excepto Patris nomine.* The same meaning has been expressed in the Trinitarian Preface: *Quod enim de tua gloria, revelante te, credimus, hoc de Filio tuo, hoc de Spiritu sancto, sine differentia discretionis sentimus.* Now such a determination of meaning is characteristically Hellenic. It is a matter of reflecting on propositions. It explains the word "consubstantial" by a second-level proposition to the effect that the Son is consubstantial with the Father, if and only if what is true of the Father also is true of the Son, except that only the Father is Father.

Let me add five observations on this typically Hellenic technique. The first is that it offers an open structure: it does not determine what attributes are to be assigned to the Father and so must be assigned to the Son as well; it leaves the believer free to conceive the Father in scriptural, patristic, medieval, or modern terms; and of course contemporary consciousness, which is historically minded, will be at home in all four.

The second is that, when reality and being are contrasted, the technique decides for being; for being is that which is; it is that which is to be known through the true proposition; and the technique operates on true propositions. On the other hand,

23

reality, when contrasted with being, denotes the evident or present that provides the remote grounds for rationally affirming being, but, unlike being, is in constant flux.

The third is that specifically Christian thought on being came into prominent existence in Athanasius' struggle against Arianism and, in particular, in his elucidation of *natum non factum*, of the difference between the Son *born* of the Father and the creature *created* by Father and Son. No doubt, such an explanation presupposes a Hellenic background for its possibility. But the problem and the content are specifically Christian. A divine Son was simply a scandal to the Hellenist Celsus; and the Christian notion of creation is not to be found in Plato or Aristotle, the Stoics or the Gnostics. When Dewart talks about the God of Greek metaphysics (p. 170), one wonders what Greek metaphysician he is talking about.

My fourth observation is that the Hellenic technique of second-level propositions is not outworn. The modern mathematician reflects on his axioms and pronounces them to be the implicit definitions of his basic terms. This technique, then, pertains not to the limitations of Hellenism antiquated by modern culture but to the achievements of Hellenism that still survive in modern culture and, indeed, form part of it.

My fifth and last observation is that the technique is not within everyone's competence. The matter seems to have been settled with some accuracy; for, in his celebrated studies of educational psychology, Jean Piaget has concluded that only about the age of twelve (if my memory is correct) do boys become able to operate on propositions. It follows that other means have to be found to communicate the doctrine of Nicea to less-developed minds. So much for my five observations.

For Dewart, "person" is a concept taken over from Hellenic thought and, though we have not managed to improve on it, we must do so (pp. 143 f.). I find this a rather inadequate account of the matter.

24

For Augustine, *persona* or *substantia* was an undefined, heuristic concept. He pointed out that Father, Son, and Spirit are three. He asked, Three what? He remarked that there are not three Gods, three Fathers, three Sons, three Spirits. He answered that there are three persons or substances, where "person" or "substance" just means what there are three of in the Trinity (*De trin.* 7, 4, 7 [*PL* 42, 939]). Obviously, such an account of the notion of "person" does no more than indicate, so to speak, the area to be investigated. It directs future development but it cannot be said to impede it. The only manner in which it could become outworn would be the rejection of the Trinity; for as long as the Trinity is acknowledged, there are acknowledged three of something.

Moreover, the original heuristic structure, while it has remained, has not remained indeterminate. It has been developed in different ways at different times. There was the stage of definitions, indeed, of the three main definitions contributed by Boethius, Richard of St. Victor, and Thomas Aquinas. There was the Trinitarian systematization that conceived the three Persons as subsistent relations and based the relations upon psychologically conceived processions. If I may cite my own views, I have maintained not only in my classes but also in a textbook that the three Persons are the perfect community, not two in one flesh, but three subjects of a single, dynamic, existential consciousness. On the other hand, I am of the opinion that the Christological systematization, from Scotus to de la Taille, had bogged down in a precritical morass. For the past thirty years, however, attention has increasingly turned to the consciousness of Christ, and my own position has been that the doctrine of one person with two natures transposes quite neatly into a recognition of a single subject of both a divine and a human consciousness.

I may be more brief on such terms as *substantia, hypostasis, natura.* All three were ambiguous. We have just seen Augustine use *substantia* in the same sense as *persona*, a usage that had vanished by the time the *Quicumque vult* was composed. Next, in the

Tomus ad Antiochenos there is the account of Athanasius reconciling those that argued for one hypostasis with those that argued for three; he asked the former if they agreed with Sabellius, and the latter if they were tritheists; both groups were astounded by the question put them, promptly disclaimed respectively Sabellianism and tritheism, and dropped their now obviously verbal dispute. "Nature," finally, which for Aristotle meant either the form or the matter, and the form rather than the matter, meant neither of these to Christians some eight centuries later. They, however, had their own ambiguous usage, and it was recognized solemnly and explicitly in the sixth and seventh centuries. In successive canons Constantinople II explained the correct meaning both of Chalcedon's two natures and of Cyril's one nature (*DS* 428 f.). More abruptly, Lateran I imposed both the Cyrillian and the Chalcedonian formulas (*DS* 505 f.).

So much for the process of Hellenizing Christian doctrine. Let us add a few words on the meaning of the technical terms; for Dewart roundly asserts that no Christian believer today (unless he can abstract himself from contemporary experience) can intelligently believe that in the one hypostasis of Jesus *two* real natures are united (p. 150). Let me put the prior question. Does Dewart's Christian believer today accept the positive part of the Nicene decree, in which neither the term "hypostasis" nor the term "nature" occurs? If so, in the part about Jesus Christ, does he observe two sections, a first containing divine predicates, and a second containing human predicates? Next, to put the question put by Cyril to Nestorius, does he accept the two series of predicates as attributes of *one and the same* Jesus Christ? If he does, he acknowledges what is meant by one hypostasis. If he does not, he does not accept the Nicene Creed. Again, does he acknowledge in the one and the same Jesus Christ both divine attributes and human attributes? If he acknowledges both, he accepts what is meant by two natures. If he does not, he does not accept the Nicene Creed.

What is true is that Catholic theology today has a tremendous task before it, for there are very real limitations to Hellenism that have been transcended by modern culture and have yet to be successfully surmounted by Catholic theology. But that task is not helped, rather it is gravely impeded, by wild statements based on misconceptions or suggesting unbelief.

V.

Prof. Dewart has treated many other topics besides those I have been able to mention, but his principal concern, no doubt, is "theism in a world come of age," for that is the subtitle of his book. The substance of his proposal here seems to come in two parts. Positively, it is that God is to be thought of, not as being or as existing, but as a reality that at times is present and at times is absent (pp. 173 ff.). Negatively, it is that atheism is fostered by unsuccessful efforts to prove God's existence, and such failures are due to the real distinction between essence and existence (pp. 156–58).

He contends, then, that one need not conceive God as being, once one gets beyond the metaphysical method grounded on Parmenides' identity. Remove that method, and "being" need no longer be identified with that-which-is. So the way is opened to giving to "being" a new meaning, and this new meaning is to be found in man. It is because he is present to himself as object that man is most truly a being; for through that presence man may transcend the subjectivity of mere objects and the objectivity of mere subjects to reach an understanding of himself as being. But to associate being with man is to dissociate being from God. As God is simply beyond man, so he is simply beyond being (pp. 173–75). By the same token, God cannot be said to exist (p. 176). He cannot because to exist is proper to being (p. 180).

We are reassured immediately, however, that the denial of being and existence to God takes away nothing of his reality and presence. To exist and to be present are quite different things. A man could be in the same room sitting beside me without being present to me, without making his presence felt. Conversely, God's real presence to us (and, therefore, His reality "in Himself") does not depend upon His being a being or an object. On the contrary, to postprimitives a reality beyond the totality of being reveals itself by its presence (pp. 176 f.).

I do not find this very satisfactory. First of all, Dewart's views on truth are not defensible. Moreover, the cultural vanguard has not yet surmounted the requirement that hypotheses be verifiable, and so Parmenides' identity still stands. It follows that "being" still is that-which-is, that intelligence still is related to reality, that "is" and "is not" are not open to reinterpretation, and that there do not exist the premises for the conclusion that "being" and "existing" are appropriate only to creatures.

Secondly, it is obvious that a person can exist without making his presence felt and that he cannot make his presence felt without existing and being present. But it is also obvious that one can have the feeling that someone is present when no one is there. Especially in a world come of age such feelings should be examined, scrutinized, investigated. The investigation may result in the judgment that someone really is there. It may result in the judgment that really no one is there. It may result only in an unresolved state of doubt. But in any case, what is decisive is not the felt presence but the rational judgment that follows upon an investigation of the felt presence.

My point here is that man's coming to know is a process, that the earlier stages of the process pertain to knowing without constituting it completely, that in each instance of coming to know it is only with the rational act of judgment that the process reaches its term. Dewart does not want propositional truth and so he does not want "being" or "existing" or "that-which-is" or assent to propositions or judgments issuing in propositions. He does very much want the reassuring sense of present reality that can be savored in the earlier phases of cognitional process and, I have no doubt, is to be savored all the more fully if the unpleasant and tiring business of questions, investigations, and possible doubts is quietly forgotten. But this seems to be less "coming of age" than infantile regression.

Thirdly, maturity is comprehensive. It does not refuse to acknowledge any part of man but embraces all from the entities of Freud's psychic embryology to the immanent norms of man's intellectual, rational, existential consciousness. As it does not deny propositional truth, so it does not disregard or belittle religious experience. On the contrary, it is quite ready to claim with Karl Rahner that a mystagogy will play a far more conspicuous role in the spirituality of the future (*Geist und Leben*, 39 [1966], 335), and it is fully aware that spiritual advance brings about in prayer the diminution and at times the disappearance of symbols and concepts of God, Still, this differentiation and specialization of consciousness does not abolish other, complementary differentiations and specializations, whether social, sexual, practical, aesthetic, scientific, philosophic, historical, or theological. Nor is this multiplicity in any way opposed to integration. For in each of such diverse patterns of conscious operation one is oneself in accord with some facet of one's being and some part of one's universe; and while one lives in only one pattern at a time in some cycle of recurrence, still the subject is over time, each pattern complements, reinforces, liberates the others, and there can develop a differentiation of consciousness to deal explicitly with differentiations of consciousness. That pattern is, of course, reflective subjectivity in philosophy and in theology. It follows the Hellenic precept "Know thyself." It follows the example of Augustinian recall, scrutiny, penetration, judgment, evaluation, decision. It realizes the modern concern for the authenticity of one's existing without amputating one's own rational objectivity expressed in propositional truth.

Fourthly, maturity understands the immature. It has been through that, and it knows what it itself has been. It is aware that in childhood, before reaching the age of reason, one perforce works out one's quite pragmatic criteria for distinguishing between the "really real" and the merely imagined, desired, feared, dreamt, the sibling's trick, joke, fib. Still more clearly is it aware of the upset of crisis and conversion that is needed to purge oneself of one's childish realism and swing round completely and coherently to a critical realism. So it understands just how it is that some cling to a naive realism all their lives, that others move on to some type of idealism, that others feel some liberation from idealism in a phenomenology or an existentialism while, at the opposite extreme, there is a conceptualist extrinsicism for which concepts have neither dates nor developments and truth is so objective that it gets along without minds.

Such is the disorientation of contemporary experience, its inability to know itself and its own resources, the root of not a little of its insecurity and anxiety. Theology has to take this fact into consideration. The popular theology devised in the past for the *simplices fideles* has to be replaced. Nor will some single replacement do; for theology has to learn to speak in many modes and on many levels and even to minister to the needs of those afflicted with philosophic problems they are not likely to solve.

There remains, finally, the contention that "the ultimate epistemological consequence of the real distinction between essence and existence in creatures is to render the *intellect* incompetent for knowing the actual existence of *any* essence, be it created or uncreated, necessary or contingent" (p. 158). In this statement the emphasis seems to lie not on the reality of the distinction but on the mere existence of any, even a notional, distinction. For the author has just argued:

> ... the doctrine that there is in God *no real* distinction between essence and existence implies that none the less there is a conceptual distinction between them. We *cannot* empirically intuit the real indistinction of essence and existence in God. We *must* none the less conceive the two as distinct. There is, therefore, an unbridgeable difference between

the way in which God is in *himself* and the way in which he is *in our knowledge*. Therefore, unless God were the object of empirical intuition, our concepts are *in principle* unable to make known to us the actual existence of God. For, as Kant was to conclude. . . . (p. 158).

Now this argument has a certain validity if in fact human knowing consists in concepts and empirical intuitions. But empirical intuition is just a misleading name for the givenness of the data of sense and of consciousness. In linking data to conception, there are inquiry and gradually developing understanding. The result of all these together is not knowledge but just thinking. To reach knowledge, to discern between astronomy and astrology, chemistry and alchemy, history and legend, philosophy and myth, there are needed the further activities of reflection, doubting, marshalling and weighing the evidence, and judging, Finally, this process of judging, in an important because clear instance, is like scientific verification, not as verification is imagined by the naive to be a matter of looking, peering, intuiting, but as verification in fact is found to be, namely, a cumulative convergence of direct and indirect confirmations any one of which by itself settles just nothing.

I quite agree, then, that our concepts are in principle unable to make known to us the actual existence of God. I would add that they are in principle unable to make known to us the actual existence of anything. For concepts are just thinking; thinking is not knowing; it is only when we reach judgment that we attain human knowledge of anything whatever, whether of essence or existence, whether of creature or Creator.

There is, however, a further point; for Dewart asserts an unbridgeable difference between the way in God is in himself and the way in which he is in our knowledge. This, of course, while absolutely possible, is not possibly known within our knowledge, and so the reader may wonder how Dewart got it into his knowledge. The fallacy seems to be Dewart's confusion of thinking and knowing. In our thinking we may distinguish a concept of divine existence from a concept of divine essence. In our knowing we may affirm (1) that we think in the above manner and (2) that there is no distinction between the reality of the divine essence and the reality of the divine existence. The contrast is, then, not between God in Himself and God in our knowledge, but between God in our knowledge and God in our thinking. Nor is there anything unbridgeable about this contrast or difference; for the thinking and judging occur within one and the same mind, and the whole function of our judging may be described as determining how much of our thinking is correct.

But let me conclude. On the dust cover of *The Future of Belief* Harvey Cox is credited with the opinion: "A mature, highly erudite, and utterly radical book. It could be epoch-making." If for my part I have made certain reservations about the first two epithets, I must express the hope that the book will be epoch-making in the sense that it will contribute forcefully to the removal from theology of the many limitations of Hellenism. To that topic I shall in due time return.

THEORIES OF INQUIRY: RESPONSES TO A SYMPOSIUM[1]

I am extremely grateful to the chairman, Fr. Nash, and to the three contributors for their interest in my work and, no doubt, I can express this best by attempting to answer the questions they have raised. I shall begin with the series Professor Reck has listed at the end of his paper and then go on to Professor Novak's and Father Burrell's.

Response to Professor Reck

Insight and Inquiry: How specifically are insight and inquiry related?

I think it will be helpful to draw a distinction, at least for present purposes, between inquiry and investigation. By investigation I would mean the process that is initiated in the subject by intellectual wonder or curiosity, that methodically seeks, accumulates, classifies possibly relevant data, that gradually through successive insights grows in understanding and so formulates hypotheses that are expanded by their logical presuppositions and implications to be tested by further observation and perhaps experiment.

Within this process there occur both insight and inquiry, with

[1] Responses to questions raised in a symposium on "Bernard Lonergan's Theory of Inquiry vis-à-vis American Thought," held at the University of Notre Dame, Indiana, as part of the American Catholic Philosophical Association's annual convention, March 28–29, 1967. Participants in the symposium were Rev. Peter W. Nash, S. J., Campion College, Chairman; Prof. Michael Novak, Stanford University; Prof. Andrew J. Reck, Tulane University; Rev. David B. Burrell, C.S.C., University of Notre Dame. Excerpted from *Proceedings of the American Catholic Philosophical Association*, 41 (1967). © 1967 by American Catholic Philosophical Association.

insight responding to inquiry, and further insight to further inquiry. Inquiry is the active principle. It takes one beyond whatever is given, perceived, known, ascertained. It does so, not by perceiving or knowing anything more, but simply by intending something more. What it intends is an unknown. By the intending it becomes a to-be-known. An unknown that is to be known may be named. In algebra it is named "x"; in physics it will be some indeterminate function such as "F $(X, Y, Z, T) =$ O"; in common English usage it is named "nature"; so we may speak of the nature of light or the nature of life, not because we know these natures, but because we name what we would know if we understood light or life.

Now this intending is also a striving, a tending, and its immediate goal is insight. When insight occurs, the immediate goal is reached, and so the striving for insight, the tending to insight, ceases or, perhaps better, it is transformed. It becomes a striving to formulate, to express in concepts and in words, what has been grasped by the insight. Once this is achieved, it is again transformed. It becomes a striving to determine whether or not the insight is correct.

Inquiry, then, and insight both occur within the larger process that is learning or investigating. Inquiry is the dynamic principle that gradually assembles all the elements in the compound that is human knowing. Among these elements insight is the most central. Like the others, insight too responds to inquiry. But it is not the total response.

May I add a final word on definition? All defining presupposes undefined terms and relations. In the book *Insight* the undefined terms are cognitional operations and the undefined relations are the dynamic relations that bind cognitional operations together. Both the operations and their dynamic relations are given in immediate internal experience, and the main purpose of the book is to help the reader to discover these operations and their dynamic relations in his own personal experience.

Pattern(s) of inquiry: *Is there one valid pattern of inquiry or several patterns? If one, what are its stages? If several, what have they in common?*

The question regards what, no doubt arbitrarily, I have wished to name, not inquiry, but investigation.

I should say that if one considers simply the cognitional operations and prescinds from the objects under investigation, then there is just a single pattern of investigation. This pattern relates different kinds of operations on different levels: so on a first level there are experiencing, imagining, saying; on a second there are inquiry, understanding, defining or conceiving; on a third there are reflection, weighing the evidence, judging. In general, the second level presupposes the first, and the third presupposes the second. But this is not to be thought to preclude any amount of traffic back and forth.

However, when one considers not simply the operations and their internal relations but also the various classes of objects to which they may be applied, there begin the differentiation of methods and the variety of types of investigation. In this variety, however, I think that the basic pattern remains, though now it occurs over and over within higher and more complex patterns.

Eros of the Mind: *In view of the scientific evidence concerning the biological basis of thought, how can the conception of the Eros of the mind be justified?*

The biological basis of thought, I should say, is like the rubber-tire basis of the motor car. It conditions and sets limits to functioning, but under the conditions and within the limits the driver directs operations.

Sensitive operations are immanent in sense organs. The sensation may be simply experiencing the organ, but again it may not. Visual experience is experiencing not our eyeballs but more or less distant colors and shapes. Again, inquiry is about all experience, whether of our own bodies or of the objects we see, hear, touch, taste, smell. What is true of inquiry, also is true of understanding and judgment. They are concerned not only with the biological but also with the physical, the chemical, the psychic, the human. Nor was it because Einstein differed biologically from Newton that he proposed Special Relativity. Nor does biological variation account for the existence of the Quantum theorists.

This is recognized in the very question. For the question affirms the biological basis of thought, not because of some biological basis in the questioner, but because of scientific evidence on the matter. But there is a demand for evidence on this matter and on any other matter, only if there exists and functions the Eros of the mind. Similarly the evidence is accumulated, evaluated, accepted or rejected, precisely in virtue of the Eros of the mind.

It is true that biological factors can interfere with the Eros of the mind, but to admit that fact is simply to acknowledge one of the many ways in which men happen to err. On the other hand, to claim that all mental operations are controlled by biological factors is the self-destructive claim that all claims are erroneous.

Subjectiveness of Insights: Is not the insight, signalized by a silent or expressed cry of Eureka, too subjective, too personal? How are we to know that is is not uttered by lesser men to hail mental aberrations and fantasies? Are we not required to employ some social and experimental method to avoid self-deception?

Certainly, insights are a dime a dozen. Any insight, by itself, is quite inadequate. Only the cumulative fruit of the self-correcting process of learning is significant. The really brilliant idea, the stroke of genius, seems to be simply the occurrence of a final insight that closes a long, slowly acquired, interlocking series of insights.

Not only must insights be very numerous but also they alone never constitute human knowledge. They presuppose experience. They must be subjected to testing and judgment. Such testing varies with the matter in hand. Chapter ten of *Insight* treats various kinds of judgments. Chapter eleven is devoted to a single basic judgment.

Inquiry and Philosophical System(s): In view of the incessant strife of speculative systems, does not the Eros of the mind seem a very fickle love? How can the neo-Thomist system be deemed the sole valid conclusion to which inquiry leads? Does not the fact that Father Lonergan's allegiance to neo-Thomism preceded the formulation of the cognitional theory heighten the suspicion that the conclusion desired determined the method propounded? Or can Father Lonergan's theory of inquiry properly validate other systems of philosophy?

Might I begin with a remark on the designation "speculative systems"? I should say that all human knowledge proceeds from data, and, in that sense, all human knowledge is empirical. I should add, however, that besides the data of sense there are the data of consciousness, and, among the latter, the data on our cognitional activities hold a privileged position. This position is privileged in the sense that such data provide empirical grounds for passing judgment on all human claims to knowledge.

Next, with regard to the claims of the neo-Thomist system, the procedure followed in *Insight* was to treat three linked questions: What am I doing when I am knowing? Why is doing that knowing? What do I know when I do it? The first was the question of cognitional theory, the second the question of epistemology, the third the question of metaphysics. The answer to the first was to invite the reader to discover his own cognitional operations in the data of his own experience. The answer to the second was had from the answer to the first, and the answer to the third followed from the first and second. The claim to validity for the system was derived from the impossibility of revising the main features of the cognitional theory, and this impossibility rested on the fact that it was only by actuating these main features that revision could be attempted.

In the third place, while this analysis cannot show other, opposed systems to be true, it can explain in general terms how they arise. In our childhood before reaching the age of reason we work out our pragmatic criteria of reality, knowledge, and objectivity, when we learn to distinguish what is really so from the dreamt, the imagined, the story, from the sibling's joke, trick, fib. In later life we have learnt to proceed in a far more sophisticated fashion, but philosophic reflection has to sort out the two manners, to overcome regressive tendencies to childish feelings and ways, and to achieve the analytic task of disentangling the many components in human knowing and the different strands in its objectivity. A list of the different ways one can go wrong will provide, I believe, a thumbnail sketch of most of the main philosophical systems.

Finally, there is the question whether my prior allegiance to Thomism did not predetermine the results I reached. Now it is true that I spent a great deal of time in the study of St. Thomas and that I know I owe a great deal to him. I just add, however, that my interest in Aquinas came late. As a student in the philosophy course at Heythrop College[2] in the twenties, I shared the common view that held the manuals in little esteem, though I read J.B.W. Joseph's *Introduction to Logic* with great care and went through the main parts of Newman's *Grammar of Assent* six times. In the early thirties I began to delight in Plato, especially the early dialogues, and then went on to the early writings of Augustine. Only later in that decade, when studying theology, did I discover the point to the real distinction by concluding the *unicum esse* from the Incarnation and by relating Aquinas' notion of *esse* to Augustine's of *veritas*. Finally, it was in the forties that I began to study Aquinas on cognitional theory, and as soon as the *Verbum* articles were completed (*Theological Studies*, 1946–49), I began to write *Insight*.

---

[2] Former Jesuit seminary in Oxfordshire, England.

Response to Professor Novak

Professor Novak has given a subtly accurate account of my position on philosophic ethics. I quite agree (1) that, as I base metaphysics, so also I base ethics not on logically first propositions but on invariant structures of human knowing and human doing, (2) that this basis leaves room for a history and, indeed a development of morals, (3) that there is a concrete level of intelligibility reached by insight but missed when universal concepts are applied to particular instances, and (4) that such concrete intelligibility is relevant not only to science but also to conduct.

I have said, however, that Professor Novak's account was not just accurate but subtly accurate. The fact is that Professor Novak is an apostle as well as a scholar and I have the feeling that he is inviting or nudging or even perhaps pushing me a little farther than I have gone on my own initiative.

He attributes to me the rejection of an "objective code of ethics out there." This is quite true inasmuch as I reject naive realism and so reject the "out there" as a measure and standard of objectivity. It is quite true inasmuch as I reject an anti-intellectual conceptualism and so reject an anti-historical immobilism. It is quite true, further, that I do not base a code of conclusions upon a code of verbal propositions named first principles. It is quite true, again, that while I assigned invariant structures as the basis for the possibility of ethics, I did not proceed to work out a code from such a basis. It is quite true, finally, as Professor Novak contends, that the basis I offer in invariant structures provides foundations for personal ethical decision and for personal concern with the concrete good in concrete situations.

Now I am completely at one with Professor Novak in his concern for personal ethical decision about the concrete good. But I wish to forestall any misapprehension about my position. Though I did not in *Insight* feel called upon to work out a code of ethics, neither did I exclude such a code. On the contrary I drew a parallel between ethics and metaphysics. In metaphysics I not only assigned a basis in invariant structures but also derived from that basis a metaphysics with a marked family resemblance to traditional views. A similar family resemblance, I believe, would be found to exist between traditional ethics and an ethics that, like the metaphysics, was explicitly aware of itself as a system on the move.

Finally, with regard to the interpretation of St. Thomas, I had noted in my reading some of the points that Professor Novak has brought forward, but my study of this precise issue has not gone far enough for me to offer any pronouncement on the matter.

Response to Father Burrell

Father Burrell has given a most helpful account of my position and he has followed it up with a forcefully presented objection to an argument for the existence of God. The argument began: If the real is completely intelligible, God exists.

The objection is to the expression "completely intelligible." He grants that anything we know is known through its intelligibility, so that any reality we know must be intelligible. But he urges that we have no acquaintance with complete intelligibility; indeed, we cannot know it since knowing it would be enjoying an unrestricted infinite act of understanding. It follows that the minor premise must be mistaken. If we cannot know complete intelligibility, then we cannot know that the real is completely intelligible.

My answer would be that, besides knowing, there is intending. Whenever one asks a genuine question, one does not know the answer. Still, one does intend, desire, ask for the answer; one is able to tell when one gets an appropriate answer; and one is able to judge whether the appropriate answer is also correct. So between not knowing and knowing there is the process of coming to know. That process is intentional. It starts from experience but goes beyond it to understanding and judgment. Such going beyond is not blind. It is aware of itself as a going beyond the given, the incompletely known. This awareness consists in a conscious intending of an unknown that is to be known.

Now such intending has to be channelled and controlled. A fool can ask more questions than a wise man can answer. Even the wise man has to advert to the strategy that asks questions in a proper order, that selects the questions that can be answered now, that prefers the questions that once solved, lead to the solution of other questions.

Behind this need for control and planning is the fact that the intending is of itself unrestricted. Our libraries are too small, yet more books keep being published. Our numerous and vast research projects only open the way for further research. To answer questions only gives rise to still further questions, and there is no prospect of this stream drying up from lack of further questions.

Moreover, while questions can and must be criticized, they may not be arbitrarily brushed aside. Such arbitrary refusal is obscurantism, and to be an obscurantist is to cease to be an authentic human being.

It follows that our intending intends, not incomplete, but complete intelligibility. If it intended no more than an incomplete intelligibility, there would be a point where further questions could arise but did not, where the half-answer appeared not a half-answer but as much an answer as human intelligence could dream of seeking. If the dynamism of human intellect intended no more than incomplete intelligibility, the horizon not merely of human knowledge but also of possible human inquiry would be bounded. Whether or not there were anything beyond that horizon, would be a question that could not even arise.

It follows that to say that being is completely intelligible is not an idle empty phrase. It is true that we have no immediate knowledge of complete intelligibility, for we have no immediate knowledge of God. It remains that our intelligence, at its living

41

root, intends intelligibility but not incomplete intelligibility and so complete intelligibility. Further, since intending is just another name for meaning, it follows that complete intelligibility, so far from being meaningless to us, is in fact at the root of all our attempts to mean anything at all.

THE FUTURE OF THOMISM[1]

When the Very Reverend Donald Kraus[2] so kindly invited me to address you, I asked him what might be a suitable topic and he suggested, among others, the one I have chosen, The Future of Thomism. However, in accepting this task, despite the title which refers to the future, I am not presuming to don the mantle of a prophet and so I beg you to excuse me if I devote my time, first, to some account of the work of St. Thomas himself, secondly, to the Thomism developed to meet the needs of the classicist period and, thirdly, to the transpositions that are necessary for a contemporary Thomism to be viable. I am afraid that my treatment of these three topics can be no more than sketchy, but I venture to offer such outlines because, I feel, they suggest the appropriate orientation and attitudes, neither simply rejecting the past, nor on the other hand, I trust, falling short of the exigences of the present.

The Work of St. Thomas

The more vital and efficacious religious activity is, the more it infiltrates, penetrates, purifies, transforms a people's symbols and rituals, its language, art, and literature, its social order, its cultural superstructure of science and philosophy, history and theology. So the early Christian Church set about transforming the Greco-Roman world. So the medieval Church was a principal agent in

---

[1] A lecture delivered March 15, 1968 at St. Paul's Seminary, Pittsburgh, Pa. The lecture has not hitherto been published. © 1967 by Bernard J. F. Lonergan.
[2] Msgr. Donald W. Kraus, Director of the seminary.

the formation of medieval society and culture. So the Renaissance Church took over the forms of a classicist culture. So today in a world whence classicist culture has vanished, we have before us the task of understanding, assimilating, penetrating, transforming modern culture.

Precisely because this vast problem is ours, we are in an excellent position for appreciating the work of Aquinas. It is true enough that his work commonly is thought of as a theological synthesis or a philosophic synthesis. But besides being a theologian and philosopher St. Thomas was a man of his time meeting the challenge of his time. What he was concerned to do may be viewed as a theological or philosophical synthesis but, if considered more concretely, it turns out to be a mighty contribution towards the medieval cultural synthesis. As in our day, so too in his there was a feverish intellectual ferment. As in our day we are somewhat belatedly coming to grips with the implications of the modern sciences and philosophies and bringing our theology and Christian living up to date, so too in his day Western Christendom was being flooded with the then novel ideas of Greek and Arabic science and philosophy. As in our day there is a demand for an *aggiornamento* of our thinking, so in his there was a demand for an *aggiornamento* of earlier medieval thought. Such updating, of course, cannot be the work of a single man. St. Thomas had his forerunners, his collaborators, his disciples and followers. But the magnitude and brilliance of his achievement permit us to single him out as the example, the specimen, of what was going forward in his day, namely, discovering, working out, thinking through a new mould for the Catholic mind, a mould in which it could remain fully Catholic and yet be at home with all the good things that might be drawn from the cultural heritage of Greeks and Arabs.

This effort at cultural synthesis is most evident, perhaps, in the four books of the *Contra Gentiles*. Only in the fourth book, where he presents distinctively Christian doctrines on the Trinity, the

44

Incarnation, original sin, the sacraments, the resurrection of the body, hell fire, the general judgment, does he proceed deductively from Scripture and tradition. Even there he is careful to add the profound analogies that yield some imperfect understanding of the truths of faith and so save the dogmas from being formulae that must be repeated, though no one need understand them. But in the first three books deduction from Scripture and tradition generally is absent. There speaks the voice of Christian wisdom on God, on creation, on the distinction of creatures, on angels and men, on the last end, the beatific vision, divine providence and divine law, on sin and grace. It is a voice that constantly quotes Scripture, but it usually does so, not to posit a premiss from which conclusions are to be drawn, but to confirm a position for which many reasons already have been given, whether demonstrative reasons, when demonstration is possible, or *rationes convenientiae*, convergent probabilities, where human reason cannot demonstrate.

The goal at which Aquinas explicitly aimed in this work was the manifestation of Catholic truth and the exclusion of opposite errors. But it is obvious that he was showing his contemporaries that one could be a master of Greek and Arabic thought and yet use it to present Christian doctrine; that the presentation could extend over five hundred pages of fine print in double columns; that it could be always coherent, always up to the minute, always persuasive and, when the occasion permitted, even demonstrative. St. Thomas wrote against the Gentiles, but he used their own weapons, and used them so skilfully that he provided his age with a concrete instance in which essential features of Catholic truth and of Greek and Arabic culture were fused into a single organic whole.

What is conspicuous in the *Contra Gentiles*, is no less to be discerned in his other works. His commentaries on Aristotle not merely reveal his mastery of the text but also bring to light the manner in which Aristotle can be transposed from his Hellenic to a Christian context. His commentaries on Scripture are theological:

they express Scriptural doctrine in the categories of the theology he was doing so much to develop. The endless *quaestiones* raised in his work on Peter Lombard's *Sentences,* in his numerous *Quaestiones disputatae,* and in his *Summa theologiae* put him in the mainstream of medieval thought. For that stream was a stream of *quaestiones.* Peter Abelard in his *Sic et Non* had taken over a technique of the canonists. He listed about one hundred and fifty-eight propositions and with respect to each he adduced authorities to prove from Scripture, from the fathers, or from reason both the affirmative and the negative. Gilbert of la Porrée had defined that a *quaestio* exists if and only if authorities and arguments can be adduced for both sides of a contradiction; so *quaestiones* traditionally began with a proof of their existence, with a *Videtur quod non* and a *Sed contra est.* Each question called for a statement of principles of solution and for the application of the principles to each of the authorities invoked. But a series of questions on a single topic, such as *De Veritate, De Potentia, De Malo,* demanded a coherent set of principles for all solutions on that topic, while a *Summa* needed a single coherent set relevant to every question that might be raised.

So it was that the development of medieval theology along the lines laid down by the technique of the *quaestio* created a need and an exigence for a coherent set of theoretical terms and relationships that would make possible coherent solutions to all the problems created by the apparent inconsistencies in Scripture and in tradition. This need was met in two steps. The first was to take over Aristotle's organized knowledge of this world. The second was to distinguish between the natural and the supernatural and to conceive the supernatural on the analogy of the naturally known.

I have been endeavoring to depict the work of St. Thomas in its historical setting. It was concerned to carry forward the vast task, initiated over a century previously, of organizing coherently all the date from Scripture and tradition. Because it was an organizing of data, of an enormous array of data, it had a marked empirical character; there were no *quaestiones* unless there was established a conflict between authorities or between authority and reason. On the other hand, the task was not merely empirical; there was sought a coherent organization, and this could be achieved only by the exercise that took the form of taking over Aristotle for things natural and extending Aristotle analogously for things supernatural. Finally, this solution not only enabled theology to attain the goal of *intelligentia fidei* but also enabled medieval culture to maintain its identity while taking over the products of Greek and Arabic culture.

Classical Thomism

Classical Thomism prided itself on its fidelity to St. Thomas. It met new questions by extending medieval solutions, and it could do so all the more confidently because of its classicist presuppositions. Truth is immutable. Human nature does not change. God has revealed Himself once for all in Christ Jesus. It is true enough that times change and that circumstances alter cases. But all that change is accidental. The same eternal principles are equally valid and equally applicable despite the flux of accidental differences.

Along with other Scholastic schools, Thomism cultivated logic. It distinguished different meanings of the same term, and it defined each meaning. It reduced propositions to their presuppositions and worked out their implications. With meanings fixed by definitions, with presuppositions and implications fixed by the laws of logic, there resulted what used to be called eternal verities but today are known as static abstractions.

It derived its notion of science from Aristotle's *Posterior Analytics*. There is science properly so called, and there is science in some weaker, analogous sense. Properly so called, science consists in the conclusions that follow necessarily from self-evident, necessary principles. In some weaker, analogous sense, science consists in conclusions that follow not necessarily but probably; or its principles may be necessary without being evident to us; or they be not even necessary but only what is fitting, convenient, suitable.

Thomism had much to say on the metaphysics of the soul, but it was little given to psychological introspection to gain knowledge of the subject. Behind this fact there did not lie any neglect of introspection on the part of Aristotle and Aquinas; I believe they hit things off much too accurately for that to be true. The difficulty was, I think, that while Aristotle did practise introspection, his works contain no account of introspective method. In his *De anima* Aristotle employed one and the same method for the study of plants, animals, and men. One was to know acts by their objects, habits by acts, potencies by habits, and the essences of souls by their potencies. The procedure was purely objective, and made no explicit mention of direct introspection of acts and of their subjects.

Human nature was studied extensively in a metaphysical psychology, in an enormous and subtle catalogue of virtues and vices, in its native capacities and proneness to evil, in the laws natural, divine, and human to which it was subject, in the great things it could accomplish by God's grace. But such study was not part of some ongoing process; everything essential had been said long ago; the only urgent task was to find the telling mode of expression and illustration that would communicate to the uneducated of today the wisdom of the great men of the past. As the study of man was static, so, too, man was conceived in static fashion. There was no notion that man had existed on earth for hundreds of thousands of years; or that there had been, and still was going forward, an ascent from crude primitive cultures, through the ancient high civilizations, to the effective emergence of critical intelligence in the first millennium B.C., and to the triumph of scientific intelligence in the last few centuries.

Finally, classical Thomism stressed first principles. It did not undertake to give an exhaustive list of all first principles, each of them defined with complete accuracy. But its commitment to logic and to the Aristotelian notion of science was such that to deny first principles was to involve oneself in skepticism, while to ignore them was to condemn oneself to superficiality.

Thomism for Tomorrow

A Thomism for tomorrow will involve, in my opinion, first a shift from the emphases of classical Thomism and, secondly, a revision of the results obtained by medieval theology.

To begin from the second point, the technique of the *quaestio* aimed at a logically coherent reconciliation of conflicting authorities. It met the demands of human intelligence seeking some understanding of its faith, and it did so in the grand manner. But its scrutiny of the data presented by Scripture and tradition was quite insufficient. On the whole it was unaware of history: of the fact that every act of meaning is embedded in a context, and that over time contexts change subtly, slowly, surely. A contemporary theology must take and has taken the fact of history into account. Inasmuch as it does so, St. Thomas ceases to be the arbiter to whom all can appeal for the solution of contemporary questions; for, by and large, contemporary questions are not the same as the questions he treated, and the contemporary context is not the context in which he treated them. But he remains a magnificent and venerable figure in the history of Catholic thought. He stands before us as a model, inviting us to do for our age what he did for his. And, if I may express a personal opinion of my own, a mature Catholic theology of the twentieth century will not ignore him; it will learn very, very much from him; and it will be aware of its debt to him, even when it is effecting its boldest transpositions from the thirteenth century to the twentieth.

What are such transpositions? I have prepared my answer to that question by my list of five emphases of classical Thomism. A

49

Thomism for tomorrow has to move from logic to method; from science as conceived in the *Posterior Analytics* to science as it is conceived today; from the metaphysics of the soul to the self-appropriation of the subject; from an apprehension of man in terms of human nature to an apprehension of man through human history; and from first principles to transcendental method. Before considering these transitions singly, let me remark in general that they are not exclusive; a transition from logic to method does not drop logic, and similarly in most of the other cases.

First, then, from logic to method. Today we frequently hear complaints about metaphysics as static. But what is static is not metaphysics as such but a logically rigorous metaphysics. Indeed, anything that is logically rigorous is static. Defined terms are abstract and abstractions are immobile. Presuppositions and implications, if rigorous, cannot shift a single iota. Logic embodies an ideal of clarity, coherence, and rigor. It is an ideal that we must ever pursue, but the pursuit is a matter not of logic but of method. A method is a normative pattern of related and recurrent operations. There are operations: for instance, to take the simplest example, in natural science there are observing, describing, defining problems, making discoveries, formulating hypotheses, working out their presuppositions and implications, devising experiments, testing hypotheses by experiments, determining whether the hypothesis so far is satisfactory or already is unsatisfactory, and so proceeding to new questions or to a revision of the hypothesis already made. All such operations are related, for each leads to the next. They are recurrent, for they form a circle that is repeated over and over and cumulatively extends the mastery of human intelligence over ever broader fields of data. The pattern of such related and recurrent operations is normative, for that is the right way to do the job. Finally, while this pattern includes all logical operations, it also includes many operations that lie outside a formal logic, such as observing, discovering, experimenting, verifying.

Secondly, from the conception of science in the *Posterior Analytics* to the modern conception of a science. On point after point the two conceptions are opposed. In the Aristotelian notion necessity was a key category; in modern science it is marginal; it has been replaced by verifiable possibility. For the Aristotelian, science is certain; for the modern, science is no more than probable, the best available scientific opinion. For the Aristotelian, causality was material, formal, efficient, exemplary, or final; for the modern, causality is correlation. For the Aristotelian, a science was a habit in the mind of an individual; for the modern, science is knowledge divided up among the scientific community; no one knows the whole of modern mathematics, of modern physics, of modern chemistry, or modern biology, and so on.

Thirdly, from soul to subject. I do not mean that the metaphysical notion of the soul and of its properties is to be dropped, any more than I mean that logic is to be dropped. But I urge the necessity of a self-appropriation of the subject, of coming to know at first hand oneself and one's own operations both as a believer and as a theologian. It is there that one will find the foundations of method, there that one will find the invariants that enable one to steer a steady course, though theological theories and opinions are subject to revision and change. Without such a basis systematic theology will remain what it has been too often in the past, a morass of questions disputed endlessly and fruitlessly.

Fourthly, from human nature to human history. The point here is that meaning is constitutive of human living. Just as words without sense are gibberish, so human living uninformed by human meaning is infantile. Next, not only is meaning constitutive of human living but also it is subject to change; cultures develop and cultures decline; meaning flowers and meaning becomes decadent. Finally, Christianity is an historical religion; it is a statement of the meaning of human living; it is a redeeming statement that cures decadence and fosters growth.

Fifthly, from first principles to transcendental method. First principles, logically first propositions, are the foundations for a mode of thought that is inspired by logic, by necessity, by objectivity, by nature. But the contemporary context, the tasks and problems of a theology that would deal with the issues of today, call for method, verified possibility, full awareness of the subject, and a thorough grasp of man's historicity. Its foundations lie, not in abstract propositions called first principles, but in the structural invariants of the concrete human subject. When the natural and the human sciences are on the move, when the social order is developing, when the everyday dimensions of culture are changing, what is needed is not a dam to block the stream but control of the river-bed through which the stream must flow. In modern science, what is fixed is not the theory or system but the method that keeps generating, improving, replacing theories and systems. Transcendental method is the assault on the citadel: it is possession of the basic method, and all other methods are just so many extensions and adaptations of it.

Finally, let me note that, when such transpositions are effected, theology will be more strictly theology than it has been. The development of method makes an academic discipline stick to its own business. Religion is one thing, and theology is another. Religion is necessary for salvation and theology is not. It is the office of the bishop to teach religious truth. It is the task of the theologian to reflect on the religious fact, and it is the task of the Christian theologian to reflect on the Christian religious fact.

Conclusion

You may ask, however, whether after the introduction of the five transpositions just outlined there would be anything left of Thomism. And at once I must grant that the five emphases I attributed to classical Thomism would disappear. One may doubt, however, whether such emphases are essential to the thought of St. Thomas or of the great Thomists.

St. Thomas practised a method, the method of the *quaestio*. The great Thomists practised a method, the method of the commentary.

St. Thomas accepted the Aristotelian ideal of science, but he restricted a theology in accord with that ideal to the mind of God and the minds of the blessed in Heaven. His theology was content, not to demonstrate, but to show how the mysteries of faith might be manifested.

St. Thomas treated of the soul at length, but he said enough about the subject for me to be able to write my *Verbum* articles.

St. Thomas did not have the modern concern for history and for man's historicity. But St. Thomas was an extraordinarily erudite person, and if one wishes to evade history and historicity, one wishes to live in a world that no longer exists.

Finally, while Aristotle and St. Thomas did not elaborate a transcendental method, they understood its point. This may be illustrated by Aristotle's advice for dealing with skeptics, namely, get them to talk; and by St. Thomas's argument against Averroës: Averroës's position implied the conclusion that *this man does not understand* and St. Thomas concluded that therefore *this man was not to be listened to.*

has to be interpreted in the light of contemporary techniques and procedures. Where before the step from premisses to conclusions was brief, simple, and certain, today the steps from data to interpretation are long, arduous, and, at best, probable. An empirical science does not demonstrate. It accumulates information, develops understanding, masters ever more of its materials, but it does not preclude the uncovering of further relevant data, the emergence of new insights, the attainment of a more comprehensive view.

Secondly, this shift from a deductivist to an empirical approach has come to stay. One has only to glance at the bibliographies in *Biblica*, in Altaner's *Patrologie*, in the *Bulletin de théologie ancienne et médiévale*, and in *Ephemerides theologicae lovanienses*, to become aware of the massive commitment of contemporary Catholic thought to an empirical approach. But to understand this movement, to grasp the reasons for it, one must do more than glance at bibliographies; one has to get down to reading the books. Then one gradually discovers that the old dogmatic theology had misconceived history on a classicist model, that it thought not in terms of evolution and development, but of universality and permanence. Vincent of Lérins had proclaimed God's truth to be *quod semper, quod ubique, quod ab omnibus*,[7] and such a view was still quite congenial in the *grand siècle* of French literature.[8] On such assumptions it was quite legitimate to expect the theologian, if only he knew the faith of today, to be equally at home in the Old and New Testaments, in the Greek and Latin Fathers, in the writings of medieval, Renaissance, and more recent theologians. But today such an assumption appears fantastic and preposterous. In almost endless studies the writings of age after age have been examined minutely, and all along the line the notion of fixity has had to give way to the fact of development. Moreover, develop-

---

[7] *Commonitorium*, II, Cambridge, 1915, p. 10.
[8] See Owen Chadwick, *From Bossuet to Newman: The Idea of Doctrinal Development*: Cambridge, 1957, pp. 17 ff.

ment is complex, intricate, manifold. Its precise character at any time can be ascertained only through detailed studies of the resources, the problems, the tendencies, and the accidents of the time. Where once the dogmatic theologian was supposed to range over centuries, now Scripture, patristics, medieval and modern studies are divided and subdivided among classes of specialists. Where once the dogmatic theologian could lay down an overall view that echoed the conciliar *tenet atque semper tenuit sancta mater Ecclesia,* now an overall view tends to be either a tentative summary of the present state of research, or a popular simplification of issues that are really not simple at all.

Thirdly, while theology has become largely empirical in its method, it has invoked a new vocabulary, new imagery, new concepts to express its thought. The Aristotelian analyses, concepts, words, that in the Middle Ages became part of the Catholic patrimony to resist both Renaissance scoffing and Protestant condemnation, almost suddenly in the twentieth century have gone out of fashion. With equal rapidity the vacuum is being refilled with biblical words and images, and with ideas worked out by historicist, personalist, phenomenological, and existential reflection. There is so much new in Catholic speculative theology that Karl Rahner felt the need to issue a *Theological Dictionary*[9] and Heinrich Fries organized over one hundred experts to collaborate and produce a two volume *Handbuch theologischer Grundbegriffe.*[10]

As the empirical approach, so too I believe, the new conceptual apparatus has come to stay. Religion is concerned with man's relations to God and to his fellow man, so that any deepening or enriching of our apprehension of man possesses religious significance and relevance. But the new conceptual apparatus does make available such a deepening and enriching. Without denying human nature, it adds the quite distinctive categories of

[9] New York, 1965.
[10] Munich, 1962 and 1963.

THEOLOGY IN ITS NEW CONTEXT

man as an historical being. Without repudiating the analysis of man into body and soul, it adds the richer and more concrete apprehension of man as incarnate subject.

It would be far more than can be attempted within the limits of the present paper to attempt to communicate what precisely is meant by the contrast between nature and history or what is added to the couple, body and soul, by the phrase "incarnate subject." Summarily, very summarily, I may perhaps say that such terms refer to a dimension of human reality that has always existed, that has always been lived and experienced, that classicist thought standardized yet tended to overlook, that modern studies have brought to light, thematized, elaborated, illustrated, documented. That dimension is the constitutive role of meaning in human living. It is the fact that acts of meaning inform human living, that such acts proceed from a free and responsible subject incarnate, that meanings differ from nation to nation, from culture to culture, and that, over time, they develop and go astray. Besides the meanings by which man apprehends nature and the meanings by which he transforms it, there are the meanings by which man thinks out the possibilities of his own living and makes his choice among them. In this realm of freedom and creativity, of solidarity and responsibility, of dazzling achievement and pitiable madness, there ever occurs man's making of man.

The wealth, the complexity, the profundity of this modern apprehension of man might be illustrated by pointing to its implications for philosophy, for human science, for art and literature, for education and psychiatry. But what must be mentioned is its significance for the notion of divine revelation. God becomes known to us in two ways: as the ground and end of the material universe; and as the one who speaks to us through Scripture and Tradition. The first manner might found a natural religion. The second adds revealed religion. For the first, one might say that the heavens show forth the glory of God; what can mere words add? But for the second, one must answer that, however

61

trifling the uses to which words may be put, still they are the vehicles of meaning, and meaning is the stuff of man's making of man. So it is that a divine revelation is God's entry and his taking part in man's making of man. It is God's claim to have a say in the aims and purposes, the direction and development of human lives, human societies, human cultures, human history.

From this significance for revealed religion there follows a significance for theology. In the medieval period theology became the queen of the sciences. But in the practice of Aquinas it was also the principle for the moulding and transforming of a culture. He was not content to write his systematic works, his commentaries on Scripture and on such Christian writers as the Pseudo-Dionysius and Boethius. At a time when Arabic and Greek thought were penetrating the whole of Western culture, he wrote extensive commentaries on numerous works of Aristotle to fit a pagan's science within a Christian context and to construct a world view that underpinned Dante's *Divine Comedy*. To this paradigm theology today must look if it is to achieve its *aggiornamento*. Its task is not limited to investigating, ordering, expounding, communicating divine revelation. All that is needed, but more must be done. For revelation is God's entry into man's making of man, and so theology not only has to reflect on revelation, but also it has somehow to mediate God's meaning into the whole of human affairs. It is not a small task, but because it is not—in a culture in which God is ignored and there are even theologians to proclaim that God is dead—it is all the more urgent.

My reflections have come full circle. Not only does the cultural context influence theology to undo its past achievements, but theology is also called upon to influence the cultural context, to translate the word of God and so project it into new mentalities and new situations. So a contemporary Catholic theology has to be not only Catholic but also ecumenist. Its concern must reach not only Christians but also non-Christians and atheists. It has to learn to draw not only on the modern philosophies but also on the relatively new sciences of religion, psychology, sociology, and the new techniques of the communication arts.

I have been speaking of our renewed theology and now I must add that a renewed theology needs a renewed foundation. The old foundation will no longer do. But we cannot get along with no foundation at all. So a new foundation and, I should say, a new type of foundation is needed to replace the old.

First, some foundation is needed. If change is to be improvement, if new tasks are to be accomplished fruitfully, discernment is needed and discrimination. If we are to draw on contemporary psychology and sociology, if we are to profit from the modern science of religions, if we are to revise scholastic categories and make our own the concepts worked out in historicist, personalist, phenomenological, or existentialist circles, then we must be able to distinguish tinsel and silver, gilt and gold. No less important than a critique of notions and conclusions is a critique of methods. The new largely empirical approach to theology can too easily be made into a device for reducing doctrines to probable opinions. A hermeneutics can pretend to philosophic neutrality yet force the conclusion that the content of revelation is mostly myth. Scientific history can be so conceived that a study of the narrative of salvation will strip it of matters of fact. If our renewed theology is not to be the dupe of every fashion, it needs a firm basis and a critical stance.

Secondly, the old foundations will no longer do. In saying this I do not mean that they are no longer true, for they are as true now as they ever were. I mean that they are no longer appropriate. I am simply recalling that one must not patch an old cloak with new cloth or put new wine in old wineskins. One type of foundation suits a theology that aims at being deductive, static, abstract, universal, equally applicable to all places and to all times. A quite different foundation is needed when theology turns from deductivism to an empirical approach, from the static to the dynamic, from the abstract to the concrete, from the universal to the historical totality of particulars, from invariable rules to intelligent adjustment and adaptation.

Thirdly, I shall no doubt be asked to give some indication of the nature or character of the new foundation. To this topic I have elsewhere given considerable attention, first, to assure historical continuity, in a study of cognitional theory in the writings of St. Thomas,[11] then in a study of contemporary development entitled *Insight*,[12] to take into account the fact of modern science and the problems of modern philosophy. On the present occasion I may be permitted, perhaps, to offer no more than a few brief approximations.

As a first approximation, to be corrected and complemented shortly by further approximations, let us consider the foundation of a modern science. It does not consist in any part of the science itself, in any of its conclusions, in any of its laws, in any of its principles. All of these are open to revision, and it is in the light of the foundation that the revision would take place. What, then, is the foundation? It is the method that will generate the revision of conclusions, laws, principles that are accepted today. It is the method that will generate the revision of conclusions, laws, principles of tomorrow. What the scientist relies on ultimately is his method.

Now one might be inclined to think of method as a set of verbal propositions enouncing rules to be followed in a scientific investigation and, of course, it is true that there are the hodmen of science who carry out the routines prescribed to them by those who understand the purpose of an investigation and the manner in which it might advance scientific knowledge. But I wish here to use the word "method" to denote not the prescriptions given the

---

[11] Originally published in *Theological Studies* (1946–1949), and recently revised and reissued by David Burrell, C.S.C., under the title *Verbum, Word and Idea in Aquinas*, Notre Dame, 1967, and London, 1968.

[12] *Insight. A Study of Human Understanding*, London and New York, 1957.

hodmen, but the grounds that governed the prescribing. Such grounds, though perfectly familiar to the director, usually are not objectified or verbalized by him. Indeed, he cannot achieve such objectification with any accuracy, unless he is ready to devote as much time and effort to cognitional theory as he has already devoted to his physics, or chemistry, or biology. This does not happen. But, were it to happen, there would result the account of a normative pattern that related to one another the cognitional operations that recur in scientific investigations. There would be listed, described, illustrated, compared such operations as inquiring, observing, describing, problem defining, discovering, forming hypotheses, working out presuppositions and implications, devising series of experiments, performing them, and verifying. The greatest stress would be placed on the importance of personal experience of the operations, of identifying them within one's experience, and of finding within that experience not only the operations, but also the dynamic and normative relations that bind them to one another. In this fashion, you will agree, the subject as scientist would come to know himself as scientist. But the subject as scientist is the reality that is principle and foundation of science, of science as it has been, of science as it is, of science as it will be.

So much for our first approximation. It illustrates by an example what might be meant by a foundation that lies not in a set of verbal propositions named first principles, but in a particular, concrete, dynamic reality generating knowledge of particular, concrete, dynamic realities. It remains that we have to effect the transition from natural science to theology, and so we turn to our second approximation.

Fundamental to religous living is conversion. It is a topic little studied in traditional theology since there remains very little of it when one reaches the universal, the abstract, the static. For conversion occurs in the lives of individuals. It is not merely a change or even a development; rather, it is a radical transformation on which follows, on all levels of living, an interlocked series of changes and developments. What hitherto was unnoticed becomes vivid and present. What had been of no concern becomes a matter of high import. So great a change in one's apprehensions and one's values accompanies no less a change in oneself, in one's relations to other persons, and in one's relations to God.

Not all conversion is as total as the one I have so summarily described. Conversion has many dimensions. A changed relation to God brings or follows changes that are personal, social, moral and intellectual. But there is no fixed rule of antecedence and consequence, no necessity of simultaneity, no prescribed magnitudes of change. Conversion may be compacted into the moment of a blinded Saul falling from his horse on the way to Damascus. It may be extended over the slow maturing process of a lifetime. It may satisfy an intermediate measure.

In a current expression, conversion is ontic. The convert apprehends differently, values differently, relates differently because he has become different. The new apprehension is not so much a new statement or a new set of statements, but rather new meanings that attach to almost any statement. It is not new values so much as a transvaluation of values. In Pauline language, "When anyone is united to Christ, there is a new world; the old order has gone, and a new order has begun" (2 Cor. 5: 17).

Though conversion is intensely personal, utterly intimate, still it is not so private as to be solitary. It can happen to many and they can form a community to sustain one another in their self-transformation, and to help one another in working out the implications, and in fulfilling the promise of their new life. Finally, what can become communal can become historical. It can pass from generation to generation. It can spread from one cultural milieu to another. It can adapt to changing circumstance, confront new situations, survive into a different age, flourish in another period or epoch.

When conversion is viewed as an ongoing process, at once

66

personal, communal, and historical, it coincides with living religion. For religion is conversion in its preparation, in its occurrence, in its development, in its consequents, and also, alas, in its incompleteness, its failures, its breakdowns, its disintegration.

Now theology, and especially the empirical theology of today, is reflection on religion. It follows that theology will be reflection on conversion. But conversion is fundamental to religion. It follows that reflection on conversion can supply theology with its foundation and, indeed, with a foundation that is concrete, dynamic, personal, communal, and historical. Just as reflection on the operations of the scientist brings to light the real foundation of the science, so too reflection on the ongoing process of conversion may bring to light the real foundation of a renewed theology.

I met the question of theological renewal, of its *aggiornamento*, by asking how far we are behind the times. I went back three centuries, for it was then that dogmatic theology had its beginnings, and it has been towards a total transformation of dogmatic theology that the developments of this century have worked. A normative structure that was deductivist has become empirical. A conceptual apparatus that at times clung pathetically to the past is yielding place to historicist, personalist, phenomenological, and existentialist notions.

I have urged that so great a transformation needs a renewed foundation, and that the needed renewal is the introduction of a new type of foundation. It is to consist not in objective statement, but in subjective reality. The objective statements of a *de vera religione, de Christo legato, de ecclesia, de inspiratione scripturae, de locis theologicis*, are as much in need of a foundation as are those of other tracts. But behind all statements is the stating subject. What is normative and foundational for subjects stating theology is to be found, I have suggested, in reflection on conversion, where conversion is taken as an ongoing process, concrete and dynamic, personal, communal, and historical.

THE SUBJECT[1]

There is a sense in which it may be said that each of us lives in a world of his own. That world usually is a bounded world, and its boundary is fixed by the range of our interests and our knowledge. There are things that exist, that are known to other men, but about them I know nothing at all. There are objects of interest that concern other men, but about them I could not care less. So the extent of our knowledge and the reach of our interests fix a horizon. Within that horizon we are confined.

Such confinement may result from the historical tradition within which we are born, from the limitations of the social milieu in which we were brought up, from our individual psychological aptitudes, efforts, misadventures. But besides specifically historical, social, and psychological determinants of subjects and their horizons, there also are philosophic factors, and to a consideration of such factors the present occasion invites us.

The Neglected Subject

In contemporary philosophy there is a great emphasis on the subject, and this emphasis may easily be traced to the influence of

[1] The Aquinas Lecture for 1968, under the sponsorship of the Wisconsin-Alpha Chapter of Phi Sigma Tau, the National Honor Society for Philosophy at Marquette University. Delivered March 3, 1968 in the Peter A. Brooks Memorial Union. © 1968 by Wisconsin-Alpha Chapter of Phi Sigma Tau.

Hegel, Kierkegaard, Nietzsche, Heidegger, Buber.[2] This fact, however, points to a previous period of neglect, and it may not be amiss to advert to the causes of such neglect, if only to make sure that they are no longer operative in our own thinking.

A first cause, then, is the objectivity of truth. The criterion, I believe, by which we arrive at the truth is a virtually unconditioned.[3] But an unconditioned has no conditions. A subject may be needed to arrive at truth, but, once truth is attained, one is beyond the subject and one has reached a realm that is non-spatial, atemporal, impersonal. Whatever is true at any time or place, can be contradicted only by falsity. No one can gainsay it, unless he is mistaken and errs.

Such is the objectivity of truth. But do not be fascinated by it. Intentionally it is independent of the subject, but ontologically it resides only in the subject: *veritas formaliter est in solo iudicio*. Intentionally it goes completely beyond the subject, yet it does so only because ontologically the subject is capable of an intentional self-transcendence, of going beyond what he feels, what he imagines, what he thinks, what seems to him, to something utterly different, to what is so. Moreover, before the subject can attain the self-transcendence of truth, there is the slow and laborious process of conception, gestation, parturition. But teaching and learning, investigating, coming to understand,

---

[2] One should, perhaps, start from Kant's Copernican revolution, which brought the subject into technical prominence while making only minimal concessions to its reality. The subsequent movement then appears as a series of attempts to win for the subject acknowledgement of its full reality and its functions. For a careful survey of the movement and its ambiguities, see James Brown, *Subject and Object in Modern Theology*, New York: 1955.

[3] The formally unconditioned has no conditions whatever; it is God. The virtually unconditioned has conditions but they have been fulfilled. Such, I should say, is the cognitional counterpart of contingent being and, as well, a technical formulation of the ordinary criterion of true judgment, namely, sufficient evidence. See my book, *Insight*, London and New York, 1957, chapter ten, for more details.

marshalling and weighing the evidence, these are not independent of the subject, of times and places, of psychological, social, historical conditions. The fruit of truth must grow and mature on the tree of the subject, before it can be plucked and placed in its absolute realm.

It remains that one can be fascinated by the objectivity of truth, that one can so emphasize objective truth as to disregard or undermine the very conditions of its emergence and existence. In fact, if at the present time among Catholics there is discerned a widespread alienation from the dogmas of faith, this is not unconnected with a previous one-sidedness that so insisted on the objectivity of truth as to leave subjects and their needs out of account.

Symptomatic of such one-sidedness was the difficulty experienced by theologians from the days of Suarez, de Lugo, and Bañez, when confronted with the syllogism: What God has revealed is true. God has revealed the mysteries of faith. Therefore, the mysteries of faith are true.[4] There is, perhaps, no need for me to explain why this syllogism was embarrassing, for it implied that the mysteries of faith were demonstrable conclusions. But the point I wish to make is that the syllogism contains an unnoticed fallacy, and the fallacy turns on an exaggerated view of the objectivity of truth. If one recalls that truth exists formally only in judgments and that judgments exist only in the mind, then the fallacy is easily pinned down. What God reveals is a truth in the mind of God and in the minds of believers, but it is not a truth in the minds of nonbelievers; and to conclude that the mysteries of faith, are truths in the mind of God or in the minds of believers in no way suggests that the mysteries are demonstrable. But this simple way out seems to have been missed by the theologians. They seem to have thought of truth as so objective as

[4] See H. Lennerz, De Virtutibus Theologicis, Rome: Gregorian Press, 1947, pp. 98 f., 103, No. 196, 204. L. Billot, De Virtutibus Infusis, Rome, 1928, pp. 191ff, 313.

to get along without minds. Nor does such thinking seem to have been confined to theoretical accounts of the act of faith. The same insistence on objective truth and the same neglect of its subjective conditions informed the old catechetics, which the new catechetics is replacing, and the old censorship, which insisted on true propositions and little understood the need to respect the dynamics of the advance toward truth.

Another source of neglect of the subject is to be found remotely in the Aristotelian notion of science, propounded in the *Posterior Analytics*, and proximately in the rationalist notion of pure reason. When scientific and philosophic conclusions follow necessarily from premises that are self-evident, then the road to science and to philosophy is not straight and narrow but broad and easy. There is no need to be concerned with the subject. No matter who he is, no matter what his interests, almost no matter how cursory his attention, he can hardly fail to grasp what is self-evident and, having grasped it, he can hardly fail to draw conclusions that are necessary. On such assumptions everything is black or white. If one happens to have opinions, one will have to defend them as self-evident or demonstrable. If one begins to doubt, one is likely to end up a complete skeptic. There is no need for concern with the subject, for the maieutic art of a Socrates, for intellectual conversion, for open-mindedness, striving, humility, perseverance.

A third source of neglect of the subject is the metaphysical account of the soul. As plants and animals, so men have souls. As in plants and animals, so in men the soul is the first act of an organic body. Still the souls of plants differ essentially from the souls of animals, and the souls of both differ essentially from the souls of men. To discern these differences we must turn from the soul to its potencies, habits, acts, objects. Through the objects we know the acts, through the acts we know the habits, through the habits we know the potencies, and through the potencies we know the essence of soul. The study of the soul, then, is totally objective. One and the same method is applied to study of plants, animals, and men. The results are completely universal. We have souls whether we are awake or asleep, saints or sinners, geniuses or imbeciles.

The study of the subject is quite different, for it is the study of oneself inasmuch as one is conscious. It prescinds from the soul, its essence, its potencies, its habits, for none of these is given in consciousness. It attends to operations and to their centre and source which is the self. It discerns the different levels of consciousness, the consciousness of the dream, of the waking subject, of the intelligently inquiring subject, of the rationally reflecting subject, of the responsibly deliberating subject. It examines the different operations on the several levels and their relations to one another.

Subject and soul, then, are two quite different topics. To know one does not exclude the other in any way. But it very easily happens that the study of the soul leaves one with the feeling that one has no need to study the subject and, to that extent, leads to a neglect of the subject.[5]

The Truncated Subject

The neglected subject does not know himself. The truncated subject not only does not know himself but also is unaware of his ignorance and so, in one way or another, concludes that what he does not know does not exist. Commonly enough the palpable facts of sensation and speech are admitted. Commonly also there is recognized the difference between sleeping and waking. But if universal, daytime somnambulism is not upheld, behaviorists would pay no attention to the inner workings of the subject; logical positivists would confine meaning to sensible data and the structures of mathematical logic; pragmatists would divert our attention to action and results.

[5] For a contrast of Aristotle and Augustine and their relations to Aquinas, see the Introduction in my *Verbum, Word and Idea in Aquinas*, Notre Dame, 1967 and London, 1968. The same material appeared also in *Philippine Studies*, 13 (1965), 576–585, under the title "Subject and Soul."

But there are less gross procedures. One can accept an apparently reasonable rule of acknowledging what is certain and disregarding what is controverted. Almost inevitably this will lead to an oversight of insight. For it is easy enough to be certain about concepts; their existence can be inferred from linguistic usage and from scientific generality. But it is only by close attention to the data of consciousness that one can discover insights, acts of understanding with the triple role of responding to inquiry, grasping intelligible form in sensible representations, and grounding the formation of concepts. So complex a matter will never be noticed as long as the subject is neglected, and so there arises conceptualism: a strong affirmation of concepts, and a skeptical disregard of insights. As insights fulfil three functions, so conceptualism has three basic defects.

A first defect is an anti-historical immobilism. Human understanding develops and, as it develops, it expresses itself in ever more precise and accurate concepts, hypotheses, theories, systems. But conceptualism, as it disregards insight, so it cannot account for the development of concepts. Of themselves, concepts are immobile. They ever remain just what they are defined to mean. They are abstract and so stand outside the spatio-temporal world of change. What does change, is human understanding and, when understanding changes or develops, then defining changes or develops. So it is that, while concepts do not change on their own, still they are changed as the mind that forms them changes.

A second defect of conceptualism is an excessive abstractness. For the generalities of our knowledge are related to concrete reality in two distinct manners. There is the relation of the universal to the particular, of *man* to *this man*, of *circle* to *this circle*. There is also the far more important relation of the intelligible to the sensible, of the unity or pattern grasped by insight to the data in which the unity or pattern is grasped. Now this second relation, which parallels the relation of form to matter, is far more intimate than the first. The universal abstracts from the particular, but the

74

intelligibility, grasped by insight, is immanent in the sensible and, when the sensible datum, image, symbol, is removed, the insight vanishes. But conceptualism ignores human understanding and so it overlooks the concrete mode of understanding that grasps intelligibility in the sensible itself. It is confined to a world of abstract universals, and its only link with the concrete is the relation of universal to particular.

A third defect of conceptualism has to do with the notion of being. Conceptualists have no difficulty in discovering a concept of being, indeed, in finding it implicit in every positive concept. But they think of it as an abstraction, as the most abstract of all abstractions, least in connotation and greatest in denotation. In fact, the notion of being is not abstract but concrete. It intends everything about everything. It prescinds from nothing whatever. But to advert to this clearly and distinctly, one must note not only that concepts express acts of understanding but also that both acts of understanding and concepts respond to questions. The notion of being first appears in questioning. Being is the unknown that questioning intends to know, that answers partially reveal, that further questioning presses on to know more fully. The notion of being, then, is essentially dynamic, proleptic, an anticipation of the entirety, the concreteness, the totality, that we ever intend and since our knowledge is finite never reach.

The neglected subject, then, leads to the truncated subject, to the subject that does not know himself and so unduly impoverishes his account of human knowledge. He condemns himself to an anti-historical immobilism, to an excessively jejune conjunction between abstract concepts and sensible presentations, and to ignorance of the proleptic and utterly concrete character of the notion of being.

The Immanentist Subject

The subject is within but he does not remain totally within. His knowing involves an intentional self-transcendence. But while his knowing does so, he has to know his knowing to know that it does so. Such knowledge is denied the neglected and the truncated subject and so we come to the merely immanent subject.

The key to doctrines of immanence is an inadequate notion of objectivity. Human knowing is a compound of many operations of different kinds. It follows that the objectivity of human knowing is not some single uniform property but once more a compound of quite different properties found in quite different kinds of operation.[6] There is an experiential objectivity in the givenness of the data of sense and of the data of consciousness. But such experiential objectivity is not the one and only ingredient in the objectivity of human knowing. The process of inquiry, investigation, reflection, coming to judge is governed throughout by the exigences of human intelligence and human reasonableness; it is these exigences that, in part, are formulated in logics and methodologies; and they are in their own way no less decisive than experiential objectivity in the genesis and progress of human knowing. Finally, there is a third, terminal, or absolute type of objectivity, that comes to the fore when we judge, when we distinguish sharply between what we feel, what we imagine, what we think, what seems to be so and, on the other hand, what is so.

However, though these three components all function in the objectivity of adult human knowing, still it is one thing for them to function and it is quite another to become explicitly aware that they function. Such explicit awareness presupposes that one is not a truncated subject, aware indeed of his sensations and his speech, but aware of little more than that. Then, what is meant by "object" and "objective," is something to be settled not by an scrutiny of one's operations and their properties, but by picture-thinking. An object, for picture-thinking, has to be something one looks at; knowing it has to be something like looking, peering, seeing, intuiting, perceiving; and objectivity, finally,

[6] For a fuller statement, *Insight*, chapter thirteen, and for something more compendious, *Collection*, New York and London, 1967, pp. 227–231.

has to be a matter of seeing all that is there to be seen and nothing that is not there.

Once picture-thinking takes over, immanence is an inevitable consequence.[7] What is intended in questioning, is not seen, intuited, perceived; it is as yet unknown; it is what we do not know but seek to know. It follows that the intention of questioning, the notion of being, is merely immanent, merely subjective. Again, what is grasped in understanding, is not some further datum added on to the data of sense and of consciousness; on the contrary, it is quite unlike all data; it consists in an intelligible unity or pattern that is, not perceived, but understood; and it is understood, not as necessarily relevant to the data, but only as possibly relevant. Now the grasp of something that is possibly relevant is nothing like seeing, intuiting, perceiving, which regard only what is actually there. It follows that, for picture-thinking, understanding too must be merely immanent and merely subjective. What holds for understanding, also holds for concepts, for concepts express what has been grasped by understanding. What holds for concepts, holds no less for judgments, since judgments proceed from a reflective understanding, just as concepts proceed from a direct or inverse understanding.

This conclusion of immanence is inevitable, once picture-thinking is admitted. For picture-thinking means thinking in visual images. Visual images are incapable of representing or suggesting the normative exigences of intelligence and reasonableness, and, much less, their power to effect the intentional self-transcendence of the subject.

The foregoing account, however, though it provides the key to doctrines of immanence, provides no more than a key. It is a general model based on knowledge of the subject. It differs from actual doctrines of immanence, inasmuch as the latter are the work of truncated subjects that have only a partial apprehension of their

---

[7] Provided, of course, one's account of human intellect is not more picture-thinking, with human intelligence a matter of looking.

own reality. But it requires, I think, no great discernment to find a parallel between the foregoing account and, to take but a single example, the Kantian argument for immanence. In this argument the effective distinction is between immediate and mediate relations of cognitional activities to objects. Judgment is only a mediate knowledge of objects, a representation of a representation.[8] Reason is never related right up to objects but only to understanding and, through understanding, to the empirical use of reason itself.[9]

Since our only cognitional activity immediately related to objects is intuition,[10] it follows that the value of our judgments and our reasoning can be no more than the value of our intuitions. But our only intuitions are sensitive; sensitive intuitions reveal not being but phenomena; and so our judgments and reasoning are confined to a merely phenomenal world.[11]

Such, substantially, seems to be the Kantian argument. It is a quite valid argument if one means by "object" what one can settle by picture-thinking. "Object" is what one looks at; looking is sensitive intuition; it alone is immediately related to objects; understanding and reason can be related to objects only mediately, only through sensitive intuition.

Moreover, the neglected and truncated subject is not going to find the answer to Kant, for he does not know himself well enough to break the hold of picture-thinking and to discover that human cognitional activities have as their object being, that the activity immediately related to this object is questioning, that other activities such as sense and consciousness, understanding and judgment, are related mediately to the object, being, inasmuch

---

[8] Kant, *Kritik der reinen Vernunft*, A 68, B 93.
[9] *Ibid.*, A 643, B 671.
[10] *Ibid.*, A 19, B 33.
[11] See F. Copleston, *A History of Philosophy*, 8 vols, Glen Rock, 1946–1962, Vol. 6, chapter 12, Nos. 1 and 8. Paperback (Image Books, Doubleday) VI-2, pp. 30 ff., 60 ff. Contrast with E. Gilson and E. Coreth in *Collection*, pp. 202–220.

as they are the means of answering questions, of reaching the goal intended by questioning.

There is a final point to be made. The transition from the neglected and truncated subject to self-appropriation is not a simple matter. It is not just a matter of finding out and assenting to a number of true propositions. More basically, it is a matter of conversion, of a personal philosophic experience, of moving out of a world of sense and of arriving, dazed and disorientated for a while, into a universe of being.

The Existential Subject

So far, our reflections on the subject have been concerned with him as a knower, as one that experiences, understands, and judges. We have now to think of him as a doer, as one that deliberates, evaluates, chooses, acts. Such doing, at first sight, affects, modifies, changes the world of objects. But even more it affects the subject himself. For human doing is free and responsible. Within it is contained the reality of morals, of building up or destroying character, of achieving personality or failing in that task. By his own acts the human subject makes himself what he is to be, and he does so freely and responsibly; indeed, he does so precisely because his acts are the free and responsible expressions of himself.

Such is the existential subject. It is a notion that is overlooked on the schematism of older categories that distinguished faculties, such as intellect and will, or different uses of the same faculty, such as speculative and practical intellect, or different types of human activity, such as theoretical inquiry and practical execution. None of these distinctions adverts to the subject as such and, while the reflexive, self-constitutive element in moral living has been known from ancient times, still it was not coupled with the notion of the subject to draw attention to him in his key role of making himself what he is to be.

Because the older schemes are not relevant, it will aid clarity if I indicate the new scheme of distinct but related levels of consciousness, in which the existential subject stands, so to speak, on the top level. For we are subjects, as it were, by degrees. At a lowest level, when unconscious in dreamless sleep or in a coma, we are merely potentially subjects. Next, we have a minimal degree of consciousness and subjectivity when we are the helpless subjects of our dreams. Thirdly, we become experiential subjects when we awake, when we become the subjects of lucid perception, imaginative projects, emotional and conative impulses, and bodily action. Fourthly, the intelligent subject sublates the experiential, i.e., it retains, preserves, goes beyond, completes it, when we inquire about our experience, investigate, grow in understanding, express our inventions and discoveries. Fifthly, the rational subject sublates the intelligent and experiential subject, when we question our own understanding, check our formulations and expressions, ask whether we have got things right, marshal the evidence *pro* and *con*, judge this to be so and that not to be so. Sixthly, finally, rational consciousness is sublated by rational self-consciousness, when we deliberate, evaluate, decide, act. Then there emerges human consciousness at its fullest. Then the existential subject exists and his character, his personal essence, is at stake.

The levels of consciousness are not only distinct but also related, and the relations are best expressed as instances of what Hegel named sublation, of a lower being retained, preserved, yet transcended and completed by a higher.[12] Human intelligence goes beyond human sensitivity yet it cannot get along without sensitivity. Human judgment goes beyond sensitivity and intelligence yet cannot function except in conjunction with them. Human action finally, must in similar fashion both presuppose and complete human sensitivity, intelligence, and judgment.

It is, of course, this fact of successive sublations that is denoted

[12] This omits, however, the Hegelian view that the higher reconciles a contradiction in the lower.

by the metaphor of levels of consciousness. But besides their distinction and their functional interdependence, the levels of consciousness are united by the unfolding of a single transcendental intending of plural, interchangeable objectives.[13] What promotes the subject from experiential to intellectual consciousness is the desire to understand, the intention of intelligibility. What next promotes him from intellectual to rational consciousness, is a fuller unfolding of the same intention: for the desire to understand, once understanding is reached, becomes the desire to understand correctly; in other words, the intention of intelligibility, once an intelligible is reached, becomes the intention of the right intelligible, of the true and, through truth, of reality. Finally, the intention of the intelligible, the true, the real, becomes also the intention of the good, the question of value, of what is worthwhile, when the already acting subject confronts his world and adverts to his own acting in it.

I am suggesting that the transcendental notion of the good regards value. It is distinct from the particular good that satisfies individual appetite, such as the appetite for food and drink, the appetite for union and communion, the appetite for knowledge, or virtue, or pleasure. Again, it is distinct from the good of order, the objective arrangement or institution that ensures for a group of people the regular recurrence of particular goods. As appetite wants breakfast, so an economic system is to ensure breakfast every morning. As appetite wants union, so marriage is to ensure life-long union. As appetite wants knowledge, so an educational system ensures the imparting of knowledge to each successive generation. But beyond the particular good and the good of order, there is the good of value. It is by appealing to value or values that we satisfy some appetites and do not satisfy others, that we approve some systems for achieving the good of order and disapprove of

[13] These objectives are approximately the Scholastic transcendentals, *ens*, *unum*, *verum*, *bonum*, and they are interchangeable in the sense of mutual predication, of *convertuntur*.

others, that we praise or blame human persons as good or evil and their actions as right or wrong.

What, then, is value? I should say that it is a transcendental notion like the notion of being. Just as the notion of being intends but, of itself, does not know being, so too the notion of value intends but, of itself, does not know value. Again, as the notion of being is dynamic principle that keeps us moving toward ever fuller knowledge of being, so the notion of value is the fuller flowering of the same dynamic principle that now keeps us moving toward ever fuller realization of the good, of what is worth while.

This may seem nebulous, so I beg leave to introduce a parallel. There is to Aristotle's *Ethics* an empiricism that seems almost question-begging. He could write: "Actions . . . are called just and temperate when they are such as the just or the temperate man would do; but it is not the man who does these that is just and temperate, but the man who also does them *as* just and temperate men do them."[14] Again, he could add: "Virtue . . . is a state of character concerned with choice, lying in a mean, i.e. the mean relative to us, this being determined by a rational principle, and by that principle by which the man of practical wisdom would determine it."[15] Aristotle, it seems to me, is refusing to speak of ethics apart from the ethical reality of good men, of justice apart from men that are just, of temperance apart from men that are temperate, of the nature of virtue apart from the judgment of the man that possesses practical wisdom.

But, whatever may be the verdict about Aristotle, at least the approach I have just noted fits in admirably with the notion of the good I am outlining. Just as the notion of being functions in one's knowing and it is by reflecting on that functioning that one comes to know what the notion of being is, so also the notion or intention of the good functions within one's human acting and it is by reflection on that functioning that one comes to know what

[14] Aristotle, *Nicomachean Ethics*, II, iii, 4; 1105b 5–8.
[15] *Ibid.*, II, vi, 15; 1106b 36 f. Translations by W. D. Ross in R. McKeon's *Basic Works of Aristotle*, New York, 1941, pp. 956, 959.

the notion of good is. Again, just as the functioning of the notion of being brings about our limited knowledge of being, so too the functioning of the notion of the good brings about our limited achievement of the good. Finally, as our knowledge of being is, not knowledge of essence, but only knowledge of this and that and other beings, so too the only good to which we have first-hand access is found in instances of the good realized in themselves or produced beyond themselves by good men.

So the paradox of the existential subject extends to the good existential subject. Just as the existential subject freely and responsibly makes himself what he is, so too he makes himself good or evil and his actions right or wrong. The good subject, the good choice, the good action are not found in isolation. For the subject is good by his good choices and good actions. Universally prior to any choice or action there is just the transcendental principle of all appraisal and criticism, the intention of the good. That principle gives rise to instances of the good, but those instances are good choices and actions. However, do not ask me to determine them, for their determination in each case is the work of the free and responsible subject producing the first and only edition of himself.

It is because the determination of the good is the work of freedom that ethical systems can catalogue sins in almost endless genera and species yet always remain rather vague about the good. They urge us to do good as well as to avoid evil, but what it is to do good does not get much beyond the golden rule, the precept of universal charity, and the like. Still the shortcomings of system are not an irremediable defect. We come to know the good from the example of those about us, from the stories people tell of the good and evil men and women of old, from the incessant flow of praise and blame that makes up the great part of human conversation, from the elation and from the shame that fill us when our own choices and deeds are our own determination of ourselves as good or evil, praiseworthy or blameworthy.

I have been affirming a primacy of the existential. I distinguished different levels of human consciousness to place rational self-consciousness at the top. It sublates the three prior levels of experiencing, of understanding, and of judging, where, of course, sublating means not destroying, not interfering, but retaining, preserving, going beyond, perfecting. The experiential, the intelligible, the true, the real, the good are one, so that understanding enlightens experience, truth is the correctness of understanding, and the pursuit of the good, of value, of what is worthwhile in no way conflicts with, in every way promotes and completes, the pursuit of the intelligible, the true, the real.

It is to be noted, however, that we are not speaking of the good in the Aristotelian sense of the object of appetite, *id quod omnia appetunt*. Nor are we speaking of the good in the intellectual, and, indeed, Thomist sense of the good of order. Besides these there is a quite distinct meaning of the word "good"; to it we refer specifically when we speak of value, of what is worthwhile, of what is right as opposed to wrong, of what is good as opposed not to bad but to evil. It is the intention of the good in this sense that prolongs the intention of the intelligible, the true, the real, that founds rational self-consciousness, that constitutes the emergence of the existential subject.

Finally, let me briefly say that the primacy of the existential does not mean the primacy of results, as in pragmatism, or the primacy of will, as a Scotist might urge, or a primacy of practical intellect, or practical reason, as an Aristotelian or Kantian might phrase it. Results proceed from actions, actions from decisions, decisions from evaluations, evaluations from deliberations, and all five from the existential subject, the subject as deliberating, evaluating, deciding, acting, bringing about results. That subject is not just an intellect or just a will. Though concerned with results, he or she more basically is concerned with himself or herself as becoming good or evil and so is to be named, not a practical subject, but an existential subject.

The Alienated Subject

Existential reflection is at once enlightening and enriching. Not only does it touch us intimately and speak to us convincingly but also it is the natural starting-point for fuller reflection on the subject as incarnate, as image and feeling as well as mind and will, as moved by symbol and story, as intersubjective, as encountering others and becoming "I" to "Thou" to move on to "We" through acquaintance, companionship, collaboration, friendship, love. Then easily we pass into the whole human world founded on meaning, a world of language, art, literature, science, philosophy, history, of family and mores, society and education, state and law, economy and technology. That human world does not come into being or survive without deliberation, evaluation, decision, action, without the exercise of freedom and responsibility. It is a world of existential subjects and it objectifies the values that they originate in their creativity and their freedom.

But the very wealth of existential reflection can turn out to be a trap. It is indeed the key that opens the doors to a philosophy, not of man in the abstract, but of concrete human living in its historical unfolding. Still, one must not think that such concreteness eliminates the ancient problems of cognitional theory, epistemology, and metaphysics, for if they occur in an abstract context, they recur with all the more force in a concrete context.

Existential reflection, as it reveals what it is for man to be good, so it raises the question whether the world is good. Is this whole process from the nebulae through plants and animals to man, is it good, a true value, something worthwhile? This question can be answered affirmatively, if and only if one acknowledges God's existence, his omnipotence, and his goodness. Granted those three, one can say that created process is good because the creative *fiat* cannot but be good. Doubt or deny any of the three, and then one doubts or denies any intelligent mind and loving will that could justify anyone saying that this world is good, worthwhile, a value worthy of man's approval and consent. For "good" in the sense we have been using the term is the goodness of the moral agent, his deeds, his works. Unless there is a moral agent responsible for the world's being and becoming, the world cannot be said to be good in that moral sense. If in that sense the world is not good, then goodness in that sense is to be found only in man. If still man would be good, he is alien to the rest of the universe. If on the other hand he renounces authentic living and drifts into the now seductive and now harsh rhythms of his psyche and of nature, then man is alienated from himself.

It is, then, no accident that a theatre of the absurd, a literature of the absurd, and philosophies of the absurd flourish in a culture in which there are theologians to proclaim that God is dead. But that absurdity and that death have their roots in a new neglect of the subject, a new truncation, a new immanentism. In the name of phenomenology, of existential self-understanding, of human encounter, of salvation history, there are those that resentfully and disdainfully brush aside the old questions of cognitional theory, epistemology, metaphysics. I have no doubt, I never did doubt, that the old answers were defective. But to reject the questions as well is to refuse to know what one is doing when one is knowing; it is to refuse to know why doing that is knowing; it is to refuse to set up a basic semantics by concluding what one knows when one does it. That threefold refusal is worse than mere neglect of the subject, and it generates a far more radical truncation. It is that truncation that we experience today not only without but within the Church, when we find that the conditions of the possibility of significant dialogue are not grasped, when the distinction between revealed religion and myth is blurred, when the possibility of objective knowledge of God's existence and of his goodness is denied.

These are large and urgent topics. I shall not treat them. Yet I do not think I am neglecting them entirely, for I have pointed throughout this paper to the root difficulty, to neglect of the subject and the vast labor involved in knowing him.

86

BELIEF: TODAY'S ISSUE[1]

Man's coming to know is a group enterprise. It is not the work of the isolated individual applying his senses, accumulating insights, weighing the evidence, forming his judgment. On the contrary, it is the work of many, with each adding, as it were, to a common fund the fruits of his observations, the perspectives caught by his understanding, the supporting or contrary evidence from his reflection.

Moreover, this division of labor in coming to know is possible just insofar as it is possible for men to believe one another. What you see with your eyes can be contributed to a common fund of knowledge only in the measure that you can be trusted to observe accurately, to speak truthfully, to select your words precisely. What holds for ocular vision, also holds for all other cognitional operations. One man can perform them and many can profit from his performance if he is trustworthy and they believe him.

Such in general is belief. It is the condition of the possibility of a division of labor in the acquisition and development of knowledge.

Now belief is very common. Most of what any of us knows depends to a greater or less extent on belief. There are some things that we have found out for ourselves, by our own observations, our own insights, our own reflection and judgment. But usually what we find out for ourselves is enmeshed in a context of other items that we came to know, not on our own, but by believing others.

[1] A paper prepared for the Pax Romana Symposium on Faith. Synod Hall, Pittsburgh, March 16, 1968. Reprinted in *Catholic Mind*, May, 1970.

We know the shape of the United States and the relative positions of its major cities because we have seen, examined, perhaps copied maps. But are the maps accurate? We do not know that. We believe it. Perhaps no one knows it, for in all probability the map of so large an area is a compilation put together from the work of very many survey parties. Each part of the map would be known to be accurate but by a different party, so that the accuracy of the whole as a whole would be a matter only of belief.

Similarly for the rest of our common-sense knowledge. There is a narrow strip of space-time that each of us inhabits and with it we are familiar. But this narrow strip is inextricably bound up with its surroundings, with a neighborhood, a district, a city, a state, a country, a continent, a world, with series of social groups and of cultural levels. Such surroundings are much more a matter of belief than of personally acquired knowledge. Moreover, our minds are not divided into two compartments with beliefs in one and personally acquired knowledge in the other. The two intermingle. Together they form a single, more or less coherent whole, with our knowledge checking and controlling beliefs and with beliefs filling out and completing and underpinning knowledge.

Now you may be ready to grant that common-sense knowledge is of this type but that scientific knowledge is quite different, that the scientist as scientist does not believe but knows. This I do not think is so. The difference between common-sense and scientific knowledge is not a different proportion of belief but a more effective control of belief.

There is not a different proportion of belief. When an engineer whips out his slide-rule and performs a rapid calculation, he knows precisely what he is doing and can explain why the thing works. None the less, his conclusion is largely dependent on belief. The slide-rule depends on logarithmic and trigonometric tables, and the engineer never worked out such a set of tables. He does not know by his own knowledge that such tables are correct. He believes it. Again, since he has never checked the marks on his rule against a set of such tables, he does not know that his rule corresponds to the tables. He believes that too.

More generally, in so far as a scientist makes an original contribution to his subject, to that extent he knows by personally acquired knowledge. In the measure that a scientist repeats another's experiments and works out for himself the theorems on which another's discovery rests, in that measure the scientist again knows by personally acquired knowledge.

But just as engineers do not waste their time making sure that logarithmic and trigonometric and other tables are correct, so too scientists do not fritter away their lives repeating and checking the experiments performed by other scientists. On the contrary, each is eagerly endeavouring to make his modest contribution to the total fund and, to do so, each draws upon the whole of the common fund not solely through personally acquired knowledge but also through belief, through taking another's word for it.

However, if there is as large a proportion of belief in science as in common sense, it remains that there is a notable difference in the control of beliefs.

Common sense, of course, has its controls, subtle, flexible, dynamic. But we speak of them in proverbs. Live and learn. Once bitten, twice shy. You can't fool all the people all of the time.

But scientific statement is precise. It has to bear the weight of its logical presuppositions and consequences. It is vulnerable, not just at one point, but at a hundred. So it is that verification not only is direct but also indirect. So it is that the law of falling bodies was verified not merely by Galileo some four centuries ago but also on every occasion that that law was presupposed in successful experiments performed during the last four hundred years.

I have been characterizing belief. I have said it is a necessary condition if man's coming to know is to be a group enterprise, if it is to be increased and accelerated by a division of labor. I also have said that belief accounts for a major portion in the knowledge both of the man of common sense and of the individual scientist. I have submitted that the difference between science and common sense lies not in the proportion of belief but in the control of belief.

I have now to draw closer to my topic and I do so by noting that in times of little social or cultural change, beliefs are stable and little open to question, but in times of great social and cultural change, beliefs too are changing and, because they are only beliefs, because they are not personally acquired knowledge, such change leaves believers at a loss. They are disorientated. They do not know which way to turn. They feel that all they have taken for granted is menaced. They may be tempted to unbelief as a liberation or, again, they may dread it as destructive of truly human living.

Such is a major premiss, and I have only to add a minor to conclude to the contemporary issue, the contemporary dis-ease with regard to belief. The minor is that ours is a time of great social and cultural change and, further, that this is being experienced more particularly by Catholics.

First, then, ours is a time of great social change. The relation of man to nature has been transformed by the discoveries of natural science, the flood of inventions, the know-how of technicians, the enterprise of industrialists, businessmen, financiers. Earlier ways of living have been disrupted by urbanism, increasing longevity, a population explosion, built-in obsolescence, mobility, detached and functional relations between persons, universal, prolonged and continuing education, instantaneous information, increasing leisure and travel, perpetually available entertainment. There is a distinctive meaning conveyed by the phrase "modern living." It connotes a varying set of more or less established innovations in the family and in manners, in society and in education, in the state and in the law, in the economy and in technology, in the Churches and the sects. The older one is, the more lively one's memory, the more easily will one recall the many manners in which our way of living has changed in the course of the present century.

But besides a way of living, the social, there is also the cultural, and by the "cultural" I would denote the meaning we find in our present way of life, the value we place upon it, or, again, the things we find meaningless, stupid, wicked, horrid, atrocious, disastrous.

In its immediacy the cultural is the meaning already present in the dream before it is interpreted, the meaning in a work of art before it is articulated by the critic, the endless shades of meaning in everyday speech, the intersubjective meanings of smile and frown, tone and gesture, evasion and silence, the passionate meanings of love and hatred, of high achievement and wrathful destruction.

But besides the meaning and value immediately intuited, felt, spoken, acted out, there is to any advanced culture a superstructure. To art and literature there are added criticism. To artisans and craftsmen there are added inventors and technicians. To common sense there is added science. To the proverbs of wise men there are added the reflections of philosophers. Industry and commerce are complicated by economics, togetherness by sociology, the state by political theory, the law by jurisprudence, man's body by medicine and his mind by psychiatry, schools by educational theories, and religions by theologies. Besides the meanings and values immanent in everyday living there is an enormous process in which meanings are elaborated and values are discerned in a far more reflective, deliberate, critical fashion.

I have been presenting a notion of culture and, if I am to characterize contemporary cultural change, I must briefly compare modern culture with its classicist predecessor.

A basic difference, then, lies in the mere size of the superstructure. Our age is an age of specialization for other reasons, of course, but also out of sheer necessity. Modern mathematics, modern physics, modern chemistry are just too vast for any of them to be mastered entirely by a single mind. What holds of them, also holds to a greater or less extent in other fields. Today the renaissance ideal of the *uomo universale*, master of every art and science, would be a mere figment of the imagination. But in the classicist period the modern sciences were in their infancy, and there existed a liberal education that enabled anyone so inclined to assimilate the substance of the cultural superstructure and to follow intelligently and critically the work of pioneers. We as a group are immeasurably richer but as individuals we have immeasurably more that we can know only by believing.

Again, classicist culture contrasted itself with barbarism. It was culture with a capital "C." Others might participate in it to a greater or less extent and, in the measure they did so, they ceased to be barbarians. In other words culture was conceived normatively. It was a matter of good manners and good taste, of grace and style, of virtue and character, of models and ideals, of eternal verities and inviolable laws.

But the modern notion of culture is not normative but empirical. Culture is a general notion. It denotes something found in every people, for in every people there is some apprehension of meaning and value in their way of life. So it is that modern culture is the culture that knows about other cultures, that relates them to one another genetically, that knows all of them to be man-made. Far more open than classicist culture, far better informed, far more discerning, it lacks the convictions of its predecessor, its clear-cut norms, its elemental strength.

Classicist culture was stable. It took its stand on what ought to be, and what ought to be is not to be refuted by what is. It legislated with its eye on the substance of things, on the unchanging essence of human living and, while it never doubted either that circumstances alter cases or that circumstances change, still it also was quite sure that essences did not change, that change affected only the accidental details that were of no great account.

So its philosophy was perennial philosophy, its classics were immortal works of art, its religion and ethics enshrined the wisdom of the ages, its laws and its tribunals the prudence of mankind.

Classicist culture, by conceiving itself normatively and universally, also had to think of itself as the one and only culture for all time. But modern culture is culture on the move. It is historicist. Because human cultures are man-made, they can be changed by man. They not only can but also should be changed. Modern man is not concerned simply to perpetuate the wisdom of his ancestors. For him the past is just the springboard to the future and the future, if it is to be good, will improve on all that is good in the past and it will liquidate all that is evil.

The classicist was aware that men individually are responsible for the lives they lead. Modern man is aware that men collectively are responsible for the world in which they lead them.

So a contemporary humanism is dynamic. It holds forth not an ideal of fixity but a programme of change. It was or is the automatic progress of the liberal, the dialectical materialism of the Marxist, the identification of cosmogenesis and christogenesis by Pierre Teilhard de Chardin. Ours is a time that criticizes and debunks the past, that preaches an ideology, that looks forward to an utopia.

It also is a time of confusion, for there are many voices, many of them shrill, and most of them contradictory.

Such a time of confusion, as I have said, calls beliefs into question and, because they are just beliefs, because they are not personally generated knowledge, answers are hard to come by. So to confusion there are easily added disorientation, disillusionment, crisis, surrender, unbelief. But, as I also said, from the present situation Catholics are suffering more keenly than others, not indeed because their plight is worse, but because up to Vatican II they were sheltered against the modern world and since Vatican II they have been exposed more and more to the chill winds of modernity. Let me briefly explain why this is so.

Always in the past it had been the Catholic tradition to penetrate and to christianize the social fabric and the culture of the age. So it entered into the Hellenistic world of the patristic period. So it was one of the principal architects of medieval society and medieval thought. So too it was almost scandalously involved in the Renaissance. But only belatedly has it come to acknowledge that the world of the classicist no longer exists and that the only world in which it can function is the modern world.

To a great extent this failure is to be explained by the fact that modern developments were covered over with a larger amount of wickedness. Since the beginning of the eighteenth century Christianity has been under attack. Agnostic and atheistic philosophies have been developed and propagated. The development of the natural and of the human sciences was such that they appeared and often were said to support such movements. The emergence of the modern languages with their new literary forms was not easily acclaimed when they contributed so little to devotion and so much, it seemed, to worldliness and irreligion. The new industry spawned slums, the new politics revolutions, the new discoveries unbelief. One may lament it but one can hardly be surprised that at the beginning of this century, when churchmen were greeted with a heresy that logically entailed all possible heresies, they named the new monster modernism.

If their opposition to wickedness made churchmen unsympathetic to modern ways, their classicism blocked their vision. They were unaware that modern science involved quite a different notion of science from that entertained by Aristotle. When they praised science and affirmed the Church's support for science, what they meant to praise and support was true and certain knowledge of things through their causes.

But modern science is not true and certain; it is just probable. It is not fully knowledge; it is hypothesis, theory, system, the best available opinion. It regards not things but data, phenomena. While it still speaks of causes, what it means is not end, agent, matter, form, but correlation.

Further, this new notion of science introduced radically new problems in philosophy. In Aristotelian physics one ascended from the earth to the heavens and beyond the heavens to the first mover. There was no logical break between knowledge of this world and knowledge of ultimate causes.

But modern science is specialized. It is knowledge of this world and only of this world. It proceeds from data and to data it adds only verifiable hypotheses. But God is not a datum of human experience for, in this life, we do not know God face to face. Again, between this world and God there is no relationship that can be verified, for verification can occur only between data, only with regard to objects that lie within this world and so can present us with data.

Now no one will be surprised that modern science, precisely because it is methodically geared to knowledge of this world, cannot yield knowledge of God. But we come to the catch when we ask the further questions. How do we know about God? What do we mean by God? Anything else we know or talk about is known or meant through experience, understanding, and judgment, where judgment rests on some type of verification. Knowledge of God, then, is a singular case. It is not immediate knowledge: there are no data on the divine itself. It is not verifiable knowledge: there are no verifiable hypotheses or principles without data. What kind of knowledge, then, is it?

Now I believe that question can be answered and I attempted to do so in a book, *Insight*. But I wish to draw your attention to the nature of the question. It is not a question that could be asked about knowledge at any time or place; on the contrary it is a question that arises only after modern science has been developed. So, if one wishes to meet that question, one will not talk metaphysics and, much less, will one talk medieval metaphysics. But the classicist did not advert to the real novelty of modern science, and so he could not conclude to the real novelty in modern philosophic problems and, particularly, in the problems concerning God.

There was a further blind spot. I have already noted that the classicist conceives culture not empirically but normatively and that this approach leads him to exaggerate the stability and the universality of his culture. Now this exaggeration had the gravest consequences for theology, for it precluded any proper sense of history and, indeed, it did so precisely when historical studies of religion and theology were undergoing their greatest development.

Since the beginning of the century theologians have been incorporating more and more historical study into their theology. The structures of the previous theology, designed by classicist mentality, here were quietly stretched and strained, there had to be broken and abandoned. But mere history is not theology, and the task of doing genuine history and on that basis proceeding to theology confronts contemporary Catholic theologians with the most basic and far-reaching of problems, the problem of method in theology. Once some progress is made there, we can begin methodically to pick up the pieces and construct a contemporary theology.

I have been attempting to outline the contemporary issue. I spoke of belief in its relation to personally acquired knowledge, of belief in tranquil times and of belief in times of great social and cultural change, of the social changes that have occurred in this century, of the transition from classicist to modern culture, of the belated acknowledgement by churchmen of this transition, and of the enormous problems suddenly thrust upon theologians and, more generally, upon all carriers of Catholic culture. I must now attempt, upon this background, to treat the issue somewhat more concretely and practically.

First, then, I have spoken very generally of human belief. But religious faith goes beyond human belief. It includes it, for the living tradition of the Church down the centuries was the handing on from generation to generation of the word first spoken in Palestine. But faith is not in man's word but in God. It is admitting the possibility and acknowledging the fact that God could and did enter into the division of labor by which men come to know, that his contribution was one that could not be replaced by human effort, that in accepting the truths of faith we are believing not just man but ultimately God.

Secondly, religion is one thing, and theology is another. Most saints were not theologians, and most theologians were not saints. Theology stands to religion, as economics does to business, as biology to health, as chemistry to du Pont industries. To revert to a distinction drawn earlier, theology pertains to the cultural superstructure, while religion pertains to its day-to-day substance. Because of this difference Cardinal Newman was quite right in saying that ten thousand difficulties do not make a doubt: the ten thousand difficulties are in the superstructure, but doubt is in one's personal life.

By this, of course, I do not mean that theology and religion are totally independent of each other. Each does depend on the other, but before this dependence can function, they must be acknowledged as distinct, as each possessing its own proper features and modes of operation. To say that ten thousand difficulties in theology do not make one doubt in religion is like saying that ten thousand difficulties in economic theory are no reason for business firms immediately declaring bankruptcy.

Thirdly, the changes going forward are primarily social and cultural. They call for adjustment and adaptation in theology and in religion. But such adjustment and adaptation are in forms and structures much more than in content. Theology has to operate within a different context; it will have to operate differently; but it will not therefore be a different theology. As medieval theology differed from the theology of the patristic period, as Renaissance theology differed from both patristic and medieval, so modern theology will differ from its predecessors as much as but perhaps no more than they did from theirs.

Fourthly, the analysis I am offering of our contemporary

situation differs notably from simpler views that are more frequently heard. It is said that the Church had become a ghetto, that it had gone to excess in defensiveness and in rigidity, that it has to break away from its Byzantine and medieval trappings, that it has to speak to the people of today, and so forth.

Now I do not think that these views are simply false, but I do think the truth they contain is expressed more politely, more accurately, and more helpfully, by noting that the Church, if it is to operate in the world, has to operate on the basis of the social order and cultural achievements of each time and place, that consequently its operation has to change with changes in its social and cultural context, that at present we have the task of a disengagement from classicist thought-forms and viewpoints, and, simultaneously, of a new involvement in modern culture.

In brief, the contemporary issue is, not a new religion, not a new faith, but a belated social and cultural transition.

Fifthly, my own endeavors in this matter are of an extremely technical nature and I shall not go into them here. But I would like to say that the contrast I have drawn between classicist and modern is not based on some *a priori* typology or periodization. It is a summary of a whole set of conclusions concerning the defects of our theological inheritance and the remedies that can be brought to bear.

I did not think things wrong because they were classicist; on the contrary, I found a number of things that I thought wrong, and, on putting them together, I found what I have named classicism. Again, I do not think things are right because they are modern, but I did find a number of things I thought right and they are modern at least in the sense that they were overlooked in the nineteenth-century Catholic theological tradition.

Here I should like to stress that our disengagement from classicism and our involvement in modernity must be open-eyed, critical, coherent, sure-footed. If we are not just to throw out what is good in classicism and replace it with contemporary trash, then we have to take the trouble, and it is enormous, to grasp the strength and the weakness, the power and the limitations, the good points and the shortcomings of both classicism and modernity.

Nor is knowledge enough. One has to be creative. Modernity lacks roots. Its values lack balance and depth. Much of its science is destructive of man. Catholics in the twentieth century are faced with a problem similar to that met by Aquinas in the thirteenth century. Then Greek and Arabic culture were pouring into Western Europe and, if it was not to destroy Christendom, it had to be known, assimilated, transformed. Today modern culture, in many ways more stupendous than any that ever existed, is surging round us. It too has to be known, assimilated, transformed. That is the contemporary issue.

The contemporary issue, then, is a tremendous challenge. Nor should one opt out on the speciously modest plea that one is not another Aquinas. There could have been no Aquinas without the preceding development of Scholasticism. There would have been no Aquinas if there had not been the students to whom he lectured and for whom he wrote.

Finally, there would have been a far more successful Aquinas, if human beings were less given to superficial opinions backed by passion, for in that case the work of Aquinas would not have been so promptly buried under the avalanche of the Augustinian-Aristotelian conflict that marked the close of the thirteenth century.

To grasp the contemporary issue and to meet its challenge calls, then, for a collective effort. It is not the individual but the group that transforms the culture.

The group does so by its concern for excellence, by its ability to wait and let issues mature, by its persevering efforts to understand, by its discernment for what is at once simple and profound, by its demand for the first-rate and its horror of mere destructiveness.

THE ABSENCE OF GOD IN
MODERN CULTURE[1]

I think I should begin not with modern culture but with its classical predecessor. Even as recently as fifty years ago it was still dominant in American Catholic circles. Then it was named simply culture. It was conceived absolutely, as the opposite of barbarism. It was a matter of acquiring and assimilating the tastes and skills, the ideals, virtues, and ideas, that were pressed upon one in a good home and through a curriculum in the liberal arts. This notion, of course, had a very ancient lineage. It stemmed out of Greek *paideia* and Roman *doctrinae studium atque humanitatis*, out of the exuberance of the Renaissance and its pruning in the Counter-reformation schools of the Jesuits. Essentially it was a normative rather than an empirical notion of culture, a matter of models to be imitated, or ideal characters to be emulated, of eternal verities and universally valid laws.

The defect of this notion of culture was, of course, its particularity. It referred not to the cultures of mankind but to a particular culture that may be named classicist. The need to revise one's notion of culture—to which I alluded a moment ago—was a need to generalize, to discern in the cultures of mankind their common generic function and the differences in the mode in which that function was fulfilled, whether among primitive tribes or in the ancient high civilizations or in the nations and states of historical times.

To this end I should like to recall a distinction sometimes made

[1] The Cardinal Bea Lecture at Fordham University 1968, in *The Presence and Absence of God*, Christopher F. Mooney, ed., New York, 1969, pp. 166–178. © 1968 Bernard J. F. Lonergan.

between the social and the cultural.[2] The social is conceived of as a way of life, a way in which men live together in some orderly and therefore predictable fashion. Such orderliness is to be observed in the family and in manners, in society with its classes and elites, in education, in the state and its laws, in the economy and technology, in the churches and sects. Such is the social, and it is upon it that the cultural arises. For men not only do things. They wish to understand their own doing. They wish to discover and to express the appropriateness, the meaning, the significance, the value, and the use of their way of life as a whole and in its parts. Such discovery and expression constitute the cultural and, quite evidently, culture stands to social order as soul to body, for any element of social order will be rejected the moment it is widely judged inappropriate, meaningless, irrelevant, useless, just not worthwhile.

Now if it is granted that culture is the meaning of a way of life, cultures may be divided according to the manner in which that meaning is apprehended and communicated. On all cultural levels there are rites and symbols, language and art. There meaning is felt and intuited and acted out. It is like the meaning already in the dream before the therapist interprets it, the meaning of the work of art before the critic focuses on it and relates it to other works, the endlessly nuanced and elusive and intricate meanings of everyday speech, the intersubjective meanings of smiles and frowns, speech and silence, intonation and gesture, the passionate meanings of interpersonal relations, of high deeds and great achievements, of all we admire, praise, revere, adore, and all we dislike, condemn, loathe, abominate. Such is meaning for undifferentiated consciousness, and it would seem to constitute the spontaneous substance of every culture.

Besides undifferentiated, there also is differentiated consciousness. It is not content to act out what it feels and intuits. Rather it seeks to mirror spontaneous living by analyzing it, making all its

[2] E. Rothacker, *Systematik und Logik der Geisteswissenschaften*, Bonn, 1947.

elements explicit, subjecting them to scrutiny, evaluation, criticism. So art and literature become the affair not only of artists and writers but also of critics and historians. The creations of craftsmen and artisans are supplanted by the discoveries of scientists and the inventions of technologists. The proverbs of wise men give place to the reflections of philosophers. Religions are complicated by theologies. The destinies of persons and peoples not only work themselves out but also are studied by biographers, historians, psychologists, economists, sociologists, and political theorists.

Modern culture shares with its classicist predecessor this reflexive, objectifying component. Both suppose ways of human living. Both ways have immanent meanings. In both this immanent meaning is elaborated, expanded, evaluated, justified or rejected in the criticism of art and of letters, in science and philosophy, in history and theology. In both there is the disastrous possibility of a conflict between human living as it can be lived and human living as a cultural superstructure dictates it should be lived.

Beyond similarities there are differences. Of these the most fundamental was the development of the modern notion of science, a development that has been described by Prof. Herbert Butterfield as one that "outshines everything since the rise of Christianity and reduces the Renaissance and the Reformation to the rank of mere episodes, mere internal displacements, within the system of medieval Christendom."[3] For, as I should put it, what occurred towards the end of the seventeenth century was the beginning not merely of much more and much better science but, basically, of a notion of science quite different from the notion worked out by Aristotle and taken for granted by his followers. To put the matter summarily, necessity was a key

[3] H. Butterfield, *The Origins of Modern Science 1300–1800*, Revised edition, New York, 1966, p. 7.

notion for Aristotle but today it is marginal; in its place is verifiable possibility. Causality was a key notion for Aristotle but today in effect, if not in name, it is replaced by correlation. The universal and abstract were normative in Aristotelian science, but modern science uses universals as tools in its unrelenting efforts to approximate to concrete process. Where the Aristotelian claimed certitude, the modern scientists disclaims anything more than probability. Where the Aristotelian wished to know things in their essences and properties, the modern scientist is satisfied with control and results. Finally, the prestige of this new idea of science is unquestioned, its effectiveness has been palpably demonstrated, its continuing necessity for the survival of the earth's teeming population is beyond doubt.

It was inevitable that the success of the new idea of science should profoundly affect the rest of the cultural superstructure, that what worked in the natural sciences should have repercussions in the human sciences, in philosophy, in theology. However, the exact nature and measure of this influence have varied, and it will clarify issues, I think, if major differences are indicated.

The fields to which I referred by speaking of the human sciences are known in America as behavioral sciences and in Germany as *Geisteswissenschaften*. The American name stresses the analogy of natural and human science: in both one observes performance, proposes hypothetical correlations, and endeavors to verify one's hypotheses as probably true. The German name stresses the basic difference between natural and human science. As it was worked out by Wilhelm Dilthey, this difference lies in the very data of the two types. The data for any natural science are just given. One needs language to describe them, classify them, identify them; one needs instruments to observe and measure them; but what counts is, not the language, but just what happens to be given to this and any other observer. In the human sciences, on the other hand, there are of course data, but the data are data for a human science not simply inasmuch as they are given but only inasmuch as there attaches to them some common-sense meaning. Thus, one could send into a law-court as many physicists, chemists, and biologists as one pleased with as much equipment as they desired. They could count, measure, weigh, describe, record, analyse, dissect to their hearts' content. But it would be only by going beyond what is just given and by attending to the meaning of the proceedings that they could discover they were dealing with a court of law; and it is only in so far as the court of law is recognized as such and the appropriate meanings are attached to the sounds and actions that the data for a human science emerge.

A further consequence has to be noted. Precisely because everyday, common-sense meaning is constitutive of the data for a human science, phenomenology and hermeneutics and history assume basic importance. Phenomenology interprets our posture and movements, our acts and deeds. Hermeneutics interprets our words. History makes us aware that human meanings change with place and time. Clearly such an emphasis on meaning and such elaborate techniques for the study of meanings greatly reduce the relevance of counting, measuring, correlating, and so move the *Geisteswissenschaften* away from the ambit of natural science and towards a close connection with—or a strong reaction against—idealist, historicist, phenomenological, personalist, or existentialist thought.

I am indicating, of course, no more than broad tendencies. Sigmund Freud interpreted meanings but, although he was a Viennese, he did so in terms of a primary process modelled on energy accumulation and discharge.[4] In contrast, a group of American social scientists defined the orientation of action by the meaning which the actor attaches to it.[5] And while we have

[4] See Joseph Nuttin, "Human motivation and Freud's Theory of Energy Discharge," in Irwin Sarason, ed., *Science and Theory in Psycho-analysis*, Princeton, 1965. Also Paul Ricoeur, *De l'interprétation, Essai sur Freud*, Paris, 1965.

[5] Talcott Parsons and Edward A. Shils, ed., *Toward a General Theory of Action*, New York, 1965, p. 4.

thoroughgoing behaviorists for whom, even when awake, we are somnambulists,[6] there is also a third force in psychology that avows the insufficiency both of Freud and of straightforward experimentalists.[7] In brief, the point I am attempting to make in no way is a contrast between peoples or nations. Rather it has to do with a radical dilemma in modern culture. Is science to be conceived and worked out in total independence of philosophy or is it not?

Historically, then, modern science grew out of an opposition to Aristotle. Further, its development and its success are to a great extent due to the ground rule of the Royal Society that excluded from consideration questions that could not be settled by an appeal to observation or experiment. Finally, philosophy is not the name of some one thing, such as are physics, chemistry, biology. On the contrary, it is the name of a shifting multitude of conflicting things. At least, until philosophers reach, if not agreement, then comprehensiveness in their disagreements, it would be suicidal for scientists not to insist on their autonomy.

Still, this is only one side of the picture. For the moment the scientist ceases to speak of the objects in his field and begins to speak of his science itself, he is subscribing to some account to human cognitional activity, to some view of the relation between such activity and its objects, to some opinion on the possible objects to be reached through that relation. Whether he knows it or not, whether he admits it or not, he is talking cognitional theory, epistemology, and metaphysics.[8] Molière depicted the *médecin malgré lui*, the doctor despite himself. The modern scientist with a claim to complete autonomy is the *philosophe malgré lui*.

---

[6] F. W. Matson, *The Broken Image*, New York, 1964, pp. 38–65.

[7] See Abraham Maslow, *Toward a Psychology of Being*, Princeton, 1962.

[8] For a distinction between the scientific and the philosophic elements in the Principle of Complementarity, see Patrick Heelan, *Quantum Mechanics and Objectivity*, The Hague, 1965, pp. 55–80.

I have been attempting to characterize the reflexive, objectifying superstructure in modern culture, and I may now draw closer to my topic and observe that the modern notion of science tends to replace theology, which treats of God and all other things in their relation to God, with religious studies, which treat of man in his supposed dealings with God or gods or goddesses.

For a modern science is an empirical science. Whether it studies nature or man, whether it is orientated by behaviorism or by the *Geisteswissenschaften*, it begins from data, it discerns intelligible unities and relationships within data, and it is subject to the check of verification, to the correction and revision to be effected by confrontation with further relevant data. Now such procedures cannot lead one beyond this world. The divine is not a datum to be observed by sense or to be uncovered by introspection. Nor will any intelligible unity or relationship verifiable within such data lead us totally beyond such data to God. Precisely because modern science is specialized knowledge of man and of nature, it cannot include knowledge of God. God is neither man nor nature. It would only be the idolatry of identifying God with man or with nature if one attempted to know God through the methods of modern science.

Religion, however, is very human. So we have histories of religion, phenomenologies of religion, psychologies of religion, sociologies of religion, philosophies of religion and, to unite these many parts into a whole, the science of religion. These disciplines cannot, of course, escape the radical dilemma confronting modern science. In the measure that they follow the model provided by natural science, they tend towards a reductionism that empties human living and especially human religion of all serious content. In the measure that they insist on their specific difference from the natural sciences, they risk losing their autonomy and becoming the captive of some fashion or fad in philosophy. But whichever way they tend, at least this much is certain: they cannot make scientific statements about God. As long as they remain within the boundaries specified by the methods of a modern science, they cannot get beyond describing and explaining the multiplicity and the variety of human religious attitudes.

God, then, is absent from modern science. Even the modern science of religion, though it bears witness to the divine, speaks not of God but of man. This, of course, is simply the inevitable result of specialization, of distinguishing different fields of investigation, of working out appropriate methods in each field, and of excluding conflicts of methodical precepts by pursuing different subjects separately. In the writings of St. Anselm there is no systematic distinction between theology and philosophy, and so his ontological argument is not what later would be desired, a strictly philosophic argument. In the writings of St. Thomas philosophy and theology are distinguished, but the distinction does not lead to a separation; so his celebrated five ways occur within a theological *Summa*. With Descartes occurs the effort to provide philosophy with its proper and independent foundations, and so not only to distinguish but also separate philosophy and theology. Still Descartes did not attempt to separate philosophy and science; on the contrary, he attempted to prove the conservation of momentum by appealing to the immutability of God. Such a separation was effected materially when Newton did for mechanics what Euclid had done for geometry. It was effected formally by the rule that, if a hypothesis is not verifiable, it is not scientific.

But if increasing specialization prevents modern science from speaking of God, one would expect it to enable modern theology to speak of God all the more fully and effectively. However, while I hope and labor that this will be so, I have to grant that it is not yet achieved. Contemporary theology and especially contemporary Catholic theology are in a feverish ferment. An old theology is being recognized as obsolete. There is a scattering of new theological fragments. But a new integration—and by this I mean, not another integration of the old type, but a new type of integration—is not yet plainly in sight. Let me describe the situation briefly under five headings.

First, the modern science or discipline of religious studies has undercut the assumptions and antiquated the methods of a theology structured by Melchior Cano's *De locis theologicis*. Such a theology was classicist in its assumptions. Truth is eternal. Principles are immutable. Change is accidental. But religious studies deal meticulously with endless matters of detail. They find that the expressions of truth and the enunciations of principles are neither eternal nor immutable. They concentrate on the historical process in which these changes occur. They bring to light whole ranges of interesting facts and quite new types of problems. In brief, religious studies have stripped the old theology of its very sources in Scripture, in patristic writings, in medieval and subsequent religious writers. They have done so by subjecting the sources to a fuller and more penetrating scrutiny than had been attempted by earlier methods.

Secondly, there is the new demythologization of Scripture. The old demythologization took place at the end of the second century. It consisted in rejecting the Bible's anthropomorphic conception of God. It may be summed up in Clement of Alexandria's statement: "Even though it is written, one must not so much think of the Father of all as having a shape, as moving, as standing or seated or in a place, as having a right hand or a left."[9] Now to this old philosophic critique of biblical statement there has been added a literary and historical critique that puts radical questions about the composition of the gospels, about the infancy narratives, the miracle stories, the sayings attributed to Jesus, the accounts of his resurrection, the origins of Pauline and Joannine *theologoumena*.

Thirdly, there is the thrust of modern philosophy. Theologians

[9] Clemens Alexandrinus, *Stromateis* V, 11; 71, 4. Stählin II, 374, 15. MG 9, 110 a.

not only repeat the past but also speak to people of today. The old theology was content, for the most part, to operate with technical concepts derived from Greek and medieval thought. But the concreteness of modern science has imposed a similar concreteness on much modern philosophy. Historicism, phenomenology, personalism, existentialism belong to a climate utterly different from that of the *per se* subject with his necessary principles or processes and his claims to demonstration. Moreover, this movement of philosophy towards concreteness and especially to the concreteness of human living has brought to light a host of notions, approaches, procedures, that are proving very fertile and illuminating in theology.

Fourthly, there is the collapse of Thomism. In the thirties it seemed still in the ascendant. After the war it seemed for a while to be holding its ground. Since Vatican II it seems to have vanished. Aquinas still is a great and venerated figure in the history of Catholic thought. But Aquinas no longer is thought of or appealed to as an arbiter in contemporary Catholic thought. Nor is the sudden change really surprising. For the assumption on which Thomism rested was typically classicist. It supposed the existence of a single perennial philosophy that might need to be adapted in this or that accidental detail but in substance remained the repository of human wisdom, a permanent oracle, and, like Thucydides' history, a possession for all time. In fact, there are a perennial materialism and a perennial idealism as well as a perennial realism. They all shift and change from one age to the next, for the questions they once treated become obsolete and the methods they employed are superseded.

Fifthly, there is a notable softening, if not weakening, of the dogmatic component once so prominent in Catholic theology. Nor can this be described as simply the correction of a former exaggeration, the advent of charity, ecumenism, dialogue, in place of less pleasant attitudes. The new philosophies are not capable of grounding objective statements about what really is so.

But dogmas purport to be such objective statements. Accordingly, if one is to defend dogmas as meaningful, one has to get beyond historicism, phenomenology, personalism, existentialism. One has to meet head-on the contention that the only meaningful statements are scientific statements. One has to do so not partially and fragmentarily but completely and thoroughly.

Further it is not only dogmas that are at stake, for it is not only dogmas that lie outside the range of a modern science. Not only every statement about God but also every statement about scientific method, about hermeneutics, about historiography, supposes a reflective procedure quite distinct from the direct procedures sanctioned by the success of modern science.

To conclude, Catholic theology at present is at a critical juncture. If I may express a personal view, I should say that the contemporary task of assimilating the fruits both of religious studies and of the new philosophies, of handling the problems of demythologization and of the possibility of objective religious statement, imposes on theology the task of recasting its notion of theological method in the most thoroughgoing and profound fashion.

I have been speaking, not of the whole of modern culture, not of its most vital part, but of its superstructure. I have said that God is absent from modern science precisely because such science systematically and exclusively is directed to knowledge of this world. Further I have said that Catholic theology is going through an unsettling period of transition in which older procedures are being repudiated and newer ones yield only incomplete and fragmentary benefits. But I have yet to ask whether God is absent not from the superstructure of modern culture but from the everyday, familiar domain of feeling, insight, judgment, decision.

On this more concrete level modern culture involves a reinterpretation of man and his world, a transformation of the ordering of society and of the control over nature, and a new sense of power and of responsibility. All three have a bearing on the absence of God in modern culture.

First, there is the reinterpretation of man in his world. This reinterpretation primarily occurs in the cultural superstructure, in the natural and the human sciences, in philosophy, history, and theology. But it is not confined to the superstructure. It is popularized, schematized, simplified. It is transposed from technical statement through simile and metaphor, image and narrative, catch-phrase and slogan, to what can be understood without too much effort and is judged to be, for practical purposes, sufficiently accurate.

Now it is quite conceivable that in a process of great cultural change all parts of the superstructure should keep in step and the popularizations of the several parts should be coherent. Such, however, has not been the transition from classicist to modern culture. For, in the first place, the classicist believed that he could escape history, that he could encapsulate culture in the universal, the normative, the ideal, the immutable, that, while times would change, still the changes necessarily would be minor, accidental, of no serious significance. In the second place, the classicist judged modern science in the light of the Aristotelian notion of science and by that standard found it wanting, for modern science does not proceed from self-evident, necessary principles and it does not demonstrate conclusions from such principles. In the third place, classicist churchmen found that the natural sciences frequently were presented in a reductionist version that was materialistic and, if not atheistic, at least agnostic, while the historical sciences were the locus of continuous attacks on traditional views of the Church in its origins and throughout its development. In brief, so far were churchmen from acknowledging the distinctive character of modern culture that they regarded it as an aberration that had to be resisted and overcome. When they were confronted with a heresy, which they considered to be the sum and substance of all heresy, they named it modernism. So far were they from seeking to enrich modern culture with a religious interpretation that they had only mistrust for a Pierre Teilhard de Chardin.

Today the pendulum has swung to the opposite extreme. Whatever is old, is out. Whatever is new, is in. But a mere swing of the pendulum, while it involves plenty of novelty, falls far short of *aggiornamento*. For *aggiornamento* is not some simple-minded rejection of all that is old and some breezy acceptance of everything new. Rather it is a disengagement from a culture that no longer exists and an involvement in a distinct culture that has replaced it. Christians have been depicted as utterly other-worldly, as idly standing about awaiting the second coming of Christ without any interest or concern or commitment for the things of this life of ours on earth. But the fact of the matter is that the ancient Church set about transforming Greek and Roman culture, that the medieval Church was a principal agent in the formation of medieval culture, that the Renaissance Church was scandalously involved in Renaissance culture. If the modern Church has stood aloof from the modern world, the fact is not too hard too explain. On the one hand, the Church's involvement in classicist culture was an involvement in a very limited view that totally underestimated the possibilities of cultural change and so precluded advertence to the need for adaptation and zeal to effect it. On the other hand, modern culture with its many excellences and its unprecedented achievements nonetheless is not just a realm of sweetness and light. The suffering, the sins, the crimes, the destructive power, the sustained blindness of the twentieth century have disenchanted us with progress and made us suspicious of development and advance. *Aggiornamento* is not desertion of the past but only a discerning and discriminating disengagement from its limitations. *Aggiornamento* is not just acceptance of the present; it is acknowledgement of its evils as well as of its good; and, as acknowledgement alone is not enough, it also is, by the power of the cross, that meeting of evil with good which transforms evil into good.

Besides its reinterpretation of man in his world, modern culture transforms man's control over nature and in consequence involves a reordering of society. The new scene is one of technology, automation, built-in obsolescence, a population explosion, increasing longevity, urbanism, mobility, detached and functional relations between persons, universal, prolonged, and continuing education, increasing leisure and travel, instantaneous information, and perpetually available entertainment. In this ever changing scene God, when not totally absent, appears an intruder. To mention him, if not meaningless, seems to be irrelevant. The greatest of financial powers, the power to increase gross national income by taxing and spending for worthy purposes, is restricted to non-religious ends, so that pluralism is given lip-service while secularism is the religion—or, perhaps, the anti-religion—by law established. At the same time, a rigorously codified religious organization finds itself ever less capable of moving with ever fluid situations, to enter meaningfully into people's lives, significantly to further all good causes, effectively to help the weak, heal the hurt, restore and reinvigorate the disheartened. Here, perhaps, as Father Karl Rahner argued in his paper at the Toronto Congress last summer, the difficulty has been an integrism in the sense that it was believed possible for authority to solve problems by laying down principles and deducing conclusions. However true such principles, however accurate such conclusions may be, it remains that they can become relevant to concrete situations only through familiarity with the situation, only through adequate insight into its causes and its potentialities, only through the ingenuity that discovers lines of solution and keeps developing and adapting them in accord with an ongoing process of change. Once more, then, we have to move beyond the classicist position and operate in the modern world. Ideals and principles and exhortations have not been antiquated. But the crying need is for the competent man on the spot free to deal with real issues as they arise and develop.

Besides a reinterpretation of man in his world, a transformation of man's control over nature, and a consequent reordering of society, modern culture has generated a new sense of power and responsibility. Superficially the sense of power might be illustrated by space-exploration, and the sense of responsibility by concern over nuclear bombs. But the matter goes far deeper. Modern culture is the culture that knows about itself and other cultures. It is aware that they are man-made. It is aware that the cultural may sustain or destroy or refashion the social. So it is that modern man not only individually is responsible for the life he leads but also collectively is responsible for the world in which he leads it. So modern culture is culture on the move. It is not dedicated to perpetuating the wisdom of ancestors, to handing on the traditions it has inherited. The past is just the springboard to the future. It is the set of good things to be improved and of evils to be eliminated. The future will belong to those who think about it, who grasp real possibilities, who project a coherent sequence of cumulative realizations, who speak to man's longing for achievement more wisely than the liberal apostles of automatic progress and more humanly than the liquidating Marxists.

Now this concern with the future of humanity is a concern for humanity in this world; so it has been thought to be purely secular. Such a conclusion is, I believe, mistaken. It is true that concern for the future is incompatible with a blind traditionalism, but a blind traditionalism is not the essence of religion. It is true that concern for the future will work itself out by human means, by drawing on human experience, human intelligence, human judgment, human decision, but again this is quite compatible with a profoundly religious attitude. It was St. Ignatius Loyola who gave the advice: act as though results depended exclusively on you, but await the results as though they depended entirely on God. What is false is that human concern for the future can generate a better future on the basis of individual and group egoism. For to know what is truly good and to effect it calls for a self-transcendence that seeks to benefit not self at the cost of the group, not the group at the cost of mankind, not present mankind at the cost of mankind's future. Concern for the future, if it is not just high-sounding hypocrisy, supposes rare moral attainment. It calls for what Christians name heroic charity. In the measure that Christians practise and radiate heroic charity they need not fear they will be superfluous either in the task of discerning man's true good in this life or in the task of bringing it about.

I have been speaking of the absence of God in modern culture. I have dwelt at length on the many ways in which he is absent both in the superstructure and on the day-to-day level of that culture. But every absence is also a potential presence, not indeed in the sense that the past is to be restored, but in the sense that our creativity has to discover the future and our determination has to realize it. Nor is God's presence only potential. Evidently, almost palpably, it is actual. Pope John spoke to the whole world. Vatican II stirred it profoundly. For the Spirit of God is moving the hearts of many and, in Paul Tillich's phrase, ultimate concern has grasped them.

NATURAL KNOWLEDGE OF GOD[1]

By natural knowledge of God I shall understand the knowledge of God intended by the dogmatic constitution *Dei Filius* of the first Vatican Council. Chapter two of the constitution begins with the words:

> Eadem sancta mater Ecclesia tenet et docet, Deum, rerum omnium principium et finem, naturali humanae rationis lumine e rebus creatis certo cognosci posse ... (DS 3004, DB 1785).

The corresponding canon reads:

> Si quis dixerit, Deum unum et verum, creatorem et Dominum nostrum, per ea, quae facta sunt, naturali rationis humanae lumine certo cognosci non posse: anathema sit. (DS 3026, DB 1806).

My interpretation of these statements will be based on Dr. Hermann J. Pottmeyer's study of the history of *Dei Filius*.[2]

First, then, there is asserted the possibility of certain knowledge, *certo cognosci posse*. Explicitly in the *Acta* there is envisaged not any

---

[1] *Proceedings of the Twenty-Third Annual Convention*, Washington, D.C., 1968 (Yonkers, N.Y., 1969), pp. 54–69. © 1969 by Catholic Theological Society of America.

[2] H. J. Pottmeyer, *Der Glaube vor dem Anspruch der Wissenschaft. Die Konstitution 'Dei Filius' des 1. Vatikanischen Konzils.* Freiburg: Herder, 1968. Pp. 168–204.

quaestio facti but only a *quaestio iuris*. What is claimed is not fact but possibility, not act but potency.

Secondly, the potency in question is not moral but physical. The natural light of human reason is part of man's physical make-up. It is not asserted that this light is sufficient for fallen man to come to certain knowledge of God; on the contrary, the words *ab homine lapso* once were in the decree and later were removed from it.[3] Again, it is not asserted that man without some tradition can reach the full development of his rational powers and so come to certain knowledge of God; on the contrary, that was the doctrine of the so-called moderate traditionalism.[4] What was condemned was an outright traditionalism that flatly denied the possibility of the light of reason reaching certain knowledge of God.

Thirdly, the knowledge in question is not immediate but mediated, and it is mediated not by revelation but by creation. It is not immediate, face to face, but through a glass darkly. It is not mediated by revelation but shortly contrasted with revelation. Explicitly it is mediated by creatures, *e rebus creatis, per ea quae facta sunt.*

Fourthly, the object of this possible knowledge is God as principle and end of all things, and, again, in the canon, as the one true God, our Creator and Lord. However, the council settled nothing about the extent of possible natural knowledge. Its

---

[3] The third schema of *Dei Filius*, composed by Father Joseph Kleutgen, read in the canon "... *per ea quae facta sunt, naturali ratione ab homine lapso certo cognosci et demonstrari posse: a. s.*" See J. D. Mansi, *Sacrorum Conciliorum Nova et Amplissima Collectio.* 53:168.

[4] The third schema had excluded the need of a religious tradition for man to arrive at natural knowledge of God. The chapter read: "... *naturali humanae rationis lumine e rebus creatis certo cognosci posse, neque ad hoc traditam de Deo doctrinam omnino necessariam esse* ..." Mansi, *ibid.*, 165.

Cardinal Franzelin's *votum*, preparatory to the council, was a chief source on the errors to be confuted and the doctrines to be proposed. His account of traditionalism is available in Pottmeyer, *op. cit., Anhang*, pp. 31* ff., 34* note 1. See also *Sachregister, s. v.* Traditionalismus.

position amounted to the assertion that man can form a true concept of the true God and know his existence with certainty.

Finally, the general intention of the council was to take a stand on the questions of the day. The stand it took was the traditional stand that defended both reason and faith, reason against fideists and outright traditionalists, faith against rationalists and semi-rationalists.

Difficulties with this doctrine are widespread today and they are not confined to those outside the church. A first question would be about the relevance of the doctrine. It springs from what seems to be an excessive objectivism, an objectivism that just leaves subjects out of account. It tells what can be done by the natural light of human reason, but it does not commit itself either to saying that the possibility ever was realized or to predicting that it ever would be realized. A contemporary would want to know what there is about this possibility that makes any difference to human life or human society.

Secondly, the context of the doctrine is the distinction between faith and reason, grace and nature, supernatural and natural. This distinction has a long history in Catholic theology, but that history is complex, abstruse, difficult, Scholastic. A contemporary is quite ready to speak with the Bible and the Fathers about God's grace and man's sinfulness. But he will ask whether things must be complicated with the notion of human nature or the natural light of human reason.

Thirdly, what the doctrine means is that there exists, at least in principle, some valid and certain argument accessible to the human mind that concludes with an affirmation of God's existence. But any such procedure would treat God as an object. Now for very many today God is not and cannot be an object. Consequently, they would repudiate any attempt to prove God's existence.

Fourthly, there are those that would admit the possibility of establishing the existence of a merely metaphysical object, an *ens a se*, but they would argue with Max Scheler that God is a person, and that no person can be known as an object but only inter-subjectively through co-operation and, so to speak, co-performance (*Mitvollzug*).[5]

Fifthly, there are all those very religious persons to whom philosophy means little or nothing. They know about God in a very real way and they know that this knowledge is something quite different from the logical business of premises and con-clusions. With Pascal they will distinguish between the *Dieu des philosophes* and *le Dieu d'Abraham, d'Isaac, et de Jacob*. So by a simpler route they reach much the same conclusion as the phenomenologist, Max Scheler. The god concluded from pre-mises is not the God Christians worship.

Sixthly, in our day the obvious instance of valid knowledge is science. Science is empirical. It proceeds from data and it develops by returning again and again to the data. Moreover, it never adds to data any intelligibility, any unity or relationship, that is not verifiable in the data. Now there are no data on the divine. God is not among the data of sense and he is not among the data of human consciousness. God, then, is not a possible object of modern science.

Further, there is no verifiable principle by which we might conclude from this world to God's existence. For a principle is verifiable only if there are data on both the terms related by the principle. There are no data on God, and so there are not the data for a principle relating this world to God. Hence, to affirm natural knowledge of God in the contemporary context is to lay oneself open to the question, By what unverifiable principle do you propose to conclude from this world to God's existence?

One might answer, By an analytic principle. But then one has to meet the distinction between analytic propositions and analytic principles.[6] Analytic propositions are to be achieved by merely verbal definitions. Analytic principles are analytic propositions

[5] See M. Frings, *Max Scheler*, Pittsburgh and Louvain, 1965, pp. 135 f.
[6] See B. Lonergan, *Insight*, New York, 1957, pp. 304 ff.

whose terms in their defined sense have been verified. With this distinction one once more is met by the demand for verifiability.

Seventhly, ontological and moral judgments pertain to quite different domains. In other words "ought" cannot occur in a conclusion, when "ought" does not occur in the premisses. To state that God is good in the moral sense presupposes moral judgments. Such moral judgments proceed not from an abstract ontology but from a morally good person.[7] Now the God of religion is the good God, and his goodness is mysteriously in contrast with the evils and suffering of this world. To acknowledge God as good is not just a conclusion; it is to adopt a whole *Weltanschauung*; it is to make an existential decision. So once more we come to the conclusion that draws a distinction between the God of the philosophers and the God of religion.

Such, very summarily, are difficulties perhaps commonly felt about the doctrine of natural knowledge of God. I propose to discuss them, not in the order in which I raised them, but in the order that will best serve to clarify the issues.

First, then let us consider two meanings of the word "object." On the one hand, there is the etymological meaning of the word, which was systematized by Kant, and remains in various subsequent philosophies that have not broken loose from Kant's basic influence. On the other hand, there is the meaning implicit in all discourse: an object is what is intended in questioning and becomes known by answering questions.

The Greek word for object, *to antikeimenon*, means what lies opposite. The Latin, *obiectum*, whence are derived our word "object," the French, *objet*, the Italian, *oggetto*, means what is put or set or lies before or opposite. The German, *Gegenstand*, means what stands opposite. In all cases, then, "object" connotes something sensible, localized, locally related presumably to a spectator or sensitive subject.

[7] I have explained this sentence in *The Subject*, above pp. 82 ff.

In full accord with the etymological meaning of "object" is one of the key sentences in Kant's *Critique of Pure Reason*. It occurs at the very beginning of the *Transcendental Aesthetic*, and it asserts that the one way in which our cognitional activities are related to objects immediately is by *Anschauung*, by intuition. Since for Kant our only intuitions are sensitive, it follows that the categories of the understanding and the ideals of reason of themselves are empty; they refer to objects only mediately, only inasmuch as they are applied to the objects intuited by sense. Accordingly, our cognitional activity is restricted to a world of possible experience and that a world not of metaphysical realities but of sensible phenomena.[8]

Substantially the same position recurs in logical atomism, logical positivism, logical empiricism.[9] Inasmuch as there is an insistence on the significance of the logical, discourse is admitted. But this admission is restricted by the affirmation of an atomism, positivism, or empiricism, for the only discourse considered meaningful is discourse that can be reduced to, or be verified in, or at least be falsifiable by sensible objects.

However, the nineteenth and twentieth centuries have witnessed a series of attempts to get beyond Kant and, in one way or another, these attempts have consisted in an insistence on the subject to offset and compensate for Kant's excessive attention to sensible objects. This was already apparent in the absolute idealisms of Fichte, Schelling, and Hegel. It took a more personal form with Kierkegaard's emphasis on the contingently existing subject and with the emphasis on will in Schopenhauer and Nietzsche. The phenomenological studies of intersubjectivity by Edmund Husserl and Max Scheler and the various forms of

[8] See F. Copleston, *A History of Philosophy*, Westminster, 1969, Vol. VI, chap. 12, nn. 1 and 8. I have treated this topic both in *Collection*, New York and London, 1967, p. 208, and in *The Subject*, above p. 78.
[9] See chapter two in J. A. Martin, *The New Dialogue Between Philosophy and Theology*, New York, 1966.

existentialism have set up against the objectivist world of impersonal science a not-to-be-objectified inner world of subjects striving for authenticity.

Now it is clear that God is not and cannot be an object in the etymological sense, in the Kantian sense, in the sense acceptable to a logical atomism, positivism, or empiricism. Moreover, as long as such a notion of object prevails, phenomenology and existentialism may allow us some access to God as a subject to whom we are subjectively orientated. (Our hearts are restless till they rest in thee), but any procedure that regards God as an object will remain excluded.

So much for a first meaning of the word "object." There is, however, a second quite different meaning. On this view, objects are what are intended in questioning and what become better known as our answers to questions become fuller and more accurate.

Objects are what are intended in questioning. What is this intending? It is neither ignorance nor knowledge but the dynamic intermediary between ignorance and knowledge. It is the conscious movement away from ignorance and towards knowledge. When we question, we do not know the answer yet, but already we want the answer. Not only do we want the answer but also we are aiming at what is to be known through the answer. Such, then, is intending and, essentially, it is dynamic. It promotes us from mere experiencing to understanding by asking what and why and how. It promotes us from understanding to truth by asking whether this or that is really so. It promotes us from truth to value by asking whether this or that is truly good or only apparently good. As answers accumulate, as they correct, complete, qualify one another, knowledge advances. But answers only give rise to still further questions. Objects are never completely, exhaustively known, for our intending always goes beyond present achievement. The greatest achievement, so far from drying up the source of questioning, of intending, only provides a broader base whence ever more questions arise. Intending then is comprehensive. Though human achievement is limited, still the root dynamism is unrestricted. We would know everything about everything, the whole universe in all its multiplicity and concreteness, *omnia*, *to pan*, and, in that concrete and comprehensive sense, being. To that object our cognitional operations are related immediately, not by sensitive intuition, but by questioning.

Now if God cannot be an object in the etymological or Kantian or equivalent meanings of the word "object" it would be only a fallacy to conclude that he cannot be an object in the quite different meaning just indicated. Moreover, it has always been in the context, at least implicit, of this meaning that the question of God and arguments for God's existence have been presented. Nor is this meaning of the word "object" limited to philosophers and theologians. On the contrary, every serious scientist that ever existed was concerned with the advancement of science, with coming to know more than at present is known, with the object to which we dynamically are orientated by our questions but which we only partially know.

Secondly, let us consider the nature of the unverifiable principle by which we proceed from knowledge of this world to knowledge of God. Four points need to be touched upon, namely, What is verification? What principles need to be verified? Are there principles that do not need to be verified? Will these principles take us beyond this world to knowledge of God?

First, what is verification? Vulgarly, verification seems to be conceived as a matter of taking a look, of making an observation. In fact, while verification includes observations, it includes not one but indefinitely many, and it includes them within a very elaborate context. That context divides into two parts, direct and indirect verification. Direct verification is a matter of working out the logical presuppositions and implications of a very carefully formulated hypothesis, devising experiments that will yield data that conform or do not conform with the implications of the hypothesis and, when hypotheses conflict, devising crucial experiments that will resolve the conflict. Indirect verification is more massive and, ultimately, more significant. All hypotheses, theories, systems of a science are linked together proximately or remotely in logical interdependence. So, for instance, the law of falling bodies was verified directly by Galileo, but it also has been verified indirectly every time in the last four centuries that that law was among the presuppositions of a successful experiment or a successful application. Similarly, any other law of principle wins an ever securer position by the far-flung and almost continuous process of indirect verification whether in laboratories or in the applications of science to industry. Nonetheless, not even the cumulative evidence assembled by the all but countless observations of direct and prolonged indirect verification suffice to exempt a scientific hypothesis from liability to revision. Unlike the everyday statements of common sense, such as "I now am here speaking to you," they do not meet the requirements for a certain judgment set by the natural light of human reason. They are merely probable, and everyone enjoying the use of the natural light of human reason knows that they are merely probable.

Incidentally, may I remark that I should like to see greater attention paid by certain types of analytic philosophy to the notable gaps between an observation and a process of verification and, on the other hand, true and certain knowledge.

Secondly, what needs to be verified? What is the need for verification? It is a need disclosed to us by what Vatican I referred to as the natural light of human reason, by what I should name our power to ask and answer questions. The first type of question, the question for intelligence, asks what or why or how. The question is put with respect to data, but the answer that is sought goes beyond the data; it is not just some other datum but something quite different from data, namely, a possibly relevant intelligible unity or relationship. Such possibly relevant intelligible unities or relationships are grasped by insights and expressed in hypothetical statements. From the nature of the case there arises, then, the further question, Is the possibly relevant unity or relationship the one that is actually relevant to this case or to this type of case? Common sense meets such questions by what I called in my book *Insight* the self-correcting process of learning. Natural science meets them by the process of direct and indirect verification.

Thirdly, are there principles that do not need to be verified? Here I would distinguish two meanings of the word "principle." Commonly it is understood as a logically first proposition, an ultimate premiss. More generally, principle has been defined as what is first in any ordered set, *primum in aliquo ordine*. In this more general sense, an originating power is a principle, and, specifically, our power to ask and answer questions is such an originating power and so a principle. Now obviously this principle, which is the human mind itself, does not need verification for its validation. It is only by the actual use of our minds that any inquiry and any process of verification can be carried out. Hence, every appeal to verification as a source of validation presupposes a prior and more fundamental appeal to the human mind as a source of validation.

However, besides the mind itself, besides our originating power to ask and answer questions, there is the objectification of this power in concepts and principles. Besides the notion of being, which is the intending behind all our questions, there is also the concept of being, which is an objectification of the notion. Besides the native procedures of the mind in asking and answering questions, there is the objectification of these procedures in such principles as identity, contradiction, sufficient reason and, more fully, in logics and methods. Now these objectifications are historically conditioned. They can be incomplete or erroneous, and they can be corrected, revised, developed. Consequently, they have to be scrutinized, checked, verified. But the process of verification appeals, not to the data of sense, but to the data of consciousness, not to any data whatever of consciousness but to the data on the process of asking and answering questions.

Fourthly, do these principles suffice to take us beyond the visible universe to knowledge of God? The answer to that question depends on the answer to our prior question about knowledge and its object. On Kantian and positivist views our knowledge is confined to a world of experience. On some subjectivist views, while we cannot know God as an object, still we can enter into some subject-to-subject relation with him in religious experience. But if human knowing consists in asking and answering questions, if ever further questions arise, if the further questions are given honest answers then, as I have argued elsewhere at some length, we can and do arrive at knowledge of God.[10]

If I have said something to clarify the ambiguities of the term "object," and the process, verification, let me now draw attention to the continuity of the intellectual with the moral and the religious, of the mind with the heart.

Our conscious and intentional operations occur on four interlocked levels. There is a level of experiencing, a level of understanding and conception, a level of reflection and judgment, a level of deliberation and decision. We are moved, promoted from one level to the next by questions; from experiencing to understanding by questions for intelligence; from understanding to judging by questions for reflection; from judging to deciding by questions for deliberation. So the many operations are linked together both on the side of the subject and on the side of the object. On the side of the subject there is the one mind putting the many questions in pursuit of a single goal. On the side of the object there is the gradual cumulation and conjoining of partial elements into a single whole. So insight grasps the intelligibility of what sense perceives. Conception unites what separately sense perceives and intelligence grasps. Judgment pronounces on the

[10] *Insight*, chapter 19.

truth of the conceiving and on the reality of the conceived. Decision acknowledges the value of actuating potentialities grasped by intelligence and judged to be real. So the transcendentals, the intelligible, the true, the real, the good, apply to absolutely every object for the very good reason that they are grounded in the successive stages in our dealing with objects. But they are one in their root as well as in their application. For the intending subject intends, first of all, the good but to achieve it must know the real; to know the real he must know what is true; to know what is true he must grasp what is intelligible; and to grasp what is intelligible he must attend to the data of sense and to the data of consciousness.

Now this unity of the human spirit, this continuity in its operations, this cumulative character in their results, seem very little understood by those that endeavor to separate and compartmentalize and isolate the intellectual, the moral, and the religious. They may, of course, be excused inasmuch as the good work they happen to have read is mostly critical while the constructive work they happen to have come across is mostly sloppy. But the fact remains that the intellectual, the moral, and the religious are three successive stages in a single achievement, the achievement of self-transcendence; and so attempts to separate and isolate the intellectual, the moral, and the religious are just so many efforts to distort or to entirely block authentic human development.

What is the intellectual but an intentional self-transcendence? It is coming to know, not what appears, not what is imagined, not what is thought, not what seems to me to be so, but what is so. To know what is so is to get beyond the subject, to transcend the subject, to reach what would be even if this particular subject happened not to exist.

Still the self-transcendence of knowledge is merely intentional. With the moral a further step is taken, for by the moral we come to know and to do what is truly good. That is a real self-transcendence, a moving beyond all merely personal satisfactions and interests and tastes and preferences and becoming a principle of benevolence and beneficence, becoming capable of genuine loving.

What, finally, is religion but complete self-transcendence? It is the love of God poured forth in our hearts by the Holy Spirit that is given to us (Rom. 5: 5). It is the love in Christ Jesus St. Paul described when he wrote: "For I am convinced that there is nothing in death or life, in the realm of spirits or superhuman powers, in the world as it is or the world as it shall be, in the forces of the universe, in heights or depths—nothing in all creation that can separate us from the love of God in Christ Jesus our Lord" (Rom. 8: 38f.). That love is not this or that act of loving but a radical being-in-love, a first principle of all one's thoughts and words and deeds and omissions, a principle that keeps us out of sin, that moves us to prayer and to penance, that can become the ever so quiet yet passionate center of all our living. It is, whatever its degree, a being-in-love that is without conditions or qualifications or reserves, and so it is other-worldly, a being-in-love that occurs within this world but heads beyond it, for no finite object or person can be the object of unqualified, unconditional loving. Such unconditional being-in-love actuates to the full the dynamic potentiality of the human spirit with its unrestricted reach and, as a full actuation, it is fulfilment, deep-set peace, the peace the world cannot give, abiding joy, the joy that remains despite humiliation and failure and privation and pain.

This complete being-in-love, the gift of God's grace, is the reason of the heart that reason does not know. It is a religious experience by which we enter into a subject-to-subject relation with God. It is the eye of faith that discerns God's hand in nature and his message in revelation. It is the efficacious reality that brings men to God despite their lack of learning or their learned errors. It is in this life the crown of human development, grace perfecting nature, the entry of God into the life of man so that man comes to love his neighbor as himself.[11]

I have been contending, then, that the intellectual, the moral, and the religious are quite distinct but not at all disparate. They are three distinct phases in the unfolding of the human spirit, of that eros for self-transcendence that goes beyond itself intentionally in knowledge, effectively in morality, totally in religion. With the affirmation of this continuity our efforts at basic clarification come to an end, and we turn to meeting explicitly some of the questions that were raised initially but so far have not been treated.

First, however, let us note very briefly our position. It is not the naive realist, Kantian, positivist view of the object. It is not the mixed view that leaves science to naive realists, Kantians, and positivists to add for humanist or religious reasons an insistence on the subjectivity of the subject. It is the view that man's spirit, his mind and his heart, is an active power, an eros, for self-transcendence; consequently, the subject is related intrinsically and indeed, constitutively to the object towards which it transcends itself; finally, knowledge, morality, and religion are the three distinct phases in which such self-transcendence is realized.

Next, it was asked what is the relevance of the doctrine of natural knowledge of God, what difference does it make to human living and human society. Obviously, I cannot attempt to treat this question in any but a very summary fashion. There are those today for whom any thought about, any mention of, either theism or atheism is just meaningless, for whom all religion at best is just a comforting illusion. Such opinions involve a profound ignorance of man's real nature, and such ignorance cannot but have a gravely distorting effect on the conduct of human affairs. The doctrine of natural knowledge of God means that God lies within the horizon of man's knowing and doing, that religion represents a fundamental dimension in human living.

[11] As described in 1 Cor. 13.

Thirdly, it was urged that we have to drop the words, "nature," "natural," that we should be content to speak with Scripture and the Fathers of God's grace and man's sinfulness. Now I have no doubt that such words as "nature" and "natural," no less than object and verification, can be abused. But I also have no doubt that if we are not only going to speak about God's grace and man's sinfulness but also we are going to say what precisely we mean by such speaking, then we are going to have to find some third term over and above grace and sin.[12]

Fourthly, can a person be an object? A person cannot be an object if "object" is taken in a naive realist, Kantian, or positivist sense. But if "object" means that towards which self-transcending heads, obviously persons are objects: we know them and we love them.

But, it will be urged, according to Max Scheler, we know other persons only intersubjectively. I would grant that such a conclusion follows from Scheler's cognitional theory but, at the same time, I would point out that, just as we pass from consciousness of the self as subject to an objectification of the self in conception and judging, so too we pass from intersubjectivity to the objectification of intersubjectivity. Not only do we (two subjects in a subject-to-subject relation) speak and act. We speak about ourselves; we act on one another; and inasmuch as we are spoken of or acted on, we are not just subjects, not subjects as subjects, but subjects as objects.

Fifthly, is not philosophy totally different from religion, and is not the God of the philosophers totally different from the God of Abraham, Isaac, Jacob?

On my analysis philosophy and religion are quite distinct but they are not totally different; they are two of the three phases of that single thrust by which the human spirit moves towards self-transcendence. What gives rise to the appearance of total difference,

---

[12] See my *Grace and Freedom*, London and New York 1971, pp. 2–19; or the original article, *Theol. Stud.*, 2 (1941) 290–306.

I should say, is a failure to distinguish between undifferentiated and differentiated consciousness. Undifferentiated consciousness is global; it is at once intellectual, moral, and religious; it does not sort out different types of issues, specialize now in one type and later in another, seek the integration of separate, specialized developments. Differentiated consciousness results precisely from this process of distinguishing, specializing and, eventually, integrating. As intellectual, it becomes technical. As moral, it concentrates on moral development. As religious, it heads towards mysticism. Now while differentiated consciousness understands undifferentiated, undifferentiated consciousness finds differentiated incomprehensible, totally different; not only does it find the technical aspects of science and philosophy simply alien to its religious piety; it also finds asceticism and mysticism equally or more alien.

There remains the further question: Is not the God of the philosophers totally different from the God of Abraham, Isaac and Jacob?

I am quite ready to grant that there are many mistaken philosophies and many mistaken notions of God. I am also ready to grant that undifferentiated consciousness has very little grasp of any philosophic notion of God, and so would find it impossible to equate the God of its piety with the God of philosophic discourse. Again, I should insist that moral and religious development vastly enrich our relations to God and our apprehension of him; in this respect I am greatly in agreement with Max Scheler and Dietrich von Hildebrand. But I should deny that our intellectual apprehension of any real object, least of all, of God is ever complete, closed, excluding further development. I should deny that the developments from moral and religious experience in any way fail to harmonize with intellectual apprehension. I should urge that just as the intellectual, the moral, and the religious are three phases in the single thrust to self-transcendence, so too moral and religious development only reveal more fully the God that can be known by the natural light of human reason.

Sixthly, natural knowledge of God is not attained without moral judgments and existential decisions. These do not occur without God's grace. Therefore, the natural light of human reason does not suffice for man's so-called natural knowledge of God.

I mention this objection, not because it is to the point, but because the point is often missed. One misinterprets Vatican I if one fancies it is speaking, not about a *quaestio iuris*, but about a *quaestio facti*. The *quaestio iuris* is (1) whether there exists a valid argument for God's existence and (2) whether the apprehension of that argument is an *actus supernaturalis quoad substantiam*. Natural knowledge of God is denied if one holds that there is no valid argument or if one holds that apprehending the argument is an intrinsically supernatural act. Natural knowledge of God is affirmed if one holds that there is a valid argument and if one holds that apprehending the argument is intrinsically natural. One goes beyond the *quaestio iuris* to the *quaestio facti*, when one turns from conditions of possibility to conditions of actual occurrence. Such conditions are always very numerous. In the present instance men must exist. They must be healthy and enjoy considerable leisure. They must have attained a sufficient differentiation of consciousness to think philosophically. They must have succeeded in avoiding all of the pitfalls in which so many great philosophers have become entrapped. They must resist their personal evil tendencies and not be seduced by the bad example of others. Such are just a few very general conditions of someone actually grasping a valid argument for God's existence. An adequate account would include every entity that conditioned the actual occurrence. Now Vatican I was not speaking of a *quaestio facti* but of a *quaestio iuris*, not of conditions of actuality but of conditions of possibility. I do not think that in this life people arrive at natural knowledge of God without God's grace, but what I do not doubt is that the knowledge they so attain is natural.

THEOLOGY AND MAN'S FUTURE[1]

The correlation between the accelerating expansion of knowledge and socio-cultural change confronts the contemporary university with a grave problem. For the university has ceased to be a storehouse whence traditional wisdom and knowledge are dispensed. It is a center in which ever-increasing knowledge is disseminated to bring about ever-increasing social and cultural change. It has a grave responsibility for the future of man, and it is the concern of St. Louis University in sponsoring the present gathering to ventilate this issue.

My paper will deal indirectly with theology, then, as it is situated in a contemporary university influenced by other disciplines, as possibly relevant to questions other disciplines raise and to problems they confront and, consequently, as making its contribution to the thought that will direct the future of man.

First, then, let me say something of the influence other disciplines have had on theology and, particularly, on Catholic theology, where the effect has been belated, more recent, and so, at least apparently, more massive. Five areas here merit attention: history, philosophy, religious studies, method, and communications.

One of the profoundest changes in Catholic theology has been brought about by modern methods of historical study. It is true,

---

[1] Reprinted from *Cross Currents*, 19 (1969), 452–61. Originally read as a paper at St. Louis University's Sesquicentennial Symposium, "Theology in the City of Man," October 15–17, 1968. © 1969 by Cross Currents Corporation.

of course, that Christianity has always been a historical religion. The Fathers appealed to the Scriptures, the medieval theologians both to the Scriptures and to the Fathers, later theologians to all their predecessors. But they did not have at their disposal the resources and the collaboration of modern scholarship with its critical editions of texts, its indices and handbooks, its specialized institutes and congresses, its ever-mounting accumulation of monographs and articles. The ideal that focused their attention was not the historical ideal of critically evaluating all available evidence with the aim of bringing back to life the societies and cultures of the past;[2] it was the theological ideal of knowing God and knowing all things in their relation to God. So they assumed not only an unbroken tradition of faith but also unchanging modes of apprehension and conception.[3] A great revolution was needed—and it is not yet completed—to make the development of doctrine an acceptable notion, to have it apprehended not merely in some abstract and notional fashion but concretely and really through exact study of relevant texts, to admit historical methods not only in the patristic and medieval and later fields but also in the scriptures, and finally—to come to the as yet unfinished task—to effect the synthesis of historical and theological aims so that we have neither history without theology nor theology without history, but both.

A second major influence has been philosophic. Catholic theology has been wedded to Aristotle. The beginnings of that wedding were auspicious enough. For medieval theology was doing two things when partly it accepted and partly it reinterpreted the Aristotelian corpus. On the one hand, it was providing itself with a conceptual system that would make it possible for it to work out coherent answers to its endless

[2] Most recently on this theme: P. Hünermann, *Der Durchbruch geschichtlichen Denkens im 19. Jahrhundert*, Freiburg i. Br., 1957.
[3] Owen Chadwick, *From Bossuet to Newman: The Idea of Doctrinal Development*, Cambridge, 1957.

quaestiones. At the same time, it was christianizing the Greek and Arabic culture that was pouring into Western Europe and threatening to engulf its faith. But what once was achievement, at a later date proved to be an obstacle to vitality and development. Aristotelian thought is unacquainted not merely with the content but also with the nature of modern science. It is not equipped to distinguish and to relate to one another the natural sciences, the human sciences, philosophy, and theology. It is unable to provide the foundations for their proper functioning and collaboration. Its conceptual system in part is to be revised and in part to be replaced by notions drawn from modern philosophy and science. So it is that contemporary theologians are drawing upon personalist, phenomenological, existential, historical, and transcendental types of philosophic thought to find the conceptual tools needed for their own thinking and writing. The results are often eclectic rather than systematic and deeply based, and here I feel there is a real danger in an age when modernist subjectivism and relativism are becoming increasingly common.

Contemporary Catholic theology, then, not only is open to philosophic influence but profoundly needs philosophy. Here I must distinguish between primary and secondary aspects of that need. The theologian will want to be acquainted with Stoicism in reading Tertullian, with middle Platonism in reading Origen, with Neoplatonism in reading Augustine, with Aristotle, Avicenna, and Averroës in reading Aquinas, with Aquinas in reading subsequent theologians. But this need is secondary. It is a matter of acquiring the necessary background for particular tasks of interpretation. Again, it is through a study of the philosophers that the theologian will be introduced to philosophic questions, that he will reach answers relevant to his primary need, that he will learn to think and speak on the level of his age and culture. But again this is secondary. It is concerned with the pedagogy of meeting the primary need. It does not define the primary need itself. The primary need is for the theologian to know what he is doing when he is doing theology. To reach such knowledge three prior questions must be answered. First is the question of cognitional theory: What am I doing when I am knowing? Second is the question of epistemology: Why is doing that knowing? Third is the question of metaphysics: What do I know when I do it? To these three questions the theologian needs full, precise, and well-grounded answers. If he has those answers, his essential needs are met. If he does not reach those answers, then he will not know what he is doing, not merely when he reads philosophers but also when he does theology, when he is interpreting a text, when he is ascertaining a historical fact, when he is reconstructing a situation or mentality, when he moves beyond reason to faith, when he determines what is and what is not a matter of faith, when he seeks an understanding of the mysteries of faith, and when he concerns himself with the problem of communicating the faith to all men of all classes and of all cultures. Briefly, theologians have minds and use them, and they had best know what they are doing when they use them. Again, to put the matter historically, to follow Aquinas today is not to repeat Aquinas today, but to do for the twentieth century what Aquinas did for the thirteenth. As Aquinas baptized key elements in Greek and Arabic culture, so the contemporary Catholic philosopher and/or theologian has to effect a baptism of key elements in modern culture.

A third major influence is the field of religious studies: the phenomenology of religion, the psychology of religion, the sociology of religion, the history of religions, and the philosophy of religion. I call this a major influence, not because the influence has been conspicuous, but because of very significant and powerful contemporary trends. The first stems from Vatican II, and it consists in the Church's concern with ecumenism, with non-Christian religions, and with the atheist negation of religion. This fact requires the theologian to reflect on his religion, not in isolation from all others, but in conjunction with others. It requires him to attend, not only to the differences separating his religion from others, but also to the similarities that connect them with one another. To meet such requirements theology will be led into the field of religious studies and, indeed, while retaining its identity, to conceive itself as a particular type of religious studies. There is a second factor leading to the same conclusion. I have already spoken of the relations of theology with history and with philosophy. But if it is to take its place in contemporary culture, it has also to be related to all the human sciences; and it is in the field of religious studies, in the phenomenology and psychology and sociology of religion, that it will find models exhibiting what can be done and accounts of what has been tried and found unsatisfactory. Finally, there is the theological doctrine that God grants all men sufficient grace for their salvation. This doctrine is relevant to religious studies; it makes them studies of the manifold ways God's grace comes to men and operates as the seed that falls on rocks or amidst thorns or by the wayside or on good ground to bring forth fruit thirty or sixty or a hundred fold.

Fourthly, there is the area of methodology. The Aristotelian notion of science is one thing, the modern notion is quite another. Contemporary Catholic theology has already in actual practice taken on the features of a modern science. But in a neurosis-like conflict with this practice there lurk in the minds of many theologians assumptions and implications that stem from Aristotle's *Posterior Analytics*. No doubt, theologians always have recognized that their subject was not a science in the Aristotelian sense, that in that sense it could be named science only by analogy. But the modern fact is that no science whatever satisfies Aristotle's requirements. To keep on thinking of theology as analogously a science is just to perpetuate a long list of misleading notions and principles.

For Aristotle science is of the necessary: we think we understand when we know the cause, know that it is the cause, and know that the effect cannot be other than it is.[4] In the modern

[4] Aristotle, *Posterior Analytics*, I, 1, 71b 10-12.

sciences necessity is a marginal notion. Their substantive concern is, not with necessity, but with verifiable possibility. The intelligibility they seek is not the intelligibility that cannot be other than it is, but the intelligibility that very well could be other than it is, and so is intrinsically hypothetical and in need of verification.

Again, for Aristotle, there was a sharp distinction between theory and practice.[5] Theory regarded the necessary; but the necessary is unchangeable; and the unchangeable cannot be changed. It lies utterly outside the whole field of practical activity. All one can do about it is contemplate it. But in the modern sciences theory and practice regard exactly the same objects; they represent successive stages in our dealings with these objects. Good theory is the possibility of efficacious practice, and practice is the application of theory.

Again, for Aristotle, science is true and certain.[6] But modern science is not true and certain. It is an ongoing process in which the range and the probability of human knowing keep increasing, but truth and certainty are just limiting concepts. This fact, of course, marks a major problem in the method of contemporary theology, for theology is the offspring not only of science but also of faith, and faith claims truth and certainty.

Finally, an Aristotelian science was a compact affair, it could be tucked into a habit in the mind of a scientist. But no modern science in its entirety is known by any individual. Modern sciences are parcelled out among the many minds of the scientific community. As they are produced by a far-flung collaboration, so they reside distributively in the minds of researchers, professors, students. And what is true of modern physics, chemistry, biology, also is true of contemporary theology. There are today no omnicompetent theologians.

Finally, there is the area of communications. The Church has

---

[5] *Ibid.*, I, 33, 88b 30 ff. *Nicomachean Ethics*, VI, 5, 1140a 24 ff.
[6] *Posterior Analytics*, I, 2, 71b 25 and 72a 37 ff.

always felt called to herald the Gospel to all men of all cultures and all classes. But the full implications of this mission were hidden by the classicist notion of culture. For that notion was not empirical but normative. It did not study the different cultures of mankind but simply set up its own as the ideal and generously offered to instruct others in its own ways. Its classics were immortal works of art, its philosophy was perennial philosophy, its assumptions were eternal truths, its laws were the depository of the wisdom and the prudence of mankind. But modern culture is the culture that knows many cultures, that studies and compares them, that knows they are all man-made and subject to development and to decay. Just as theology has to enter into the context of modern philosophy and science, so religion has to retain its identity yet penetrate into the cultures of mankind, into the manifold fabric of everyday meaning and feeling that directs and propels the lives of men. It has to know the uses of symbol and story, the resources of the arts and of literature, the potentialities of the old and the new media of communication, the various motivations on which in any given area it can rely, the themes that in a given culture and class provide a carrying wave for the message.

So much for my first topic. I have indicated five major areas in which theology has been profoundly influenced or is about to be profoundly influenced by other disciplines: history, philosophy, religious studies, method, and communications. This list, of course, is not exclusive. I have selected them simply on the basis of their enormous contribution to theology or theology's pressing need of them. I now turn to my second topic: What has theology to offer? What relevance does it possess for the concerns of other disciplines? What aid can it bring towards a solution of their problems?

These are large and difficult questions and, perhaps, I cannot do better than go back to the basic theorem in Newman's *Idea of a University*. It contains two parts, one positive, the other negative.

Positively, Newman advanced that human knowing was a whole with its parts organically related, and this accords with the contemporary phenomenological notion of horizon, that one's perceptions are functions of one's outlook, that one's meaning is a function of a context and that context of still broader contexts.[7] On the negative side, Newman asked what would happen if a significant part of knowledge were omitted, overlooked, ignored, not just by some individual but by the cultural community, and he contended that there would be three consequences. First, people in general would be ignorant of that area. Second, the rounded whole of human knowing would be mutilated. Third, the remaining parts would endeavor to round off the whole once more despite the omission of a part and, as a result, they would suffer distortion from their effort to perform a function for which they were not designed. Such was Newman's theorem.[8] In fact, theology has for some time been dropped from most university curricula. So one well may ask whether Newman's inferences have been confirmed in fact, whether there is a widespread ignorance of specifically theological areas, and whether this has resulted in a mutilation and distortion of human knowledge generally. A fair and adequate answer to these questions would have many presuppositions and would involve a very delicately nuanced survey. I cannot here expound the former nor have I been able to undertake the latter. So I must be content with having brought the matter to your attention.

But it is within this context that I should like to indicate a possible relevance of theology to a basic problem of the human sciences. For the human sciences may be and often are pursued simply on the analogy of the natural sciences. When this is done

[7] See Herbert Spiegelberg, *The Phenomenological Movement: A Historical Introduction*, 2 vols., The Hague, 1960, pp. 159 ff. Also the index of subjects, s. vv. "Horizon" and "Lebenswelt," pp. 718, 720.

[8] For this theorem I am indebted to Fergal McGrath, *The Consecration of Learning, Lectures on Newman's* "Idea of a University," Dublin, 1962.

rigorously, when it is contended that a scientific explanation of human behavior is reached if the same behavior can be had in a robot,[9] then everything specifically human disappears from the science. The human sciences become exact by ceasing to treat of man as he is. On the other hand, when human scientists reject such reductionism, and many do,[10] not only does the exactitude of the natural sciences vanish but also the human sciences risk becoming captives of some philosophy. For what the reductionist omits are the meaning and value that inform human living and acting. But meaning and value are notions that can be clarified only by painstakingly making one's way through the jungle of the philosophies.

Now the suggestion I wish to make is that theology, and in particular a theology that has carefully and accurately worked out its method, could provide the human sciences with hints or even models for tackling the type of problem I have mentioned. For theology has long worked in conjunction with philosophy. At the present time, Catholic theology is disengaging itself from Aristotle and deriving new categories from personalist, phenomenological, existential, historicist, and transcendental types of philosophic thought. It will possess a certain expertise in using the philosophies without committing itself to more of them than it intends. It is much at home with questions concerning meaning from its study of developing doctrines and its problems of demythologization. Finally, not even the natural sciences can prescind from the question of value, for the very pursuit of science is the pursuit of a value, and the contention that science

---

[9] For a sketch of such views see the first part of Floyd Matson's *The Broken Image*, New York, 1964.

[10] For the "third force" in psychology, see Abraham Maslow, *Toward a Psychology of Being*, Princeton, N.J., 1962, pp. 206 ff. In sociology there is the attention to meaning in the collective work, *Toward a General Theory of Action*, edited by Talcott Parsons and Edward Shils, New York, 1962, pp. 4 ff. Cf. Parsons's study of Max Weber in *Essays in Sociological Theory Pure and Applied*, Glencoe, Illinois, 1949, pp. 72–93.

should be value-free, *wertfrei*, if taken literally,[11] implies that science should be worthless. Theology has long been aware of conflicting judgments of value, even with radical conflicts, and a successful method of theology will have a technique for dealing competently, respectfully, and honestly with this issue.

Besides the sciences, there are the humanities, and, as I have no need to insist, much modern humanism is prone to ignore God and to ridicule religion, when it is not militantly atheistic. Whether certain youth movements indicate a significant break in this trend, I cannot say. But I venture to affirm that an authentic humanism is profoundly religious.

Man's development is a matter of getting beyond himself, of transcending himself, of ceasing to be an animal in a habitat and of becoming a genuine person in a community. The first stage of this development lies in the sensibility that enables him to perceive his surroundings and to respond to what he perceives. But man not only perceives but also wonders, inquires, seeks to understand. He unifies and relates, constructs and extrapolates, serializes and generalizes. He moves out of his immediate surroundings into a universe put together by the symbols and stories of mythic consciousness, or by the speculations of philosophers, or by the investigations of scientists. But besides such cognitional self-transcendence, there is also a real self-transcendence. Men ask not only about facts but also about values. They are not content with satisfactions. They distinguish between what truly is good and what only apparently is good. They are stopped by the question: Is what I have achieved really worthwhile? Is what I hope for really worthwhile? Because men can raise such questions, and answer them, and live by the answers, they can be principles of benevolence and beneficence, of genuine co-operation, of true love.

[11] Talcott Parsons understands Weber to have meant by *Wertfreiheit* that the values of the intellectual disciplines must be differentiated from other types of values constitutive of the culture. *Daedalus*, 94 (1965), 59.

Now there is a profound difference between particular acts of loving and the dynamic state to which we refer when we speak of falling in love and of being in love. That dynamic state, while it has its causes, conditions, occasions, none the less once it occurs and as long as it lasts, is a first principle in one's living. It is the origin and source that prompts and colors all one's thoughts and feelings, all one's hopes and fears, all one's joys and sorrows. Moreover, such being-in-love is of three kinds. There is being-in-love with the domestic community, with one's mate and one's children. There is being-in-love with the civil community, eagerly making one's contribution to its needs and promoting its betterment. There is being-in-love with God. Of this love St. Paul spoke when he wrote to the Romans: "The love of God is poured forth in our hearts by the Spirit of God who has been given to us" (Rom. 5: 5). To it he referred when he asked: "Then what can separate us from the love of Christ? Can affliction or hardship? Can persecution, hunger, nakedness, peril, or the sword?" And his answer was: "For I am convinced that there is nothing in death or life, in the realm of spirits or superhuman powers, in the world as it is or the world as it shall be, in the forces of the universe, in heights or depths—nothing in all creation that can separate us from the love of God in Christ Jesus our Lord" (Rom. 8: 35, 38, 39).

All authentic being-in-love is a total self-surrender. But the love of God is not restricted to particular areas of human living. It is the foundation of love of one's neighbor. It is the grace that keeps one ever faithful and devoted to one's mate. But it is also something in itself, something personal, intimate, and profoundly attuned to the deepest yearnings of the human heart. It constitutes a basic fulfilment of man's being. Because it is such a fulfilment, it is the source of a great peace, the peace that the world cannot give. It is a wellspring of joy that can endure despite the sorrow of failure, humiliation, privation, pain, desertion. Because it is such, a fulfilment, it removes the temptation of all that is shallow hollow, empty, and degrading without handing man over to the fanaticism that arises when man's capacity for God is misdirected to finite goals.

I have quoted St. Paul, but I would not have you think that being in love with God is to be found only among Christians. God gives all men sufficient grace for salvation. Nor is his grace without fruit. A celebrated student of religions, Friedrich Heiler, has listed seven features common to all the high religions.[12] His account runs over ten pages, and I cannot repeat it here, partly because it is too long, but also because I feel that he would recognize at least a rough equivalence between his seven features and what I have said of being in love with God.

There exists, then, in man a capacity for holiness, a capacity for love that, in its immediacy, regards not the ever-passing shape of this world but the mysterious reality, immanent and transcendent, that we name God. Deeply hidden, intensely personal, this love is not so private as to be solitary. The Spirit is given to many, and the many form a community. The community endures over generations, spreads over different nations, adapts to cultural changes. It acquires a history of its origins, its development, its successes and failures, its happy strokes and its mistakes. Its failures and its mistakes becloud its witness, but they argue not for abolition of religion but for its reform.

Long ago St. Augustine exclaimed that God had made us for himself and that our hearts are restless till they rest in him. What that restlessness is, we see all about us in the mountainous discontents, hatreds, and terrors of the twentieth century. But what it is to rest in God is not easily known or readily understood. Though God's grace is given to all, still the experience of resting in God ordinarily needs a religious tradition for it to be encouraged, fostered, interpreted, guided, developed. Though grace bestows

[12] Friedrich Heiler, "The History of Religions as a Preparation for the Cooperation of Religions," in *The History of Religions, Essays in Methodology*, edited by M. Eliade and J. Kitagawa, Chicago, 1959, pp. 142–153.

both good will and good performance, still one shrinks and draws back from the performance of denying oneself daily and taking up one's cross and following Christ. For the fulfilment that is the love of God is not the fulfilment of any appetite or desire or wish or dream impulse, but the fulfilment of getting beyond one's appetites and desires and wishes and impulses, the fulfilment of self-transcendence, the fulfilment of human authenticity, the fulfilment that overflows into a love of one's neighbor as oneself.

I have been speaking to you of religion at its best. But an organized religion, a church, is not a conventicle of saints. It is like a net cast into the sea that catches all sorts of fish. If the same ultimate goal and ideal is proposed to all, there also must be proposed the successive stages in a development towards reaching the goal. So it is that, as generation follows generation, there is always a gap between the ideal and the real, between religion as it strives to be and religion as it is in fact. But apart from cases of self-deception or insincerity, this gap or contrast does not imply that religion is phony, that religious people say one thing and do another. The very being of man is not static but dynamic; it never is a state of achieved perfection; it always is at best a striving. The striving of the religious man is to give himself to God in something nearer the way in which God has given himself to us. Such a goal is always distant, but it is not inhuman, for it corresponds to the dynamic structure of man's being, to the restlessness that is ours till we rest in God.

I have been arguing that, because religion pertains to an authentic humanism, theology has a contribution to make to the humanities. But one can go further and argue with Karl Rahner that the dogmatic theology of the past has to become a theological anthropology.[13] By this is meant that all theological questions and answers have to be matched by the transcendental questions and answers that reveal in the human subject the conditions of the

[13] Karl Rahner, "Theologie and Anthropologie," in *Schriften zur Theologie.* Einsiedeln, 1967, Vol. VIII, pp. 43–65.

possibility of the theological answers. Explicitly Father Rahner excludes a modernist interpretation of his view, namely, that theological doctrines are to be taken as statements about merely human reality. His position is that man is for God, that religion is intrinsic to an authentic humanism, that in theology theocentrism and anthropocentrism coincide. On this basis he desires all theological statements to be matched by statements of their meaning in human terms. His purpose is not to water down theological truth but to bring it to life, not to impose an alien method but to exclude the risk of mythology and to introduce into theological thinking the challenge of rigorous controls.

I must not give the impression, however, that such a theological anthropology already exists. Father Rahner has not, to my knowledge, done more than sketch how one might go about constructing it. But the mere fact that the proposal has been made reveals how closely a future theology may be related to the human sciences and to the humanities.

Let me conclude with a brief summary. I pointed to five areas in which theology has been learning or has to learn from other disciplines: history, philosophy, religious studies, methodology, and communications. Then I recalled Newman's theorem that the omission of a significant discipline from the university curriculum left a blind spot, the mutilation of an organic whole, and a distortion of the disciplines that remained and endeavored to meet real human needs. While I was not in a position to discern whether this theorem is borne out by facts, I did suggest that a theology with a properly developed method would be of some use to human scientists who, on the one hand, wished to avoid all reductionism without, on the other hand, becoming captives of some philosophic fad. Further, I added that religion was part of an authentic humanism, and so that theological reflection on religion was pertinent to the human sciences and the humanities. Finally, I referred to a paper of Father Karl Rahner's with which I am in substantial agreement, to indicate just how closely related to human studies a future theology may prove to be.

THE FUTURE OF CHRISTIANITY[1]

In a collective work on the history of religions published by the Divinity School of the University of Chicago almost a decade ago, the noted German scholar Friedrich Heiler had occasion to list seven principal areas of unity to be discerned, not only in Christian churches and congregations, but in all the religions of mankind: in Judaism, in Islam, in Zoroastrian Mazdaism, in Hinduism, Buddhism, Taoism.[2] I should like to begin this paper with a brief summary of Prof. Heiler's account. For it will draw attention away from what is outward and towards what is inner and vital in religion. It will reassure us that the Christian churches and congregations, despite their many differences, have in common something that is very profound and very dynamic, that promises Christianity a future, that constitutes a basis for serious dialogue not only among Christians but among the representatives of all the world religions. It is true, of course, that Prof. Heiler's list omits what is distinctive of Christianity, but I feel sure that that omission is something that each of us will be more than ready to remedy.

First, then, Prof. Heiler listed "the reality of the transcendent, the holy, the divine, the Other." Distinct from all things transient there is acknowledged "true being," the "reality of all realities,"

---

[1] Published in the *Holy Cross Quarterly*, Worcester, Mass. Winter, 1969, pp. 5–10. © 1969 by Bernard J. F. Lonergan.
[2] Friedrich Heiler, "The History of Religions as a Preparation for the Cooperation of Religions," in *The History of Religions, Essays in Methodology*, edited by M. Eliade and J. Kitagawa, Chicago, 1959 and 1962, pp. 142–153.

"the one without a counterpart," "the eternal truth." What is meant is what we name God. While God may be conceived rationally as the ground of the universe, and personally as the "Thou" we interiorly address, still these movements of the human mind and heart are held to be inadequate to reveal what God is.

Secondly, the divine, while transcendent, is also immanent in human hearts. St. Paul has it that our bodies are temples of the Holy Spirit. The Koran, that God is nearer than our very pulse. St. Augustine, that he is more inward than one's innermost being. The mysticism of ancient India, that man is one with Brahma.

Thirdly, this reality, transcendent and immanent, is for man the highest good, the highest truth, righteousness, goodness, beauty. There is nothing in the world of nature or spirit to compare with this Ultimate and Supreme; and so that highest good is the final goal of all the longing and striving of the world religions.

Fourthly, the reality of the divine is ultimate love. Mercy and grace are the attributes of Yahweh in the experience of the prophets of Israel. God in the gospel is outgoing and forgiving love. Goodness and all-encompassing care make up the characteristic of the Tao of Laotse. The great heart of compassion is the inmost essence of the divine in Mahayana Buddhism.

Fifthly, the way of man to God is universally the way of sacrifice. The path of salvation everywhere begins with sorrowful renunciation, resignation, the *via purgativa*, ethical self-discipline, asceticism. The path to God finds its continuation in meditation, contemplation, prayer. All pious men pray, partly in words, partly without words, partly in complete solitude, partly in the community of the faithful. And the great saints of all high religions "pray without ceasing," as Paul says. Their whole life is, as Origen said, "one single, great continuing prayer." As they advance they seek not earthly good but God himself and God's rule on earth.

Sixthly, the high religions teach not only the way to God but always and at the same time the way to the neighbor as well. All preach brotherly love, a love on which there are no limitations, a love that is to be extended even to enemies, a love that has its origin and source not in man himself but in God operating on man, a love that, as it comes from God, also returns to him, for in loving our neighbor we are loving God.

Finally, while religious experience is as manifold and various as the human condition itself, still the superior way to God is love. It is love of God that leads the high religions to conceive bliss, the highest blessedness, now as the vision of God, now as some other union with him, now as some dissolving into him.

I have been giving a brief summary of what Prof. Heiler set forth in some eleven pages. I have been doing so because such a summary seemed to me the best way of indicating realistically, though incompletely, what is meant by religion. I now propose to pursue that topic further by raising two questions. First, what is the function of religion in human living? Secondly, how may a Christian account for the great similarity in the diverse high religions without denying the uniqueness of Christianity?

First, then, what is the function of religion in human living? Let us begin by noting that human living divides into sleeping and waking. When one is asleep, one is still alive, but one's humanity is at a minimum. Religion may help people sleep more soundly, but, if it does, the reason for that has to be sought in man's waking state. Now being awake is not some simple and indivisible event. Rather it is essentially dynamic, a matter of continuous change. It begins with the flow of sensations, memories, anticipations, feelings, perceptions, movements. From such experiencing there emerges the effort to understand, to unify and to relate intelligently the data of experience; and as this effort succeeds, insights accumulate to complement and correct one another and, eventually, to constitute a grasp, a habitual understanding, of this world and of the human condition. But if we can understand, we can also misunderstand; so on experiencing and understanding there emerges a third level of operations, on which we doubt, reflect, marshal and weigh the evidence, and finally judge with certitude or probability that this or that is or is not so. There remains the fourth and final level of deliberation, evaluation, decision, action. We ask whether or not our projects are worthwhile, whether they are truly good or only apparently good. We can answer such questions and live by the answers. Because we can do so, we can be principles of benevolence and beneficence, genuine collaborators, faithful lovers.

Now I have described these four levels of man's intentional consciousness, because I wish to draw a conclusion, namely, that authentic human living consists in self-transcendence. Already on the level of experience we are going beyond ourselves in apprehending and in responding to persons and things about us. But while animals live in a habitat, man lives in a universe. He does so because he asks endless questions, because he draws on the experience and memories of his contemporaries and their predecessors, because he cannot live humanly without forming some view concerning the facts and the possibilities of human existence. With the third level of judgment there emerges a still more radical element in self-transcendence. For the judgment may be, not a simple report on what I feel, or imagine, or think, or am inclined to say, but a quite confident statement of what is or is not so. Indeed, the true statement (concerning objects) intends to state what would be so even if the subject making the statement did not exist. But self-transcendence has a still further dimension. For so far we have considered a self-transcendence that is only cognitional. Beyond it there is a self-transcendence that is real. When he pronounces a project to be worthwhile, a man moves beyond consideration of all merely personal satisfactions and interests, tastes and preferences. He is acknowledging objective values and taking the first step towards authentic human existence. That authenticity is realized when judgments of value are followed by decision and action, when knowing what truly is good leads to doing what truly is good.

Man is not an island. Our self-transcendence is not solitary. We fall in love. The love into which we fall is not some single act of loving, not some series of acts, but a dynamic state that prompts and molds all our thoughts and feelings, all our judgments and decisions. That dynamic state has its antecedent causes and conditions and occasions, but, once it occurs and as long as it lasts, it is a first principle in our living, the origin and source of the lovingness that colors our every thought, word, deed, and omission.

Such being-in-love is of many kinds. Best known is the love of husband for wife and of wife for husband. But there is also the love of one's neighbor, of one's clan or nation, of one's fellow citizens and countrymen, of mankind; for the common good, man can toil incessantly and, if need be, risk his life and die. Underpinning both love of one's family and love of one's fellowmen, there is the love of God. Of it St. Paul wrote to the Romans (5: 5): "Through the Holy Spirit given to us, God's love has flooded our hearts." To that same gift he again referred when later he asked: "What can separate us from the love of Christ? Can affliction or hardship? Can persecution, hunger, nakedness, peril or the sword?" And he answered: "I am convinced that there is nothing in death or life, in the realm of spirits or superhuman powers, in the world as it is or the world as it shall be, in the forces of the universe, in heights or depths, nothing in all creation that can separate us from the love of God in Christ Jesus our Lord" (Rom. 8: 35, 38, 39).

God's gift of his love to us is the crowning point of our self-transcendence. St. Ausustine wrote: "Thou hast made us for thyself, O Lord, and our hearts are restless till they rest in thee." But that resting in God is something, not that we achieve, but that we receive, accept, ratify. It comes quietly, secretly, unobtrusively. We know about it when we notice its fruits in our lives. It is the profoundest fulfilment of the human spirit. Because it is fulfilment, it gives us peace, the peace that the world cannot give. Because it is fulfilment, it gives us joy, a joy that can endure despite the sorrows of failure, humiliation, privation, pain, betrayal, desertion. Because it is fulfilment, its absence is revealed, now in the trivialization of human life in debauchery, now in the fanaticism with which limited goals are pursued violently and recklessly, now in the despair that condemns man and his world as absurd.

There are further aspects to the matter. Being in love with God grounds faith. St. Paul spoke of "faith active in love" (Gal. 5: 6). The Scholastic theologians considered faith without love to be incomplete, *fides informis*. If with some contemporary thinkers one distinguishes between particular items of knowing or believing or doing and, on the other hand, the total context within which these acts occur, then, I think, one will conclude that it is being in love that determines the total context, the *Weltanschauung*, the horizon; while faith is, so to speak, the eye of love, discerning God's hand in nature and his self-disclosure in revelation. Similarly, love is connected with hope, for hope is the security and the confidence of those to whom God has given his love. Above all, God's gift of his love overflows into love of one's neighbor. Just as God himself is love (1 John 4: 8, 16), and it is the overflowing of that love that creates and sustains and promotes this seething universe of mass and energy, of chemical process, of endlessly varied plant and animal life, of human intelligence and of human love; so too the love that God gives us overflows into a love of all that God has made and especially of all persons whom God wishes to love. It is a love that makes a husband love his wife with all the tenderness he has for his own body (Eph. 5: 28). It is a love that stops the good Samaritan and has him care for the traveler assaulted by thieves. It is a love that has no frontiers, for it seeks the kingdom of God, God's rule on earth, and that rule is universal.

I have been endeavoring to meet the question, What is the function of religion in human life? By now, perhaps, the answer will be plain enough. To live intelligently, reasonably, responsibly, an adult has to form some view of the universe, of man's place in the universe, of his role along with other men. He may do so by appealing to myth, or to science, or to philosophy, or to religion. He may do so explicitly, consciously, deliberately, or he may do so implicitly, inadvertently, without deliberation. He may confront what he beholds, or try to escape in debauchery and drugs, or rage fanatically against it, or collapse in existential despair. Such is the human condition and such the human problem. A mythic solution will do only for the immature. A scientific solution is impossible, for science methodically and systematically refuses to consider the issue. A philosophic solution is out-of-date, for philosophy has become existential; it is concerned with man in his concrete existing; and there the issue is authenticity. I have argued that man exists authentically in the measure that he succeeds in self-transcendence, and I have found that self-transcendence has both its fulfilment and its enduring ground in holiness, in God's gift of his love to us.

I began by asking two questions. I have said something about the significance of religion in human living, and now I must turn very briefly to the relationship between Christianity and the other world religions. Now I have been quoting St. Paul and St. Augustine and speaking in Christian terms, but I have not been doing so in any exclusive manner, for it is not Christian doctrine that the gift of God's love is restricted to Christians. The First Epistle to Timothy tells us that it is God's will that all men should find salvation and come to knowledge of the truth (1 Tim. 2: 4). From this many theologians have concluded that, since grace is necessary to salvation, grace sufficient for salvation is given to all men. That this grace does include the great grace, the gift of God's love, may be inferred, I think, from Prof. Heiler's account of the seven areas common to all the high religions.

For these seven areas are just what one would expect to result from God's gift of his love. That love itself is the seventh common area. It involves love of one's neighbor, which is the sixth. It involves loving attention to God, which is prayer, and self-transcendence, which is self-denial; prayer and self-denial are the fifth common area. Further, love of God is not love of this world or of any part of it, and so it is love of a transcendent being; yet God's love is in us, more intimate than our innermost being, and so God is immanent in human hearts; the transcendence and immanence of God were the first two common areas. Finally, God's gift of his love is fulfilment of our massive thrust to self-transcendence. But we transcend ourselves by seeking the intelligible, the true, the real, the good, love. What fulfils that seeking, the God in whom we rest, must be the summit of intelligibility, truth, reality, goodness, love; and so we conclude to the third and fourth areas. It would seem that the seven areas listed by Prof. Heiler from the viewpoint of a history of religions, may be described from a Christian viewpoint as seven effects of God's gift of his love.

To come now to what is distinctive of Christianity, let me quote the Lady Margaret Professor of Divinity in the University of Cambridge, C. F. D. Moule. In a recent series of lectures he stated: "At no point within the New Testament is there any evidence that the Christians stood for an original philosophy of life or an original ethic. Their sole function is to bear witness to what they claim as an event—the raising of Jesus from among the dead."[3] What distinguishes the Christian, then, is not God's grace, which he shares with others, but the mediation of God's grace through Jesus Christ our Lord.

In the Christian, accordingly, God's gift of his love is a love that is in Christ Jesus. From this fact flow the social, historical, doctrinal aspects of Christianity. For the gift of God's love, however intimate and personal, is not so private as to be solitary. It is given to many through Christ Jesus that they may be one in him. They need one another to come to understand the gift that has been given them, to think out what it implies and involves, to support one another in their effort to live Christian lives.

[3] C. F. D. Moule, *The Phenomenon of the New Testament*, London, 1967, p. 14.

Normally, the gift of God's love is not a sudden transformation of character or personality. It is like the seed planted in ground that needs to be tilled, like the sprout that needs sunlight and rain and protection from choking weeds, devouring insects, and roving animals. As Charlie Brown needs all the friends he can get, so Christians need all the help they can get. Great saints are rare, and even they call themselves vessels of clay. The need of teaching and preaching, of rituals and common worship, is the need to be members of one another, to share with one another what is deepest in ourselves, to be recalled from our waywardness, to be encouraged in our good intentions.

Today there is not a little talk about religionless Christianity. /While it would be a digression for me to explain what was meant by Karl Barth and by Dietrich Bonhoeffer, I think I should attempt to indicate the element of truth covered by the phrase. In the preface to her translation of Luigi Sturzo's *Church and State*, Barbara Carter sums up the author's view that:

> ... in every form of social life and in society as a whole two currents are invariably present, the "organizational" and the "mystical" or ideal, the one tending to conservation, to practical constructions that perpetuate an established order, the other to renewal, with sharpened awareness of present deficiencies and impellent aspirations towards a better future. The distinction between them (i.e., between the organizational and the mystical currents) is never absolute, for they are made up of human individuals and reflect the complexity of human minds; their action is an interweaving, the one eventually consolidating something of what the other conceives, yet they come together only to part anew; the conflict they manifest is the conflict between the ideal and its always only partial realization, between the letter that kills and the spirit that quickens. . . .[4]

[4] Luigi Sturzo, *Church and State*, trans. Barbara Barclay Carter, London, 1939, p. 6.

In brief, there are no simple, absolute distinctions. The organizational ever needs to be brought to life by the inner spirit. It has to change and adapt to new needs, new conditions, new circumstances. The changes and adaptations themselves have to show the gift of God's love. Only falteringly and imperfectly do Christians achieve these ideals. But from this it does not follow that the organizational can be jettisoned. The gift of God's love involves loving one's neighbor. It is the very opposite of some introverted and sterile individualism. Of itself it makes Christians love one another, share one another's burdens, work together to hasten the advent of the Kingdom of God, of God's rule on earth. One can investigate how much organization is opportune. One can ask what kind of organization is desirable. But to exclude all organization is just to exclude the Christian community.

Finally, with regard to the phrase, "religionless Christianity," perhaps three remarks may be made. First, there exist positivist or other reductionist studies of religion, and these engender a notion of religion that a Christian or, indeed, any religious person is not going to accept. If by religion is meant some psychological, sociological, historical, or philosophic interpretation of religion that conceives it as "nothing but this" or "nothing but that," then of course Christianity should be conceived as religionless. However, I do not believe that the word "religion" should be handed over to mere reductionists. There are many quite different students of religion with a profound understanding of the reality of religion; on their meaning of the word "Christianity" is not religionless; and the importance of their meaning is that it provides the bridge over which Christians may walk towards an understanding of non-Christian religions. Secondly, Christians can come to think of their religion as an end in itself; they can become so devoted to the Christian cause as to forget its subordination to the cause of mankind. Now if by religion one means self-centered religion, then no doubt Christianity should be religionless or, as it also is said, secular. But 1 for one would object to the identification of religion with self-centered religion; as I have already contended, the function of religion is not to make man self-centered but to complete his self-transcendence. Thirdly, because Christians are not all saints, their weaknesses and sinfulness show up in their outward behavior and their organizations. But the perpetually needed remedy is not outer but inner; it is not to abolish the community structures and thereby bring about a loveless isolation of individuals; it is the repentance and prayer that asks our Father in heaven for a more abundant gift of his Spirit.

However, to discuss or investigate church structures inevitably leads to doctrinal issues, but the doctrinal matter that, in all likelihood, you would wish me to discuss is not some particular doctrine concerning this or that structure, but rather the wind of change that appears to be blowing through Roman Catholicism. What precisely is going forward? How far will it go? I shall attempt to say something on these matters but, for me to do so, you must permit me to speak, not simply as a Christian but as a Roman Catholic.

Georg Simmel, the German sociologist, coined the phrase, *die Wendung zur Idee*, the shift to the idea, to denote the tendency and even the necessity of every large social, cultural, or religious movement, to reflect on itself, to define its goals, to scrutinize the means it employs or might employ, to keep in mind its origins, its past achievements, its failures.

Now this shift to the idea is performed differently in different cultural settings. While a historical tradition can retain its identity though it passes from one culture to another, still it can live and function in those several cultures only if it thinks of itself, only if it effects its shift to the idea, in harmony with the style, the mode of forming concepts, the mentality, the horizon proper to each culture.

But what is true of any large social, cultural, or religious movement, also is true of the Catholic religion. It expressed itself in the New Testament, but it kept adding further expressions in the Apostolic Fathers, the Apologists, the Greek and Latin Fathers. An entirely new mode made its appearance with Byzantine Scholasticism, and this recurred on a universal scale with the medieval canonists and theologians. Humanism, the Renaissance, the Counter-reformation brought in another style, a new mode of concept formation, a different mentality. From that style, that mode, that mentality Catholics have been breaking away and they have been endeavoring to effect a new shift to the idea in the style and mode and mentality of modern culture. Efforts in this direction have been going forward for over a century, but the massive breakthrough took place at the Second Vatican Council.

In general, then, what is going forward in Catholic circles is a disengagement from the forms of classicist culture and a transposition into the forms of modern culture.

This is a matter involved in considerable confusion. The confusion arises mainly because classicist culture made no provision for the possibility of its own demise. It conceived itself not empirically but normatively, not as one culture among many, but as the only culture any right-minded and cultivated person would name culture. "It was a matter of acquiring and assimilating the tastes and skills, the ideals, virtues, and ideas, that were pressed upon one in a good home and through a curriculum in the liberal arts. This notion, of course, had, very ancient lineage. It stemmed out of Greek *paideia* and Roman *doctrinae studium atque humanitatis*, out of the exuberance of the Renaissance and its pruning in the Counter-reformation schools of the Jesuits."[5] Its very antiquity, however, only reinforced its more fundamental character of immobility. It considered its classics immortal works of art, its philosophy was the *philosophia perennis*, its laws and structures were the fruit of the prudence and wisdom of mankind. Of course, one had to adapt to changing circumstances and opportunities, but neither

[5] I am quoting from an earlier paper, see above p. 101.

circumstance nor opportunity modified human nature, and so adaptation could never affect the substance of things.

While classicist culture conceived itself normatively and abstractly, modern culture conceives itself empirically and concretely. It is the culture that recognizes cultural variation, difference, development, breakdown, that investigates each of the many cultures of mankind, that studies their histories, that seeks to understand what the classicist would tend to write off as strange or uncultivated or barbaric. Instead of thinking of man in terms of a nature common to all men, whether awake or asleep, geniuses or morons, saints or sinners, it attends to men in their concrete living. If it can discern common and invariant structures in human operations, it refuses to take flight from the particular to the universal, and it endeavors to meet the challenge of knowing people in all their diversity and mutability.

There is, I am sure, no need for me to explain that this cultural change has vastly, if belatedly, enriched the historical dimension of Catholic theology, first, in patristic and medieval studies but, particularly over the past twenty-five years since *Divino afflante Spiritu*, in scriptural studies as well. But I must add that this development necessitates a complete restructuring of Catholic theology, for the deductivist approach of the past was possible only as long as accurate and detailed knowledge was lacking. Moreover, while Scholastic categories are being replaced by more relevant categories drawn from historicist, phenomenological, existentialist, and personalist trends, there is occurring a shift, in Karl Rahner's terminology, from a cosmological to an anthropological viewpoint. Where before man contemplated an objective universe and understood himself in terms of the same objective categories, now what is first to be understood is not the universe but man, even though it is man as the principle whence one can come to know the universe. Where before knowledge preceded, founded, and justified loving, now falling-in-love and being-in-love culminate and complete the process of self-transcendence, which begins with knowledge but goes beyond it, as Blaise Pascal saw when he remarked that the heart has reasons which reason does not know.

This change liberates religion and theology from rationalist tendencies, from the need or desire to prove the truths of faith simply from reason and history. For though both reason and history have their contribution to make, still that contribution is subordinate to God's gift of his love to us, to the love that discerns God's self-manifestation in nature and his self-disclosure in revelation. Nor is this somewhat metaphorical identification of faith with an eye of love something peculiar to religious knowledge. All human knowing occurs within a context, a horizon, a total view, an all-encompassing framework, a *Weltanschuung*, and apart from that context it loses sense, significance, meaning. Further, the sweep of one's horizon is proportionate to one's self-transcendence: it narrows as one fails to transcend oneself; it advances in breadth and height and depth, as one succeeds in transcending oneself. Being in love with God is the existential stance opening on the horizon in which Christian doctrines are intelligible, powerful, meaningful, in which, as the Epistle to the Hebrews puts it: ". . . the word of God is alive and active. It cuts more keenly than any two-edged sword, piercing as far as the place where life and spirit, joints and marrow, divide. It sifts the purposes and thoughts of the heart" (Heb. 4: 12).

I see, then, many changes going forward in the Catholic apprehension of Catholicism. To mention but one of their tendencies, I should say that they promote ecumenism. Scientific historical study is concerned, not to bolster controversy, but to bring to light what happened or what was going forward in the past. An existential approach reveals that fundamental differences do not lie in this or that particular doctrine but rather in one's personal stance and one's resulting outlook. It seems to follow that if we take our stand on the common stance and outlook produced within and beyond the Christian communions by God's gift of His love, there is bound to arise and to be sustained an efficacious desire for sincere and, may it please God, fruitful dialogue.

I have spoken of many changes but in closing I should recall their general nature. They are of a kind that has already occurred more than once. They are changes, not in God's self-disclosure or our faith, but in our culture. They are changes such as occurred when the first Christians moved from Palestine into the Roman Empire, changes such as occurred when the Empire succumbed to the Dark Ages, changes such as occurred when the medieval Church built its cathedrals with their schools and founded its universities, changes such as occurred when Scholasticism yielded to Humanism, the Renaissance, the Reformation and the Counterreformation. Ours is a new age, and enormous tasks lie ahead. But we shall be all the more likely to surmount them, if we take the trouble to understand what is going forward and why.

THE RESPONSE OF THE JESUIT
AS PRIEST AND APOSTLE IN THE
MODERN WORLD[1]

My remarks may be grouped under the following headings: (1) authenticity, (2) the Spirit, (3) the word, (4) sending, (5) the Renaissance Jesuit, (6) the Jesuit today.

1. *Authenticity*

First, then, authenticity. For I wish to begin from what is simply human and, indeed, from a contemporary apprehension of what it is to be human. There is the older, highly logical, and so abstract, static, and minimal apprehension of being human. It holds that being human is something independent of the merely accidental, and so one is pronounced human whether or not one is awake or asleep, a genius or a moron, a saint or a sinner, young or old, sober or drunk, well or ill, sane or crazy. In contrast with the static, minimal, logical approach, there is the contemporary, concrete, dynamic, maximal view that endeavors to envisage the range of human potentiality and to distinguish authentic from unauthentic realization of that potentiality. On this approach, being human is ambivalent: one can be human authentically, genuinely, and one can be human unauthentically. Moreover, besides ambivalence, there also is dialectic: authenticity never is

---

[1] This paper was originally presented, with a slightly different title, in the Jesuit Institute held February 6–8, 1970, at Fusz Memorial, St. Louis, on "The Jesuit Priest Today." © 1970 by the American Assistancy Seminar on Jesuit Spirituality.

some pure, serene, secure possession; it is always precarious, ever a withdrawal from unauthenticity, ever in danger of slipping back into unauthenticity.

On this view, then, the basic question is, What is authentic or genuine realization of human potentiality? In a word, my answer is that authentic realization is a self-transcending realization. So I must attempt to describe what I mean by self-transcending. I shall illustrate five different instances and conclude that the last four of the five form an ordered unity.

In dreamless sleep, we are still alive. We are operating in accord with the laws of physics, chemistry, and biology. It may be said that we are ourselves but not that we are reaching beyond ourselves and, much less, that we are rising above ourselves. But when we begin to dream, consciousness emerges. However helpless, however lacking in initiative, the dreamer is an intending subject. What is intended, commonly is obscure, fragmentary, symbolic. In so-called dreams of the night the source of the dream is one's somatic state, say, the state of one's digestion. But in dreams of the morning the dreamer is anticipating his waking state; he is recollecting his world; he is beginning to adopt a stance within that world. In the dream of the morning, then, the dreamer has got beyond himself; he is concerned with what is distinct from himself; he is anticipating his self-transcendence.

An enormously richer self-transcendence emerges when one awakes. There is the endless variety of things to be seen, sounds to be heard, odors to be sniffed, tastes to be palated, shapes and textures to be touched. We feel pleasure and pain, desire and fear, joy and sorrow, and in such feelings there seem to reside the mass and momentum of our lives. We move about in various manners, assume now this and now that posture and position, and by the fleeting movements of our facial muscles, communicate to others the quiet pulse or sudden surge of our feelings.

Still, sensations, feelings, movements are confined to the narrow strip of space-time occupied by immediate experience.

But beyond that there is a vastly larger world. Nor is anyone content with immediate experience. Imagination wants to fill out and round off the picture. Language makes questions possible, and intelligence makes them fascinating. So we ask why and what and what for and how. Our answers construct, serialize, extrapolate, generalize. Memory and tradition and belief put at our disposal the tales of travellers, the stories of clans or nations, the exploits of heroes, the treasures of literature, the discoveries of science, the reflections of philosophers, and the meditations of holy men. Each of us has his own little world of immediacy, but all such worlds are just minute strips within a far larger world, a world constructed by imagination and intelligence, mediated by words and meaning, and based largely upon belief.

If the larger world is one and the same, still there are as many different constructions of it as there are stages in human development and differences in human cultures. But such diversity only serves to bring to light a still further dimension of self-transcendence. Beyond questions for intelligence—such as what and why and how and what for—there are the questions for reflection that ask, Is that so or is it not so? Is that certain or is it only probable? Unlike questions for intelligence, these can be answered by a simple "Yes" or "No." How we can give such answers, is beside my present purpose; but what such answers mean, is very much to it. For when we say that this or that really and truly is so, we do not mean that this is what appears, or what we imagine, or what we would like, or what we think, or what seems to be so, or what we would be inclined to say. No doubt, we frequently have to be content with such lesser statements. But the point I would make is that the greater statement is not reducible to the lesser. When we seriously affirm that something really and truly is so, we are making the claim that we have got beyond ourselves in some absolute fashion, somehow have got hold of something that is independent of ourselves, somehow have reached beyond, transcended ourselves.

I have been endeavoring to clarify the notion of self-transcendence by contrasting, first, dreamless sleep with the beginnings of consciousness in the dream, secondly, the dreaming with the waking subject, thirdly, the world of immediate experience and the enormously vaster real world in which we live our lives, fourthly that larger world as constructed by intelligence with the same larger world as known to have been constructed as it really is.

There remains a still further dimension of self-transcendence. Our illustrations, so far, have mainly regarded knowledge. There remains action. Beyond questions for intelligence—what? why? how? what for?—there are questions for reflection—is that so? But beyond both there are questions for deliberation. Beyond the pleasures we enjoy and the pains we dread, there are the values to which we may respond with the whole of our being. On the topmost level of human consciousness the subject deliberates, evaluates, decides, controls, acts. At once he is practical and existential: practical inasmuch as he is concerned with concrete courses of action; existential inasmuch as control includes self-control, and the possibility of self-control involves responsibility for the effects of his actions on others and, more basically, on himself. The topmost level of human consciousness is conscience.

However, man's self-control can proceed from quite different grounds. It can tend to be mere selfishness. Then the process of deliberation, evaluation, decision, is limited to determining what is most to one's advantage, what best serves one's interests, what on the whole yields a maximum of pleasure and a minimum of pain. At the opposite pole it can tend to be concerned solely with values: with the vital values of health and strength; with the social values enshrined in family and custom, society and education, the state and the law, the economy and technology, the church or sect; with the cultural values of religion and art, language and literature, science, philosophy, history, theology;

with the achieved personal value of one dedicated to realizing values in himself and promoting their realization in others.

In the measure that one's living, one's aims, one's achievements are a response to values, in that measure self-transcendence is effected in the field of action. One has got beyond mere selfishness. One has become a principle of benevolence and beneficence. One has become capable of genuine collaboration and of true love. In the measure that self-transcendence in the field of action characterizes the members of a society, in that measure their world not only is constructed by imagination and intelligence, mediated by words and meaning, based by and large on belief; it also is a world motivated and regulated not by self-seeking but by values, not by what is only apparently good but by what truly is good.

Now if we compare the last four of our modes of self-transcendence, we find that they form an interlocking unity. Experiencing is presupposed and complemented by inquiry and understanding. Experiencing and understanding are presupposed and complemented by reflecting and judging. Experiencing, understanding, and judging, are presupposed and complemented by deliberating and deciding. The four modes are interdependent, and each later level sublates those that precede in the sense that it goes beyond them, introduces something entirely new, makes that new element a new basis of operation; but so far from crowding or interfering with its predecessors, it preserves them, perfects them, and extends their relevance and significance. Inquiry sharpens our powers of observation, understanding enormously extends the field of data one can master, reflection and judgment force inquiry to attend to ever further data and force understanding to revise its previous achievements, deliberation turns attention from what is to what can be, to what probably would be and above all, to what really is worthwhile.

To conclude, human authenticity is a matter of following the built-in law of the human spirit. Because we can experience, we should attend. Because we can understand, we should inquire. Because we can reach the truth, we should reflect and check. Because we can realize values in ourselves and promote them in others, we should deliberate. In the measure that we follow these precepts, in the measure we fulfil these conditions of being human persons, we also achieve self-transcendence both in the field of knowledge and in the field of action.

Now you may have been wondering why I have spent so much time on so remote a topic as authenticity. I have had three reasons for doing so. First, I wished to get out of the abstract and static context dictated by logical clarity, coherence, and rigor and into the concrete, open, and ongoing context dictated by attention, inquiry, reflection, and deliberation. Secondly, I wished to get out of the context of a faculty psychology with its consequent alternatives of voluntarism, intellectualism, sentimentalism, and sensism, none of which has any serious, viable meaning, and into the context of intentionality analysis that distinguishes and relates the manifold of human conscious operations and reveals that together they head man towards self-transcendence. Thirdly, I wished to have a base, a starting-point, a springboard, in people as they are and as they can discover themselves to be; for without such a base, talk about the Spirit, the Word, the apostolate, the Jesuit priesthood is all in the air; it sounds abstract, irrelevant, without substance.

2. *The Spirit*

I have said that human authenticity is a matter of achieving self-transcendence. I have said that such achievement is always precarious, always a withdrawal from unauthenticity, always in danger of slipping back into unauthenticity. This is not a cheerful picture, and you may ask whether ordinary human beings ever seriously and perseveringly transcend themselves.

I think they do so when they fall in love. Then their being becomes being-in-love. Such being-in-love has its antecedents, its causes, its conditions, its occasions. But once it has occurred and as long as it lasts, it takes over. It becomes the first principle. From it flow one's desires and fears, one's joys and sorrows, one's discernment of values, one's vision of possibilities, one's decisions and deeds.

Being-in-love is of different kinds. There is the love of intimacy, of husband and wife, of parents and children. There is the love of one's fellowmen with its fruit in the achievement of human welfare. There is the love of God with one's whole heart and whole soul, with all one's mind and all one's strength (Mk. 12: 30). It is God's love flooding our hearts through the Holy Spirit given to us (Rom. 5: 5). In it was grounded the conviction of St. Paul that ". . . there is nothing in death or life, in the realm of spirits or superhuman powers, in the world as it is or the world as it shall be, in the forces of the universe—nothing in all creation that can separate us from the love of God in Christ Jesus our Lord" (Rom. 8: 38–39).

Being in love with God, as experienced, is being in love in an unrestricted fashion. All love is self-surrender, but being in love with God is being in love without limits or qualifications or conditions or reservations. It is with one's whole heart and whole soul and all one's mind and all one's strength. Just as a total openness to all questioning is our capacity for self-transcendence, so too an unrestricted being in love is the proper fulfilment of that capacity.

Because that love is the proper fulfilment of our capacity, fulfilment brings a deep-set joy that can remain despite humiliation, privation, pain, betrayal, desertion. Again, that fulfilment brings a radical peace, the peace that the world cannot give. That fulfilment bears fruit in acts of love for one's neighbor, a love that strives mightily to bring about the kingdom of God on this earth. On the other hand, the absence of that fulfilment opens the way to the trivialization of human life in the pursuit of fun, to the harshness of human life that results from the ruthless exercise of power, to despair about human welfare springing up from the conviction that the universe is absurd.

The fulfilment that is being in love with God is not the product of our knowledge and choice. It is God's gift. Like all being in love, as distinct from particular acts of loving, it is a first principle. So far from resulting from our knowledge and choice, it dismantles and abolishes the horizon within which our knowing and choosing went on, and it sets up a new horizon within which the love of God transvalues our values and the eyes of that love transform our knowing.

Though not the product of our knowing and choosing, it is not unconscious. On the contrary, it is a conscious, dynamic state, manifesting itself in what St. Paul named the harvest of the Spirit: love, joy, peace, kindness, goodness, fidelity, gentleness, and self-control (Gal. 5:22).

To say that this dynamic state is conscious is not to say that it is known. What is conscious, indeed, is experienced. But human knowing is not just experiencing. Human knowing includes experiencing but adds to it attention, scrutiny, inquiry, insight, conception, naming, reflecting, checking, judging. The whole problem of cognitional theory is to effect the transition from operations as experienced to operations as known. A great part of psychiatry is helping people to make the transition from conscious feelings to known feelings. In like manner the gift of God's love ordinarily is not objectified in knowledge, but remains within subjectivity as a dynamic vector, a mysterious undertow, a fateful call to a dreaded holiness.

Because that dynamic state is conscious without being known, it is an experience of mystery. Because the dynamic state is being in love, the mystery is not merely attractive but fascinating: to it one belongs, by it one is possessed. Because it is an unrestricted, unmeasured being in love, the mystery is out of this world; it is otherworldly; it evokes awe. Because it is a love so different from the selfish self it transcends, it evokes fear and terror. Of itself, then, and apart from any particular religious context in which it is interpreted, the experience of the gift of God's love is an experience of the holy, of Rudolph Otto's *mysterium tremendum et fascinans*. Again, it is what Paul Tillich named a being grasped by ultimate concern. Again, it corresponds to Ignatius of Loyola's consolation without a cause, as interpreted by Karl Rahner, namely, an experience with a content but without an apprehended object.

I have distinguished different levels of consciousness, and now I must add that the gift of God's love is on the topmost level. It is not the sensitive type of consciousness that emerged with sensing, feeling, moving. It is not the intellectual type that is added when we inquire, understand, think. It is not the rational type that emerges when we reflect, weigh the evidence, judge. It is the type of consciousness that also is conscience, that deliberates, evaluates, decides, controls, acts. But it is this type of consciousness at its root, as brought to fulfilment, as having undergone conversion, as possessing a basis that may be broadened and deepened and heightened and enriched but not superseded, as ever more ready to deliberate and evaluate and decide and act with the easy freedom of those that do all good because they are in love. The gift of God's love takes over the ground and root of the fourth and highest level of man's waking consciousness. It takes over the peak of the soul, the *apex animae*.

3. The Word

Being in love is not just a state of mind and heart. It is interpersonal, ongoing; it has its ups and downs, its ecstasies and quarrels and reconciliations, its withdrawals and returns; it reaches security and serenity only at the end of a long apprenticeship. If a man and woman were to love each other yet never avow their love, then they would have the beginnings of love but hardly the real thing. There would be lacking an interpersonal component, a mutual presence of self-donation, the opportunity and, indeed, the necessity of sustained development and growth. There would not be the steady increase in knowledge of each other. There would not be the constant flow of favors given and received, of privations endured together, of evils banished by common good will, to make love fully aware of its reality, its strength, its durability, to make love aware that it could always be counted on.

What is true of the love of intimacy, also is true of the love of God. Though God is one, he is not solitary. The one God is three persons: Father, Son, and Spirit. The Father is not only the light in which there is no darkness but also love, *agápe* (1 Jn. 1: 5; 4: 8, 16). The Son is his Word, through whom all things were made (Jn. 1: 3), sent into the world to manifest the Father's love for the world (Jn. 3: 16; 1 Jn. 4: 14–16). The gift of the Spirit is what floods Christian hearts with God's love. United in Christ through the Spirit, Christians are to love one another (*koinonía*), bear witness to God's love (*marturía*), serve mankind (*diakonía*), and look forward to a future consummation when their love of God will not be just orientation to mystery but coupled with a knowledge of God similar to God's knowledge of them (1 Cor. 13: 12).

God wills all men to be saved (1 Tim. 2: 4), and theologians have concluded that he gives all men sufficient grace for salvation. Just what this sufficient grace is, commonly is not specified. But it is difficult to suppose that grace would be sufficient if it fell short of the gift of loving God above all and loving one's neighbor as oneself. So I am inclined to interpret the religions of mankind, in their positive moment, as the fruit of the gift of the Spirit, though diversified by the many degrees of social and cultural development, and distorted by man's infidelity to the self-transcendence to which he aspires.

But there is a notable anonymity to this gift of the Spirit. Like the Johannine *pneuma*, it blows where it wills; you hear the sound of it, but you do not know where it comes from or where it is going (Jn. 3: 8). What removes this obscurity and anonymity is the fact that the Father has spoken to us of old through the prophets and in this final age through the Son (Heb. 1: 1–2). His communication is twofold; it is both by linguistic meaning and by incarnate meaning. By linguistic meaning he rebuked those that give scandal, announced redemption for sinners, provided for the forgiveness of sin, established the bond of the Eucharist, promised the gift of the Spirit, and set before men the destiny of eternal life. But all such linguistic meaning was endlessly reinforced by the incarnate meaning to be contemplated in the life and ministry and, above all, in the suffering, death, and resurrection of Christ.

4. Sending

Both Christ's communication by linguistic meaning and his communication by incarnate meaning were circumscribed spatially and temporally. The gift of the Spirit can be everywhere at once, but the challenge of the Word radiates to the ends of the earth only through human mediation.

Such mediation may or may not be institutionalized. Institutionalized mediation may be discerned in New Testament statements about the Twelve, about the Seventy-two, about Apostles not among the Twelve, about their companions, helpers, deputies, about bishops and deacons, and finally about elders. On the other hand, mediation that is not institutionalized is represented by the man casting out devils in Christ's name though he was not a follower of Jesus (Mk. 9: 38), by the least of these, my little ones, that are to be loved as Christ himself (Mk. 25: 40, 45), by the duty of every Christian to express in his words and his deeds what he has received from Christ and his Spirit.

We are prone to think of the institutional as impersonal, but the institutionalized mediation of the New Testament was strictly personal. To the Twelve Matthew has Jesus saying; "To receive you is to receive me, and to receive me is to receive the one that sent me" (Mt. 10: 40). To the Seventy-two Luke has

Jesus saying: "Whoever listens to you, listens to me; whoever rejects you, rejects me. And whoever rejects me, rejects the one who sent me" (Lk. 10: 16). To those in the upper room late the first Easter Sunday John has Jesus saying: "As the Father sent me, so I send you." And "Receive the Holy Spirit. If you forgive any man's sins, they stand forgiven; and if you pronounce them unforgiven, unforgiven they remain" (Jn. 20: 21-23). In the speech made before King Agrippa Luke reports Paul to have said that ". . . the Lord replied, I am Jesus whom you are persecuting. But now rise to your feet and stand upright. I have appeared to you for a purpose: to appoint you my servant and witness, to testify both to what you have seen and what you shall yet see of me. I will rescue you from this people and from the Gentiles to whom I am sending you. I send you to open their eyes and turn them from darkness to light, from the dominion of Satan to God, so that, by trust in me, they may obtain forgiveness of sins, and a place with those whom God has made his own" (Acts 26: 15-18).

Next, the early mediators are described as wonder workers. The Twelve were sent not only to preach the kingdom but also to heal the sick, raise the dead, cleanse lepers, and cast out devils (Mt. 10: 7-8). The Seventy-two were told to announce the proximity of the kingdom and to heal the sick (Lk. 10: 8-9); they cast out devils and were able unhurt to tread underfoot snakes and scorpions (Lk. 10: 17, 19). After the coming of the Spirit, Peter cured a well-known cripple outside the "Beautiful Gate" of the temple with sensational results (Acts 3: 4). Later we are told, "In the end the sick were actually carried out into the streets and laid there on beds and stretchers, so that even the shadow of Peter might fall on one or another as he passed by; and the people from the towns around Jerusalem flocked in, bringing those that were ill or harassed by unclean spirits, and all of them were cured" (Acts 5: 15-16). Philip in Samaria exorcized devils, and cured paralytics and cripples (Acts 8: 8). Miracles by Paul at Paphos, in Lycaonia, at Philippi, at Troas, on the storm-ridden ship at sea, and on Malta are recounted in Acts (Acts 13: 11; 14: 10; 16: 18; 20: 7–12; 27: 21; 28: 3, 8). But at Ephesus ". . . through Paul God worked miracles of an unusual kind: when handkerchiefs or scarves which had been in contact with his skin were carried to the sick, they were rid of their diseases and the evil spirits came out of them" (Acts 19: 11–12). Finally, according to Paul the accompaniment of signs, marvels, and miracles is among the marks of a true apostle (2 Cor. 12: 12; cf. Rom. 15: 18–19); and this view echoes the response Jesus gave to the question put him by the disciples of the Baptist (Mt. 11: 2–6).

Thirdly, institutionalized mediation slowly developed. The sending of the Twelve during the public ministry seems to have been an incidental task. But choosing them to be his permanent companions (Mk. 3: 14) and giving them authority to cast out unclean spirits and to cure ailments of every kind (Mt. 10: 1) are the beginnings of an institution. So, after the resurrection, the Eleven could be told that they were to bear witness to Jesus to the ends of the earth (Acts 1: 8) and they decided to restore their original number by choosing another who had been with Jesus since the days of the preaching of John (Acts 1: 15–26). Finally, after the coming of the Spirit, they begin to preach and perform great deeds; the number of converts moves to three thousand and then five thousand (Acts 2: 41; 4: 4); and persecutions begin.

The sending of the Seventy-two seems to have been incidental, a task rather than an office, but at least it set a precedent to the effect that others, not of the Twelve, could perform the same mission as the Twelve performed. Of the Seven (Acts 6: 3), five are not mentioned again. Stephen soon became a martyr. Philip, after evangelizing in Samaria and in the towns from Azotus to Caesarea, seems to have settled in the latter place, where he and his four virgin and prophesying daughters were visited by St. Paul (Acts 21: 8).

After three chapters recounting mainly the activities of Stephen and Philip, Acts narrates the conversion of St. Paul. He is the clearest instance of one that is not of the Twelve yet an apostle. As he styled himself, ". . . an apostle, not by human appointment or human commission, but by commission from Jesus Christ and God the Father. . . ." (Gal. 1: 1), and again, "Am I not an apostle? Have I not seen the Lord? If others do not accept me as an apostle, you at least are bound to do so, for you are yourselves the very seal of my apostolate, in the Lord" (1 Cor. 9: 1–2). Finally, St. Paul very sharply distinguished his position from that of those with charismatic gifts. He asked the Corinthians: "Did the word of God originate with you? Or are you the only people to whom it came? If anyone claims to be inspired or a prophet, let him recognize that what I write has the Lord's authority. If he does not recognize this, he himself should not be recognized " (1 Cor. 14: 36–38).

A further step in the development may be discerned in Paul's companions, helpers, deputies. Of many of them very little is known, of others more, but best known are Timothy and Titus. Timothy's name appears in the inscriptions of the second letter to the Corinthians, of the letters to the Philippians, Colossians, and Philemon, and of the first and second letters to the Thessalonians. The Romans learn that he is Paul's companion in labor (Rom. 16: 21) and the Corinthians are told that he does the work of the Lord as does Paul himself (1 Cor. 16: 10). He was sent by Paul on various missions: from Ephesus to Macedonia (Acts 19: 22), to Corinth (1 Cor. 4: 17), from Athens to Thessalonika (1 Thes. 3: 2), and there was a project of sending him to Philippi (Phil. 2: 19). Finally, the author of the first of the pastorals instructed him on the appointment of bishops and deacons (1 Tim. 3: 1–13) and later on the treatment to be accorded elders (1 Tim. 5: 17–22). Titus accompanied Paul and Barnabas to Jerusalem where circumcision was not required of him (Gal. 2: 1, 3). He was sent on a mission to Corinth and the second letter to the Corinthians repeatedly refers to his success (2 Cor. 2: 13; 7: 7, 13, 14; 8: 6, 16, 23; 12: 18). The second letter to Timothy reports that he is in Dalmatia, while the letter to Titus himself says that Paul left him in Crete to correct abuses and to appoint elders in each of the towns (Ti. 1: 5).

After untitled companions, helpers, deputies there come titled elders and titled bishops and deacons. Of these the best attested are the elders. The synoptic gospels speak of Jewish elders and in Matthew's passion narrative they are associated with the arch-priests and the scribes. In Acts Christian elders are mentioned a number of times. There was a group of elders at Jerusalem. The alms sent to the church there were received by the elders (Acts 11: 30). At the council of Jerusalem the apostles and the elders were in charge (Acts 15: 2, 4, 6, 22–23; 16: 4). After his third journey Paul visited James in Jerusalem, and, on that occasion, recounted to James and all the elders his missionary activities (Acts 21: 18).

The existence of Christian elders also is attested for Asia Minor, Ephesus, and Crete. At the end of his first journey Paul is said to have instituted elders in the churches (Acts 14: 23). On the return from his third journey Paul asked the elders of Ephesus to come to Miletus where he addressed them at some length (Acts 20: 17–35). Titus was instructed to institute elders in each town in Crete (Ti. 1: 5).

The main function of the elders was watchfulness. Paul in his farewell discourse bade the elders from Ephesus to "Keep watch over yourselves and all the flock of which the Holy Spirit has given you charge, as shepherds of the church of the Lord, which he won for himself by his own blood. I know that when I am gone savage wolves will come in among you and will not spare the flock. Even from your own body there will be men coming forward who will distort the truth to induce the disciples to break away and follow them. So be on the alert; remember how for three years, night and day, I never ceased to counsel each of you, and how I wept over you" (Acts 20: 28–31).

The letter to Titus sets forth moral qualities to be required of elders to conclude with the prescription that an elder ". . . must adhere to the true doctrine, so that he may be well able both to move his hearers and to confute objectors. There are all too many, especially among Jewish converts, who are out of all control; they talk wildly and lead men's minds astray. Such men must be curbed, because they are ruining whole families by teaching things they should not, and all for sordid gain" (Ti. 1:9–11; cf. 1 Pt. 5:1–5).

The first letter to Timothy speaks of the elders both as leaders and as preaching and teaching (1 Tim. 5:17). It implies that they are constituted by the laying on of hands (1 Tim. 5:19). Inversely Timothy himself is said to have received grace from the laying on of hands by the college of elders (1 Tim. 4:14; cf. 2 Tim. 1:6). The letter from James states that the elders are to be summoned to pray over the sick and to anoint them (James 5:14).

A few notes are in order. The Greek word for elder is *presbúteros*. From it are derived the English, *priest*, the French, *prêtre*, the German, *Priester*, the Italian, *prete*. But while the New Testament thinks of the elder chiefly as leading and teaching, later thought gives more prominence to the priest's role as dispenser of the sacraments.

Again, while the English word, *priest*, is derived from the Greek, *presbúteros*, it also is used to translate the Greek, *hiereis*, and the Latin, *sacerdos*. Later on these terms were used to refer to members of the Christian clergy, but in the New Testament they refer to Jewish and pagan priests, or to Christ, or to all the faithful.

From this twofold use of the word, *priest*, there can arise some confusion. The priesthood of all the faithful means, not that all the faithful are elders, *presbúteroi*, but that all are *hiereis*, concerned with *to hierón*, the sacred.

Finally, the tasks performed by the elders elsewhere, were performed by untitled laborers at Thessalonika. To the Thessalonians Paul wrote: "We beg you, brothers, to acknowledge those who are working so hard among you, and in the Lord's fellowship are your leaders and counsellors. Hold them in the highest possible esteem and affection for the work they do" (1 Thes. 5: 12). But though the letter to the Romans does allude to the one that presides (Rom. 12: 8), and First Corinthians speaks of gifts of guidance (1 Cor. 12: 28), the silence about local leaders in much of St. Paul's writing suggests a gradual development.

There remain bishops and deacons. In two passages it would seem that these terms denote, not simply "overseer" and "helper," but ranks or orders in the church. The letter to the Philippians salutes all the faithful there with the bishops and the deacons (Phil. 1: 1). The first letter to Timothy lists the qualities to be required first of bishops (1 Tim. 3: 1–7) and then of deacons (1 Tim. 3: 8–13). The term "deacon" occurs elsewhere frequently enough, but it seems to mean simply a helper. The term "bishop" occurs on three other occasions: once it is applied to Christ (1 Pt. 2: 25); twice it is applied to persons who in the context have already been referred to as elders (Acts 20: 17, 28; Ti. 1: 5–9). It seems to be doubtful that those named bishops in the New Testament were bishops in the later sense: first, they are not assigned functions distinct from those of elders; secondly, there hardly could be successors to the apostles when the apostles were still around.

5. The Renaissance Jesuit

There are the constants of Christianity and the variables. The constants are man's capacity and need for self-transcendence, the Spirit of God flooding men's hearts with God's love, the efficacy of those who mediate the word of God by word and example, by linguistic and incarnate meaning, for *cor ad cor loquitur*, speak from the heart and you will speak to the heart. But there also are the variables. Early Christianity had to transpose from its Palestinian origins to the Greco-Roman world. The thirteenth century had to meet the invasion of Greek and Arabic philosophy and science, and Thomas Aquinas had the merit not merely of preventing a destruction of faith but also of using a new knowledge to develop the faith and its theological expression. So too the old Society sized up and set about meeting the problems of its day.

There were the needs of the people, and the Jesuits worked in hospitals, taught catechism, preached, and dispensed the sacraments. There were the voyages of exploration and the beginnings of colonization, and the Jesuits were in India, Malaya, Indonesia, Japan, China, and North and South America. There was the Reformation, and the Jesuits were eminent in the labors of the Counter-reformation. The renewal of Greek and Latin studies contained a threat of a revival of paganism, and the Jesuits became the schoolmasters of Europe.

If we can be proud of our predecessors, we must also note that they took on the coloring of their age and shared its limitations. The Renaissance ideal was the *uomo universale*, the man who can turn his hand to anything. In the meaure that this ideal was attained by superiors and by subjects, it was possible for subjects to be shifted from one task to another, and it was possible to have superiors who could give such orders both wisely and prudently. Again, the culture of the time was classicist. It was conceived not empirically but normatively, not as the meanings and values inherent in a given way of life, but as the right set of meanings and values that were to be accepted and respected if one was not to be a plebeian, a foreigner, a native, a barbarian. Classicist philosophy was the one perennial philosophy. Classicist art was the set of immortal classics. Classicist laws and structures were the deposit of the wisdom and prudence of mankind. This classicist outlook was a great protector of good manners and a great support of good morals, but it had one enormous drawback. It included a built-in incapacity to grasp the need for change and to effect the necessary adaptations. In my opinion this built-in incapacity is the principal cause of the present situation in the Church and in the Society. Today most of us grant the need of change, but we would not be at such a loss when it comes to saying what are the needed changes, if today's openness had existed in 1870, or 1770, or 1670.

6. The Jesuit Today

A principal function of the Society of Jesus, in its original conception, was to meet crises. There is a crises of the first magnitude today. For a principal duty of priests is to lead and teach the people of God. But all leadership and all teaching occurs within social structures and through cultural channels. In the measure that one insists on leading and teaching within structures that no longer function and through channels that no longer exist, in that very measure leadership and teaching cease to exist. The sheep are without shepherds: they are disoriented, bewildered, lost. Indeed, what is true of the sheep, can also be true of the shepherds as well: they too can be disoriented, bewildered, lost.

Perhaps the best I can attempt will be to outline three fundamental features of our time: modernity, secularism, and self-destructiveness.

By modernity I do not mean just anything that exists or functions today. I mean the basic developments out of which has come the modern world. Of these the first is empirical science. It is something quite different from the notion of science set forth in Aristotle's *Posterior Analytics*. Not only is it a new notion but also it admits application, and its application has resulted in industrialization, urbanization, automation, a population explosion, mass media, instantaneous world news, rapid transportation, guided missiles, and thermonuclear bombs.

Next, despite the Renaissance ideal of speaking Latin, writing Greek, and reading Hebrew, there developed the modern languages and literatures. In the nineteenth century new conceptions and procedures were introduced into philology, hermeneutics, and history by a phalanx of investigators following the lead of Friedrich Wolf, Friedrich Schleiermacher, August Boeckh, and Leopold von Ranke. The classicist, normative notion of culture was replaced by an empirical notion: a culture came to denote the set of meanings and values inherent in a way of life. Human studies, *Geisteswissenschaften*, set about investigating, understanding, depicting the cultures of mankind. All were found to be man-made, contingent, subject to development, propagation, alteration, decay. All were found to have their good points and their weaknesses and, when to knowledge of them was added respect for them, there resulted pluralism. The new methods, applied to Hebrew and Christian religion, made it plain that one had to dilute conciliar statements about *quod tenet atque semper tenuit sancta mater ecclesia*. Not only was development a fact that had to be acknowledged, not only were previous theological positions to be reversed, but the whole conception and method of theology has had to be overhauled.

The natural sciences and the new human studies have had their repercussions on philosophy. Positivism would drop philosophy and make sociology the queen of the sciences. Kantians offer a foundation for science, absolute idealists set forth a super-science, Kierkegaard, Schopenhauer, Nietzsche, Blondel, American pragmatists, and European existentialists turn to decision and action. The Catholic decision, promulgated by Leo XIII in *Aeterni Patris*, was "Back to Aquinas." While this movement flourished in the early part of this century, in the last decade it has completely collapsed, first, because historical studies of the medieval period made any accurate statement of Thomist thought enormously complicated and permanently open to revision and, secondly, because the infiltration of the new types of human studies into theology necessitated a far more sophisticated type of philosophy than the medieval world could furnish. However, as yet there is no generally accepted up-to-date philosophy and, until there is, we can only expect a theological pluralism far more radical than the old-style pluralism of Thomists, Scotists, Suarezians, and so on. Such pluralism is the first item on the agenda of the recently formed International Theological Commission.

The problems that Catholics finally are facing have long existed. In his book, *The Modern Schism*, Martin Marty has them splitting the West into a religious minority and a secularist majority between the years 1840 and 1870. Further, he distinguished three types of secularists. In continental Europe secularists considered religion an evil and aimed at extirpating it. In Great Britain they considered it a private affair of no importance. In the United States religious leaders themselves tended to adapt religion to the secularizing trends of the times. But where religion is persecuted or ridiculed or watered down, there is unbelief, and unbelief is contagious. When everyone believes except the village atheist, doubting is almost impossible. When few believe, doubting is spontaneous, and believing is difficult.

A third feature of contemporary society is the consequence of secularism. It was Newman's theorem in *The Idea of a University* that to suppress a part of human knowledge has three effects: first, it results in ignorance of that part; secondly, it mutilates what of itself is an organic whole; thirdly, it causes distortion in the remainder in which man endeavors to compensate for the part that has been suppressed. On this showing, one is to expect that secularism not only leads to ignorance of religion but also mutilates knowledge as a whole and brings about distortion in what remains. Consider a few instances of such distortion.

Human knowledge results from a vast collaboration of many peoples over uncounted millennia. The necessary condition of that collaboration is belief. What any of us knows, only slightly results from personal experience, personal discovery, personally conducted verification; for the most part it results from believing. But the eighteenth-century Enlightenment was not content to attack religious belief. It prided itself on its philosophers. It set up a rationalist individualism that asked people to prove their assumptions or else regard them as arbitrary. In effect it was out to destroy not only the religious tradition but all tradition. Such rationalist individualism in the twentieth century seems to have infected our educationalists. Students are encouraged to find things out for themselves, to develop originality, to be creative,

A SECOND COLLECTION

to criticize, but it does not seem that they are instructed in the enormous role of belief in the acquisition and the expansion of knowledge. Many do not seem to be aware that what they know of science is not immanently generated but for the most part simply belief.

A second distortion occurs in man's apprehension of man. Positivists, naturalists, behaviorists insist that human sciences have to be conducted on the same lines as the natural sciences. But the resultant apprehension of man, if not mechanistic, is theriomorphic. Nor is this view of man as a machine or as an animal confined to some rarefied academic realm. It is applied. The applications reach out into all departments of thought and into all walks of life. They have the common feature of omitting advertence to human dignity and respect for human morality.

A third distortion is in the realm of technique. Applied science and consequent inventions have given us our vast industrial, commercial, financial, adminstrative, educational, military complex. Technicians are the people with the task of figuring out the most efficient use of currently available hardware. The more successful they are, the greater is the domain that they organize, and the less the domain under the control of old-style decision-makers, of managers, directors, mayors, governors, presidents. Again, the more brilliant they are, the less is it possible to explain to the uninitiated why things are done the way in which they are done. Finally, the more thorough the application of the principle of efficiency, the more must men adapt themselves to its dictates in all their labor hours and in all the goods and services they purchase from the technological establishment. Yet we must bear in mind that anything less than the most efficient procedures threatens the survival of the mass of mankind.

If I am correct in assuming that the Jesuits of the twentieth century, like those of the sixteenth, exist to meet crises, they have to accept the gains of modernity in natural science, in philosophy, in theology, while working out strategies for dealing with secularist views on religion and with concomitant distortions in man's notion of human knowledge, in his apprehension of human reality, in his organization of human affairs. How such strategies are to be worked out is, of course, an enormous question, and I must be content to offer no more than the briefest suggestions. First, any such strategy is not a conclusion from premises but a creative project emerging from a thorough understanding of a situation and a grasp of just what can be done about it. Secondly, it is not some static project set forth once and for all but, on the contrary, it is an ongoing project constantly revised in the light of the feedback from its implementation. Thirdly, it is not some single, ongoing project but a set of them, constantly reported to some central clearinghouse with the twofold function (1) of drawing attention to conflicts between separate parts and (2) of keeping all parts informed both of what has been achieved elsewhere and what has been tried and found wanting. Finally, all such projects must be in Christ Jesus, the work of those who take up their cross daily, who live by the Spirit in the Word, who consecrate themselves to loving, who banish all tendencies to hatred, reviling, destroying.

THE EXAMPLE OF GIBSON WINTER[1]

On the relations between religious studies and theology, in the very brief space at my disposal, I can offer not a blueprint, not a sketch, not an outline, but only a suggestion. The suggestion is to point to the example of Gibson Winter. For it seems to me that Prof. Winter has done a remarkable piece of interdisciplinary work in relating sociology to ethics[2] and that by following his example theologians could relate empirical religious studies with theology or, indeed, empirical human studies with theology. There would result, of course, only one of the various possible manners in which studies might collaborate but, I think, a manner very appropriate to our current needs.

First, then, recall Max Weber's celebrated distinction between social science and social policy. Social policy pursues goals; it proceeds from decisions; the decisions are or, at least, may be motivated by genuine values. But social science is empirical science. It is concerned, not with what is right or wrong, not with what ought or ought not to be, but with what in fact is so, what in fact is possible, what in fact is probable. Now Prof. Winter accepts Weber's distinction, but he does so to go beyond it. Between social science and social policy he inserts social ethics. The ethics adds the value judgments from which

[1] From *Social Compass*, an international review of socio-religious studies (Louvain and The Hague), (1970) 280–282. Contribution to a collection of notes on Theology and Social Sciences. © 1970 by Bernard J. F. Lonergan.

[2] Gibson Winter, *Elements for a Social Ethic. The Role of Social Science in Public Policy*, New York 1966, paperback 1968.

social science rigidly abstains and by which social policy should be guided.

Next, social science is not some single homogeneous block. Prof. Winter distinguishes four styles, which he names the physical, the functional, the voluntarist, and the intentional. The physical style considers that the methods of natural science are the only scientific methods; it is positivist, behaviorist, reductionist. The functional style understands social structures and processes by grasping the functions of parts in the whole; in America it is associated with the name of Talcott Parsons. The voluntarist style stresses power, conflict, and ideology; in America it is associated with the name of the late C. Wright Mills. The intentional style is phenomenological: its subjective dimensions are the constituting intentionalities of embodied consciousness; its objective dimensions are the forms in which the world appears for this consciousness. This style was transported from Vienna to America by Alfred Schutz who, six years before emigrating, had composed *Der sinnhafte Aufbau der sozialen Welt*.[3]

Thirdly, the divergent styles invite reflection on the possibility of social science. This is, of course, the transcendental turn. But it turns not to any isolated self but to the self as emergent within an intersubjective matrix, as discovering the meaning of its gesture in the response made by another to the gesture, as coming to consciousness of the other and the self within communication. From this basis there are worked out fundamental sociological terms and relations and there is effected a critique of the various sociological styles inasmuch as their assumptions and procedures involve a reinterpretation, often an at least apparently distorting reinterpretation, of the fundamental terms and relations. The ultimate conclusion is, however, that the different styles are appropriate in different areas of investigation and may be used intelligently if the weaknesses revealed by the critique are borne in mind.

[3] Vienna, 1932. English translation by G. Walsh and F. Lehnert, *The Phenomenology of the Social World*, Evanston, 1967.

Fourthly, ethical content is not imported from outside the *Lebenswelt* but found already existent and operative within it. It is in the light of its own effective morality that the responsible society has to screen the policies, positive and negative, that come to light through the investigations of social science. Specifically, just as the assumptions and procedures of the various styles can conflict with an acceptable social philosophy, so too they can conflict with the moral intentions of a responsible society.

The foregoing, need I insist, is only a thumbnail sketch of the contents of a densely packed, three-hundred-page book. To that book I must refer the reader desirous of a clearer and fuller grasp of the possibilities that, I believe, it reveals. Just as one can distinguish empirical social science and social policy, so too one can distinguish empirical religious studies and the policies of religious groups. Just as a social philosophy and a social ethic can be inserted between social science and social policy, so too a philosophy of religion and its extension into a theology can be inserted between empirical religious studies and the policies of religious groups.

The relevant philosophy would follow the transcendental turn: it would bring to light the conditions of the possibility of the religious studies and their correlative objects. It would survey the areas investigated and the methods employed; it would provide the ultimate basis for appropriate methods; and it would justify or criticize accepted distinctions and procedures. Next, insofar as the philosophy includes an account of genuine religious experience, it can be inserted within the perspectives of a theology and, indeed, provide the theology with a basic element for the formulation of its categories. Finally, empirical religious studies, especially as grounded in a critical philosophy and set within the perspectives of a theology, not only provide an informed, intelligent, wise, and pious source of policies for religious groups, but also can provide the feedback that reveals how the policies are working, what has to be dropped, what can be substituted, what improvements can be made. There would result a *praktische Theologie*[4] that set forth not timeless truths but the adaptations of attitudes and actions needed at each particular time and place.

It would be a notable achievement, but more is demanded. The Church in the modern world is concerned not only with itself but also with the world. What has been said about empirical religious studies has to be repeated about empirical human studies. They too need a philosophic critique and grounding. They too have to be inserted within the perspectives of a theology. They have to be an ongoing source of ever better policies guiding Christian action in the renewal and the redemption of human society.

[4] *Lexikon für Theologie und Kirche*, 8 (1963), 682–685.

PHILOSOPHY AND THEOLOGY[1]

My title, "Philosophy and Theology," is far too abrupt. It suggests an endless affair listing all the different conceptions of philosophy, all the different conceptions of theology, and all the ways in which the two might be related. I have no intention of perpetrating such a monster. My aim is far more modest, and, also, more concrete. It is to indicate a certain relevance and need of philosophy in contemporary Catholic theology, and to this end I shall develop briefly three topics: first, the change in Catholic theology, second, the key task in current theology, and third, the contribution of philosophy in the performance of that task.

The Change in Catholic Theology

Very many things have happened in Catholic theology, but the one I propose to single out, the one I consider to underpin most if not all the others, is the underlying implication of the transition from eternal truths to developing doctrines.

Aquinas (*Sum. theol.*, I. q. 16, a. 7) was quite accurate on the matter of eternal truths. They exist, but only in the eternal and unchanging mind of God. There is, however, a certain speciousness to the contrary view that eternal truths may also be found in human minds. For, what once is true, never can be truthfully denied. If Caesar crossed the Rubicon at a certain time and place then it never will be true to deny that he did so at that time and place.

[1] Medalist's Address in Proceedings of the *American Catholic Philosophical Association*, 46 (1970), 19–30. Reprinted with permission.

This certainly is plausible, but there is a slight, apparently very slight, flaw in the argument. Any statement presupposes a context within which the meaning and implications of the statement can be presented. The statement that is true at a given time and place, also will be true at other times and places, provided that the contexts are sufficiently similar. There exists then a further proviso and, it appears, there may be eternal truths in human minds only in the measure that this proviso is eternally fulfilled.

Now the issue may be argued in two manners. One may argue in the abstract and *a priori*: say, that human nature is ever the same and, therefore, the contexts of human statements will ever be substantially the same. Or one may argue in the concrete and *a posteriori*, and it was this *a posteriori* type of argument that was more and more in favour as the natural sciences progressed and, what is more to our purpose, a parallel development took place in certain human sciences, in philology, hermeneutics, and critical history.

This occurred in Germany and, as I cannot sketch the movement, I must be content to name a few of the originators. There was Friedrich Wolf who conceived classical philology to be a philosophico-historical study of human nature as exhibited in antiquity, and who brought together in his courses at Halle literature, antiquities, geography, art, numismatics, and the critical spirit that produced his *Prolegomena to Homer*.[2] There was Friedrich Schleiermacher who transformed hermeneutics from sets of rules of thumb followed by biblical or classical exegetes to a general art of avoiding misunderstanding and misinterpretation.[3]

---

[2] On Wolf, see G. P. Gooch, *History and Historians in the Nineteenth Century*, London, 1952, pp. 25–28. For a philosophical view of the movement: E. Cassirer, *The Problem of Knowledge, Philosophy, Science, and History since Hegel*, New Haven, 1950, pp. 217–325; H. G. Gadamer, *Wahrheit und Methode*, 1960.

[3] F. D. E. Schleiermacher, *Hermeneutik, Nach den Handschriften neu herausgegeben und eingeleitet von Heinz Kimmerle*, Heidelberg, 1950. Cf. Gadamer, *op. cit.*, pp. 172–185; R. Palmer, *Hermeneutics*, Evanston, 1960, pp. 81–97.

There was August Boeckh, a pupil both of Wolf and of Schleiermacher, who conceived philology as the reconstruction of the
constructions of the human spirit and wrote an *Encyclopedia and
Methodology of the Philological Sciences.*[4] There was Leopold von
Ranke, who by his seminar and his writing of history taught
historians to keep the passions of the present out of the facts of the
past, to base their facts on strictly contemporary sources, and to
determine where the authors of the sources got their information
and how they used it.[5] There was Johann Gustav Droysen, who
lectured on the method of historical investigation and composed
a text on the subject.[6] There was Wilhelm Dilthey who endeavoured
to work out the philosophical foundations for the new hermeneutics and history.[7]

There resulted an avalanche both of interpretative commentaries
on the literatures and of critical histories on the achievements of
the past. Ancient languages were deciphered, ancient cities
excavated, coins and artifacts collected, critical editions produced,
handbooks, dictionaries, encyclopedias, repertories, bibliographies,
collections composed. The movement spread to religious studies.
The Bible, patristic writers, medieval theologians, Reformation
and Counter-reformation figures were studied in a quite new
manner. Previously they had been invoked as witnesses to divine
revelation, and from that witness were sought knowledge of God
and knowledge of other things in their relation to God. But now

[4] August Boeckh, *Enzyklopädie und Methodologie der philologischen Wissen-
schaften,* hrsg. v. Ernst Bratuscheck, Leipzig, 1877. Cf. Gooch, *op. cit.,* pp.
28–32; also P. Hünermann, *Der Durchbruch geschichtlichen Denkens im 19
Jahrhundert,* Freiburg, 1967, pp. 63–68.
[5] On v. Ranke, Gooch, *op. cit.,* pp. 72–97, esp. 97; Gadamer, *op. cit.,* pp.
191–199; Cassirer, *op. cit.,* pp. 230–242.
[6] J. G. Droysen, *Historik, Vorlesungen über Enzyklopädie und Methodologie der
Geschichte,* hrsg. v. R. Hübner München, 1960. Cf. Hünermann, *op. cit.,* pp.
49–132; Gadamer, *op. cit.,* pp. 199–205; Cassirer, *op. cit.,* pp. 257 f.
[7] Cf. Hünermann, *op. cit.,* pp. 133–291; Gadamer, *op. cit.,* 205–228; Palmer,
op. cit., pp. 98–123.

aims were more pedestrian, and procedures more exigent. Nothing was to be affirmed without corroborative evidence; no evidence was to be offered without being rigorously scrutinized; and the scrutiny was allowed to overlook none of the myriad little oddities which the preconceptions of a later day are apt to dismiss as unimportant. At first, in conservative circles, the new methods were impugned. Next, they were adopted but used in an apologetic struggle against the new conclusions. Finally, methods and conclusions were to a great extent accepted in medieval and patristic and eventually, among Catholics, in biblical studies.

The new methods and conclusions do not imply a new revelation or a new faith, but certainly they are not compatible with previous conceptions of theology. In the high medieval period theology alternated between *lectio* and *quaestio*. One read the Bible and the Fathers; one noticed incoherences and contradictions; one asked for reconciliations. There emerged glossaries and commentaries to facilitate the reading, books of sentences that collected passages relevant to distinct topics, books of questions that attempted a theoretical unification of collected doctrines, and an adaptation of Aristotelian thought in an effort to construct a Christian world-view. There was an empirical basis in the Bible and the Fathers; there was a search for coherence and intelligibility; but there was not entertained the possibility that the relevant intelligibility was mediated by an ongoing historical process.

By the end of the thirteenth century the constructive impulse was stifled by the mutual denunciations of Augustinians and Aristotelians. Everyone, however, accepted Aristotle's logical works with their heavy accent on necessity and immutability. Theologians turned their attention to demonstration and, as necessary premisses for necessary conclusions are hard to come by, there was a wave of skepticism followed by decadence.

Later in the Renaissance period Cajetan and Spanish theologians produced commentaries on the *Summa theologiae* of Aquinas —a step that separated theology from its historical sources. This was only partially reversed by Melchior Cano whose *De locis theologicis* has the theologian proving medieval doctrines by arguing from Scripture, the Fathers, the councils, the theologians, the *sensus fidelium*, and so on. It was this scheme that governed much of the theological literature of the last and the present century, until the acceptance of the new, highly specialized methods made it evidently ridiculous to suppose that a single mind could master not only all the Scriptures, but also all the Fathers, councils, and theologians, not to mention the *sensus fidelium*. Such an undertaking was possible only for those that held no doubts about the accuracy of Cardinal Ottaviani's motto, *semper idem*, ever the same.

The Key Task in Current Catholic Theology

The shift from eternal truths to developing doctrines not only made theology the collaborative work of many specialists but also revealed the unreconciled antithesis of older procedures. For that older theology knew from its religious sources that faith was not a conclusion from premises but a gift of God, that the mysteries of faith could not be demonstrated but, at best, could be met with some analogous and imperfect understanding. At the same time it proposed to establish Scholastic theses from an appeal to the Bible, the Fathers, the popes and councils, the consensus of theologians, and so on. But what precisely was the nature of that appeal? Was it just rhetoric and, if so, was theology even analogously a science? Was it more than rhetoric and, if so, wherein lay the difference?

The common position (apart from the gradual acceptance of the new methods) was that theology occupied some indeterminate position between rhetoric and the science described in Aristotle's *Posterior Analytics*. Indeed, while the actual achievement tended to be rhetorical, the guiding ideal tended to be polarized by the clarity, coherence, and rigor of logic. Clarity demanded sharply defined terms, and these were abstract and so outside the realm where change occurs. Coherence demanded the absence of contradictions. Rigor demanded that conclusions follow necessarily from their premisses. All three together provided the appropriate home for eternal truths and defined the ideal that human imperfection in this life might aim at but not attain.

Now it is this outlook, this assumption, this viewpoint that is incompatible with the new methods in hermeneutics and history and with the conclusions they reach. For the new methods are ongoing. They solve problems tentatively rather than definitively, and definitive solutions, even when reached, only uncover a further range of problems as yet unsolved. Not only are the methods ongoing but so too are the realities they progressively reveal whether they are doctrines of faith or theological views.

Thus, the New Testament records the faith of the early Church. The proper meaning of that record lies within the various contexts of the several writers. The aim of contemporary exegesis is to propound that proper meaning within its own proper context. But the labors down the ages of popes and councils, of Fathers and theologians, have a quite different function. They regard the New Testament as normative for all ages. The New Testament is read in the very different contexts of the early Church, of the patristic period, of the medieval period, of the Renaissance and Reformation, and of the contemporary Church. Not only is it read but also it gives rise to questions, and these questions are vital questions. They belong to the context of their own day. They are couched in its concepts and language, arise from its perspectives, stand on the level of later times, are relevant to new problems or issues. What is to be done about these questions?

A first solution is archaism. It denies the fact of historical change, or it claims that men should not have changed. It insists that the Gospel be preached in every age as it was preached in Antioch and Ephesus, in Corinth and Rome. It refuses to answer the questions that arise, not within the context of the New

Testament, but on the later soil of Greco-Roman culture, or in medieval Paris, or at Trent, or at Vatican I or II.

A second solution is anachronism. It answers the questions, but it does not know about history. It assures everyone that these answers are already in the doctrines of the New Testament, that if they are not there explicitly, they are there implicitly. It is against such anachronism that biblical studies have had to contend.

Besides archaism and anachronism, there are development and aberration. Both development and aberration answer the questions of the day within their proper context. But development answers them in the light of revelation and under the guidance of the Holy Spirit. Aberration fails to do so in one or more respects.

Besides developments in the doctrines of faith, there also are theological developments. A discipline that is developing is advancing into the unknown. The clarity, coherence, and rigor of the logical ideal are aimed at, but only with reservations. Clarity is wanted and terms are becoming clearer, but it is not supposed that all haziness and indetermination have been removed. Coherence is desired but it is not purchased at any price; if two incompatible statements each have something in their favor, both are retained as possible facets of some truth not yet known. Rigor, finally, is welcome when it can be had, but, when it is unavailable, the merely postulated, hypothetical, probable are enough.

Let me illustrate these points from theology as in fact it has ever been. Since the Cappadocian settlement in the fourth century, the Church has acknowledged three persons in God. What, then, is meant by a person? For Augustine the meaning was merely heuristic. The term "person" denoted what there are three of in the Trinity. There are three: Father, Son, and Holy Spirit. What are there three of? Well, there are not three Gods or three Fathers or three Sons or three Spirits. So the name "person" is employed when one desires to have an answer to the question, "Three what?"[8]

[8] Augustine, De trinitate, VII, iv, 7; PL. 42, 939.

During the next nine centuries theology advanced beyond the person as heuristic notion to definitions of the person. Three definitions emerged, one by Boethius, one by Richard of St. Victor, and one by Thomas Aquinas. All three were couched in metaphysical terms, and so to compare them and make a reasonable choice, the metaphysics of the person had to be investigated. This was done with varying results by Scotus, Capreolus, Cajetan, Tiphanus, and Suarez. Next, Cartesian and subsequent attention to the psychological subject led to conceiving the person less in metaphysical and more in terms of the psychological subject and this, of course, was in harmony with the psychological theory of the trinitarian processions initiated by Augustine and, in my opinion, very highly developed by Aquinas. Recently, the phenomenologists have been scrutinizing the mutual communion of "I" and "thou" and thereby opening up the possibility of another dimension to trinitarian thought. In Catholic thought, then, the term "person" in a trinitarian context basically is a heuristic notion, a question, to which a series of answers have been given. Finally, what is true of the term "person" in general, also is true of other theological terms. Their meaning is to be known not by a definition but by a history of questions asked and answers given.

Our next illustration concerns the logical ideal of coherence. In the high Middle Ages that ideal was pursued methodically. Evidence was collected on one side of an issue, *Videtur quod non*, and contrary evidence was placed on the other, *Sed contra est*. Incoherence proved the existence of a *quaestio*, and this proof was the preliminary to offering both the general lines of a solution and its application to the adduced evidence. Next, the multiplication of *quaestiones*—there were hordes of them—gave rise to a second-level problem of coherence, namely, how is one to assure the coherence of the many solutions? It was at this point that the adoption and adaptation of some system of thought, such as Aristotle's, became not only relevant but well nigh imperative and, inasmuch as this step was taken, there emerged still further realms of *quaestiones* in a theology that had become comprehensive and systematic. Medieval theology was an ongoing process. One has only to compare the topics discussed by Aquinas in his *Scriptum super Sententias* with the supposedly corresponding topics in the work of Peter Lombard to witness the advances theology made between the middle of the twelfth and the middle of the thirteenth centuries.

The logical ideal demands rigor. Indeed, Aristotle's *Posterior Analytics* wants not only conclusions that follow necessarily from premisses but also premisses that are necessary truths.[9] Now this cult of necessity is a thing of the past. While contemporary mathematicians want conclusions that follow necessarily from premisses, they do not suppose that their premisses are necessary truths; so far from being necessary, they are freely postulated, and the problem is whether the many postulates are coherent. Again, while the nineteenth century spoke of the necessary laws of physics and even of the iron laws of economics, contemporary science does not. The laws of nature are not intelligibilities in the fashion that the necessary is intelligible; they are intelligibilities in the fashion that the possible is intelligible. The necessary could not be other than it is; but the laws of nature could be other than they are; they are intrinsically hypothetical, essentially in need of verification, and to be rejected as soon as verification fails and an alternative view is presented. In fact, the intelligibility of modern science is, in the main, the intelligibility that in traditional theology went by the name of *convenientia*.

When theology is seen as an ongoing process, its contextual structure accords not with the rules of deductive logic but with the continuous and cumulative process ruled by a method. It is a context in which similar questions are assigned successively different answers. It is a context in which incoherence is removed,

[9] Aristotle, *Post. Anal.*, 1, 2, 71 b 16 ff. See the *Introduction* in W. D. Ross, *Aristotle's Prior and Posterior Analytics*, Oxford, 1949, pp. 51–75.

not at a stroke, but only gradually, while this gradual removal only tends to bring to light broader and deeper problems. It is a context in which the intelligibility attained is, in general, that of the possible and not that of the necessary. Finally, it is a context in which developments no less than aberrations are not historically necessitated but only historically conditioned; they are the steps that *de facto* were taken in given situations and either legitimated or not by the situations and their antecedents.

Let me conclude. This second section was concerned with the question, What seems the key task in current Catholic theology? My answer has been a contrast between a rigid logical ideal alone fit to house eternal truths in a permanent synthesis and, on the other hand, the concrete, ongoing, cumulative process guided by a method. Only a theology structured by method can assimilate the somewhat recently accepted hermeneutic and historical methods and it alone has room for developing doctrines and developing theologies. The key task, then, in contemporary Catholic theology is to replace the shattered thoughtforms associated with eternal truths and logical ideals with new thought-forms that accord with the dynamics of development and the concrete style of method.

The Contribution of Philosophy to the Establishment of New Thought-Forms

One can turn on the television set and adjust it without ever having attempted to penetrate the mysteries of electronics. But if one wishes to design a new and better type of television set, the more one knows of electronics and the more fertile one is in invention, the greater the likelihood one will succeed. Similarly, one can learn the techniques of this or that branch or division of theology by repeating the performance of others revealed in their lectures, their seminars, their articles, and their books. But it is one thing to juxtapose the various techniques of the many branches. It is quite another to see how each set can be rearranged, expanded, curtailed, transformed, so that all will lock together in a single, ongoing, cumulative process. Most of all, it is in preparing that transforming and unifying view that philosophy can make a contribution to contemporary theology.

For a method guides cognitional performance. Because the performance is cognitional, there are needed full and precise answers to three basic questions. There is the question of cognitional theory: What precisely is one doing when one is knowing? There is the question of epistemology: Why is doing that knowing? There is the question of metaphysics? What does one know when one does it? When the foregoing questions are answered with philosophic generality, one is already in possession of a transcendental method, that is, of a method that is as yet not specified by any particular field or subject but, by suitable additions and adaptations, can be specified to any field or subject of human inquiry.

The foregoing is, in my opinion, the core contribution a philosophy can make to contemporary theological need. But it also can make further contributions that help theology explicate its proper adaptations of transcendental method. Let me briefly indicate the nature of such further contributions.

First, in terms of cognitional theory, epistemology, and metaphysics, there has to be worked out a foundational account both of hermeneutics and of critical history. The techniques exist and are practised. But there is needed an adequate analysis followed by an epistemological critique of the different interpretations given the techniques by naive realists, by empiricists, by positivists, by idealists, by phenomenologists, by critical realists. Without the analysis and the epistemological critique, any attempt to get beyond the "Jesus of history" to the "Christ of faith" risks being blocked by usually unacknowledged philosophic assumptions.

Secondly, let me note that the metaphysics I would envisage would not be a philosophic first. It would be a conclusion derived from epistemology and cognitional theory, and these in turn would be formulations of one's personal experience of one's own cognitional operations. In this fashion philosophy and the root of theological method would come out of the personal experience of the thinker and it would evoke the personal experience of those to whom he speaks or for whom he writes.

Thirdly, cognitional theory, epistemology, and metaphysics are needed but they are not enough. They have to be subsumed under the higher operations that integrate knowing with feeling and consist in deliberating, evaluating, deciding, acting. It is on this level that people move from unauthenticity to authenticity; it is on this level that they decide to believe; it is at the root of this level that God's love floods their hearts through the gift of the Holy Spirit (Rom. 5: 5). As before, so here too the account is not to presuppose a metaphysical framework of potencies, habits, acts, objects but basically it is to proceed from personal experience and move towards an analysis of the structures of our conscious and intentional operations. More than anywhere it is essential here to be able to speak from the heart to the heart without introducing elements that, however true in themselves, have the disadvantage of not being given in experience.

Fourthly, there exist religious studies. There are the history of religions, the phenomenology of religion, the psychology of religion, the sociology of religion, and underpinning them all and, as well, overarching them there is the philosophy of religion. Philosophy of religion reveals how basic thinking relates itself to the various branches of religious studies. Thereby it offers theology an analogous model of the way it can relate itself to religious studies, how it can profit from them, and how it can teach its own students what they will need to understand if the new secretariats, established by Vatican II, for ecumenism, for non-Christian religions, and for unbelievers, are to have competent staffs and to be properly understood, supported, and promoted by the Church and the hierarchy.

Fifthly, there is the history of philosophy. If one is to read Tertullian, one had best know Stoicism. If one is to read Origen, one has to be acquainted with Middle Platonism. If one is to read Augustine, one has to know his *Platonici*. Similarly, down the ages, theology has drawn upon the philosophers, because it has to speak both of the man that grace converts and of the world in which he lives. The historical theologian, then, has to know the philosophers relevant to his field of study; he has to be able to discern how much of the philosophers' thought the Christian writer really grasped and how much was only loosely assimilated. Finally, he must also be a critical philosopher, both capable of spotting what is misleading or inadequate in this or that philosophy, and able to reveal how philosophic defect led to theological defect. By such criticism historical theology can yield a dialectic. By revealing the philosophic sources of aberrations, it can account for differences in patristic and in theological thought. By discerning the manner in which aberrations have been overcome, it can sketch the genesis of a distinctive Catholic philosophy. For neither Plato nor Aristotle, neither Stoics nor Gnostics, anticipated the notions implied by Nicea, by Ephesus, by Chalcedon.

Sixthly, just as transcendental method can be adapted and extended into theology, into religious studies, into historical theology, so too it can be adapted and extended into sociocultural studies. Meanings, values, modes of group action have developed and diversified down the ages. There is no lack of detailed studies. There is no lack of the expertise that, through the self-correcting process of common-sense learning, comes to understand alien cultures. Besides detailed studies there exist such overall views as Bruno Snell's *The Discovery of Mind* and Ernst Cassirer's *Philosophy of Symbolic Forms*.

But something more is wanted. It is not supplied either by Aquinas' interpretation of Scripture in Aristotelian terms or by Bultmann's interpretation of the New Testament in terms of the early Heidegger. Rather what is wanted is a coming together of the fruits of historical expertise and, on the other hand, of models derived from the data of consciousness, from the different types of its differentiation and specialization, from the various structures that result from differentiation and specialization. From the interaction of detailed research, overall views, and the construction of models there would gradually emerge a phylogenetic set of schemata that would provide socio-cultural expertise with a first approximation to the notions it has to express and, on the other hand, would provide students both with an initial access to alien cultures and with an overall view of the stages and variations of human meanings, values, structures.

To this academic utility there must be added its practical utility. The Gospel is to be preached to all nations, to every class of men in every culture. As long as classicist culture was accepted, it could be thought that there existed but a single culture and that the Gospel could be preached substantially through that culture, even though accidentally certain adaptations had to be made to reach the uncultured. Now that classicist culture is a thing of the past, we can no longer suppose that classicist assumptions could succeed in preaching the Gospel to all nations. We have to learn to express the Gospel message so that it can be grasped by the members of every class within each of the cultures of the world. A philosophy of culture can make a great contribution towards the fulfilment of that task.

There is, then, a certain type of philosophy that in many ways is very relevant to Catholic theology in its current crisis. For the current crisis is a shift in horizon. The earlier horizon was a basic outlook in terms of logic and of eternal truths, with the consequence that serious change of context was assumed to be impossible and so its possibility was not investigated. The current horizon is a basic outlook in terms of method and developing doctrines. The application of hermeneutics and critical history has brought to light notable changes of context and, with them, those continuities and contrasts that we refer to as doctrinal developments. In place of eternal truths, we now have differing apprehensions of the object of faith, where the differences rise from the changing contexts within which the apprehensions occur.

A philosophy very relevant to this shift of horizon, of basic outlook, is one that centers on three questions: (1) What am I doing when I am knowing? (2) Why is doing that knowing? and (3) What do I know when I do it? With answers to those questions ascertained, one reaches the method of theology by asking and answering the specific question: What are we doing when we do theology?

The same type of philosophy also makes possible an analysis and a much needed critique both of hermeneutics and of critical history. It underpins a philosophy of action—a philosophy of deliberation, evaluation, decision, deed. It opens out upon a philosophy of religion, a dialectical history of theology, a philosophy of culture and of communications. In all these areas it blazes trails for theology to follow, enlarge, enrich.

SUMMARY COMMENTS

1. Transcendental method is transcendental both in the Scholastic sense (it is not confined to any particular genus or category of inquiry) and in the Kantian sense (it is the condition of the possibility, that is, the necessary but not sufficient condition of any categorial method).

2. Those that still cling to eternal truths may object that my position is relativist. They may argue a posteriori: hermeneutics and critical history did lead to the historicism of Ernst Troeltsch, which was just a thorough-going relativism. They may argue a priori: a truth that is not eternal is relative to some particular place and time.

To the a posteriori argument: recall that I accept hermeneutics and critical method but not without a soundly based analysis and an epistemological critique. Troeltsch's relativism springs from a philosophic inadequacy.

To the a priori argument: note that truths that are not eternal are relative, not to a place and time, but to the context of a place and time; but such contexts are related to one another; history includes the study of such relations; in the light of history it becomes possible to transpose from one context to another; by such transpositions one reaches a truth that extends over places and times.

3. While the paper sets forth problems in contemporary theology, it can make no attempt to solve them on the theological level. That is a task for a separate book. Our concern is limited to the contribution that philosophy might make to the solution of theological problems.

AN INTERVIEW WITH
FR. BERNARD LONERGAN, S. J.[1]

Edited by
PHILIP McSHANE

The First International Lonergan Congress was held in Florida during Easter, 1970, sponsored by Mr. Joseph Collins of New York. During the Congress Fr. Lonergan was interviewed in public session by three participants: Frs. Joseph Flanagan, Matthew Lamb and Philip McShane. The following is an edited version of that interview.[2] The editing left Fr. Lonergan's statements virtually unchanged but cut down the questions for brevity's sake.

Asked to comment on the present cultural crisis in relation to his own more recent interests and to Jaspers' *The Origin and Goal of History*, Fr. Lonergan remarked:

"I won't go back to Jaspers (it is some time since I read his book). The crisis comes to me this way. When I was sent to boarding school when I was a boy, there were no local high schools—that sort of thing didn't exist, you were sent out to a boarding school—the one I went to in Montreal, in 1918, was organized pretty much along the same lines as Jesuit schools had been since the beginning of the Renaissance, with a few slight

---

[1] Published in *The Clergy Review*, 56 (1971), 412–431.

[2] A selection of the papers from the Congress, edited by Philip McShane was published under the titles *Foundations of Theology* and *Language, Truth, and Meaning*, Dublin and Notre Dame, 1971 and 1972, respectively.

modifications. So that I can speak of classical culture as something I was brought up in and gradually learned to move *out of*. The Renaissance period was the period of the *uomo universale*, the man who could turn his hand to anything. The command of all that there was to be known at that time was not a fantastic notion. There was one culture, culture with a capital C: a normative notion of culture. That you could acquire it—a career opened to talent, and so on—was fairly well understood in various ways, and either you got it or did not. Communication, fundamentally, occurred *within* that one culture. You made slight adaptations to the people who were uncultured—and they were also not expected to expect to understand things.

"At the present time we don't have only to speak Latin, write Greek, and read Hebrew. We have all the modern languages with their modern literatures; the modern nations and the different worlds; instantaneous communication, perpetually available entertainment; terrific development in industry, in finance and all this sort of thing. No mathematician knows all mathematics, no physicist knows all physics, no chemist, all chemistry; and, least of all, no theologian knows all theology. With this transformation that has taken place, the world is a world of specialization. I think the Catholic Church has put up more resistance to it than anyone else and consequently is coming on the scene with too little and too late: Churchill's famous phrase."

To the question whether *Method in Theology* was restricted to theology or to a particular theology Fr. Lonergan replied:

"Karl Rahner, in his paper, remarked he thought it could be applied to any human science that was fully conscious of itself as depending on the past and looking towards the future. I think that's true. But I'm not working it out in those terms. I'm working it out in terms of a theology. That chapter on functional specializations is not going to be chapter two (as was said a year and a half ago when I sent this paper to *Gregorianum*) it's chapter five now. The four background chapters are: 'Method,' 'The Human Good,'

'Meaning,' and 'Religion.' So it's a theology because it's a reflection on religion, as said in *Functional Specialties*.

"Now it is doing *method* in theology; it is *not* doing theology. It aims at avoiding settling any theological question. Is it the Koran? Or the Old Testament? Or the Old and the New? Or the Old and the New and the Fathers? Or does it include the whole Christian tradition? Those are questions that theologians have to settle. I'm not going to settle them. So it's a structure, and you can have an analogy to it in Piaget's *Le Structuralisme*—a very thin little book in which he conceives this structuralism as a matter of interdependent, self-regulating, ongoing process.

"The eight functional specialties are a set of self-regulative, ongoing, interdependent processes. They're not stages such that you do one and then you do the next. Rather you have different people at all eight and interacting. And the interaction is not logical. It's attentive, intelligent, reasonable, responsible, and religious. The responsibility includes the element not only of morality but also of religion. I conceive religion as total commitment.

"For example: Lyonnet does a new exegesis of Romans 5: 12 and people say, 'Oh, you're a heretic,' Well, it's too fast. That's true if theology is just one plain deductive system. But with an onging process that is interdependent, once there is a new exegesis of 5: 12, then you can no longer argue for original sin from that text the way you could before that interpretation. You have a new situation. You haven't got a new heretic."

The Classic Treatises

Questions were raised as to the relation of Fr. Lonergan's Latin treatises *De Verbo Incarnato* and *De Deo Trino* to this method.

"Well—those things are practical chores, that you have to do if you're teaching a class of 650 people. They're not going to get it on the wing out of lectures. One of the techniques of getting them to come to the lectures and get something out of them is to provide them with a thick book so that they'll be glad to have some map as to what's important in it and what you can skip. It belongs to a period in which the situation I was in was hopelessly antiquated, but had not yet been demolished—it has since been demolished. But to be a professor in dogmatic theology was to be a specialist in the Old Testament—not just in the Pentateuch or something like that—the Old Testament, the New, the Apostolic Fathers, the Greek Fathers, the ante-Nicene, Greek and Latin, the post-Nicene, the medieval Scholastics, the Renaissance period, the Reformation, contemporary philosophy and so on. There's no one who is a specialist in all that; but that was the sort of thing you had to handle. And you did what you could—(as Damon Runyon's characters put it: 'How are you doing?' 'I'm doing what I can.').

"It was a matter of doing that—and also of introducing what I could. For example my analysis of the ante-Nicene period on trinitarian doctrine: I was developing there also what I consider something permanently valid, namely this type of interpretation that is concerned with things that the thinkers themselves didn't think about. Tertullian has a stoic background, Origen has a middle Platonist background, Athanasius' account of Nicea is something totally new that you can't reduce to anything Platonic, Aristotelian, Gnostic, or Stoic and so on; a new situation is created. It's second-level thinking, the sort of thing that is possible within a Hellenistic culture. But that comparison of all three, revealing their different backgrounds—the different ways in which they conceived the Son to be divine, totally different ways—is an understanding of the process from the New Testament to Nicea. That, I think, is something valid. There are chunks in those books that I think are permanently valid. But having to write the book at all was totally invalid—yet necessary concretely.

"Doing method fundamentally is distinguishing different tasks, and thereby eliminating totalitarian ambitions. Systematic theologians for a couple of centuries thought they were the only ones who were theologians, then, positive theologians thought they were the only ones. This other stuff was all out.

"What I want is eight different tasks distinguished. It isn't that one can't do all eight. One extraordinary person may very well do all eight—but he's doing eight different things, not just one and the same thing over and over again. That's a fundamental concern for method, eliminating totalitarian ambitions. On the other hand, it's making tasks not intolerably difficult. If you're trying to do one thing, and people are asking you why aren't you doing the other seven, and you're constantly explaining, you never get anywhere. And that's the way things were. My *De Deo Trino* comes in two parts. In the first part I manage to separate what I call systematics from doctrines. In the second I manage to separate what I call systematics and doctrine on the one hand and on the other positive studies, positive research, historical research. Well, I've moved on from those three to eight entirely different tasks."

Insight

Questions were put regarding the book *Insight*, whether it was a *way* or a *theory*, and how the exercise of self-appropriation to which it invites one generates horizons.

"Now with regard to the business of *Insight*, *Insight* happened this way: my original intention was method in theology. *Insight* was an exploration of methods in other fields, prior to trying to do method in theology. I got word in 1952 that I was to go to the Gregorian and teach in 1953, so I cut down my original ambition to do method in theology and put this book together. It's both a way and something like a theory. Fundamentally it's a way. It's asking people to discover in themselves what they are. And as Fr. Heelan put it, 'There's something liberating about that.' The word *Lonerganian* has come up in recent days. In a sense there's no such thing. Because what I'm asking people is to discover themselves and be themselves. They can arrive at conclusions different from mine on the basis of what they find in themselves. And in that sense it is a way.

"But that self-appropriation can be objectified. It's a heightening of consciousness—as one moves from attention to intelligence, to reasonableness, to responsibility, to religious experience. Those modalities of consciousness, the *a priori* that they constitute, *that* can be objectified. Not in the sense of subject-object—in here now, out there now—but in the sense that objectivity is the fruit of authentic subjectivity. That self-appropriation can be objectified and its objectification is theory.

"But it is not theory in exactly the same way physics is. Its basic elements—mass, temperature, electromagnetic field—are *not* within the field of experience. They are, all of them, constructs. Temperature is not what feels hot or cold. You put your hand on something metal, on something wood and one feels warmer than the other. They're both the same temperature—they're in the same room for a sufficient length of time. These fundamental concepts in physics are not data of experience.

"But the fundamental terms and relations in cognitional theory are *given* in consciousness. The relations are the dynamisms of consciousness and the terms are the operations that are related through the dynamisms. So it is theory—but in a sense as totally different from theory (in physics) as Eddington's two tables. On one you can put your hands, rest your weight; you find it solid, brown, it weighs so much. The other consists mostly of empty space, and where the space isn't empty you have a wavicle; but what it's doing is very hard to say.

"The exercise of self-appropriation gives you the structure that generates horizons. And because you have the structure that's generating horizon, because that structure is heuristic, you're anticipating. If the intelligible, being, the good—what you mean by those terms—is what is correlative to the desire to understand, to be reasonable, to be responsible; then, in yourself, you have the subjective pole of an objective field. You have also, in intelligent reasonable responsibility, norms, built-in norms, that are yourself. They are not propositions about yourself; but yourself, in your spiritual reality, to guide you in working out what that objective horizon is, the objective pole of the horizon. It's normative, it's potential. Not absolute, in the sense that you have it all tucked away. But you have the machinery for going at it, and you know what happens when you do."

To the objection that the structure is invariant and therefore not open, Lonergan replied:

"Well, it can happen that any particular person does get caught in some sort of cul-de-sac and that's his misfortune.

"But how do you get him out of it?

"By asking further questions.

"And the thing I'm talking about is dynamic and it is precisely the dynamic of asking further questions. And while there are restricted topics, on which you can say, 'Well, I don't think there are any further relevant questions with regard to that' (as in the chapter on judgment I talked about the man who leaves his beautiful, neat, perfect home in the morning to go to work, comes back in the evening and finds the windows broken, water on the floor and smoke in the air—and he doesn't say 'There was a fire.' That could be all faked, but he says 'Something happened.' He might ask 'Where's my wife?' and that would be a further question on a different topic. Still, with regard to the statement 'Something happened' there are no further relevant questions)."

Theology and the Social Sciences

A question as to the relation of theology to the social sciences brought the following reply:

"Well, that is inter-disciplinary. I had a note from Fr. Houtart, who edits *Social Compass* and represents a large number of sociological students. There was a remark I made about the religious sciences in 'Theology and Man's Future.' I spoke of their increasing relevance to theology and he asked me to expand on that in a thousand words. He's asking other people to do something similar.

"I answered by a paper, a short note, on the example of Gibson Winter. Gibson Winter, in *Elements for a Social Ethic*, took Max Weber's distinction between social science and social policy. He found that social science, in America at the present time, was either behaviorist, or functionalist like Talcott Parsons, or voluntarist like C. Wright Mills *et alii*, or—with the intentionality analysis of the new school of social research—phenomenological. Also that the middle two disagreed rather vigorously with one another. He put the question, 'Is this difference scientific or ideological?' Consequently he had the transition from social science to social philosophy; and drew on George Mead to do a beautiful thing on the social construction of meaning. (You find out what you mean by your gesture or your words from the other person's reaction to it. So that meaning has a common origin, a social origin.) Winter went on from that—to build up something in the way of a philosophy, a social philosophy, and added on a social ethic. When you put these two on top of empirical social science, you could go on to an enlightened social policy.

"Similarly you can have empirical psychology of religion, and empirical sociology of religion and so on. Add on to it a philosophy of religion and if it contains an account of genuine religious experience it will be open to a theology and a moral theology, and you can go on to religious policy. Such policy is psychological in schools—in teaching, preaching and so on, and in sociological group action. Then the empirical scientists could see the results, give you the feedback, and have an ongoing process. That's one scheme of the way in which theology and the social sciences or religious sciences might co-operate.

"Now there is also a relevance of religion to sociology in the broader sense—not simply the sociology of religion. I think you can see how it could extend that way too. But it is a more complicated matter."

216

Questioned further on the distinction mentioned, "scientific or ideological," Fr. Lonergan continued:

"Well, Talcott Parsons' functional analysis is a beautiful and terrific analysis; but when it is applied it seems to favor the *status quo*. C. Wright Mills' analysis, which is in terms of will, power, struggle and so on, gives you an alternative view of the situation. Now that's what emerges when you start applying them, eh? And the real question is the ideological element that comes in when you start applying. But it's really a springboard for Winter to move out of their context into a philosophic context on society. This is just my impression. I'm not speaking for Winter."

Regarding the present state of the relationship of sociology, philosophy and religion Fr. Lonergan's comment was:

"Well, *de facto*, religious studies are: research, interpretation, history, with a bit of dialectic with the other people who are in the field; but not dialectic worked out in any very systematic fashion. 'So and so has written this book and I think he's a little wrong on that.' "

Conversion

On the fact that conversion is outside the functional specialties —a fact objected to by some:

"Well, it is. It's a personal event, and it occurs in all sorts of contexts. Religious conversion is transferring oneself into the world of worship; theology is in the academy, the classroom, the seminar, it isn't in the Church but about the Church.

"Again, with regard to the openness of the method, the functional specialties do not set up conditions of membership. Anyone can do research, interpretation, history and enter into the dialectic. Non-religious people, also religious people. You start sorting the thing out when you get to the dialectic—that's what the dialectic is for, sorting things out. Consequently, insofar as non-religious people are reflecting on religion, they'll have rather negative views, reductionist views. But insofar as religious people are, they needn't. There's no necessity of having Bultmann's notion of what science is, in doing interpretation or history. The reason for writing chapters, and the setting up specific chapters on each one of these things, is the fact that at the end of the nineteenth century the positivists did capture critical history and give their interpretations to it. Droysen's handbook is far more intelligent, fundamentally, than Bernheim, and Bernheim much more intelligent than Langlois and Seignobos.

"You have a reaction against that positivist invasion of history: in Carl Becker in the States, in Collingwood in England, Marrou in France. *Insight* is very relevant to working out, from a critical philosophic basis, just what critical history is, just what objective interpretation is. I think you *need* that philosophic critique before you're going to be able to handle questions like the 'Jesus of history' and the 'Christ of faith' without being blocked by unconscious philosophic assumptions."

The question of objectivity was raised in relation to the remark in *Insight*, p. xxviii, that "there is an intelligent and reasonable realism between which and materialism the half-way house is idealism."

"I think I have a better start in Professor Johann's paper. Professor Johann found that my notion of judgment and Dewey's were extremely similar. But he agreed, when I spoke to him, that the contexts were entirely different. Being, for me, is the universe, the world mediated by meaning. It's the answer to what you know when you answer questions that regard everything about everything. Dewey's world fundamentally is the nonproblematic. There are problems here and there, and you solve them. But the world principally is what is taken for granted. You solve some problems; and when you get them solved, well, they come into what you can now take for granted. It's a world—the world-of-the-taken-for-granted.

"Now the criteria, with regard to the two worlds, are totally different. The taken-for-granted is the already-out-there-now-real. It's 'already'—prior to any questions; 'out'—extroverted consciousness; 'there'—spatial sense organs have spatial objects; 'now'—the time of the observer is the time of the observed; 'real'—well, that's what we mean by reality, we're defining it. But you can have an entirely different world—the world mediated by meaning—the world that is most known through belief. Ninety-eight per cent of what a genius knows, he believes. It isn't personally independently acquired knowledge. Human knowledge is an acquisition that goes on over centuries and centuries, and if we want to accept nothing, that we don't find out for ourselves, we revert to the palaeozoic age. At that period they found out for themselves everything they knew.

"That world, mediated by meaning, is what most of us mean by the real world. And the criteria for knowing it, for being objective *there*, are the criteria of being attentive, of being intelligent, being reasonable, being responsible. An entirely different set of criteria. Now those two can be confused. The naive realist knows the world mediated by meaning. But he knows it by taking a look. The naive idealist says '*esse est percipi.*' Esse—it is—the affirmation of reality, in the world mediated by meaning, is the *percipi*—the taking a look. The rigorist empiricist eliminates from the world mediated by meaning everything that isn't in the world you take for granted. The critical idealist—he doesn't attend to data and understand and judge. He sees the appearances of things in themselves that you can't know but can talk about by using a limiting concept. He adds to these appearances the categories of understanding and the ideals of reason. So he has valid knowledge on this side, and the impossibility of knowledge on the other. His unconditioned at one stage is the totality of conditions —and it was Hegel who conceived the universe as the totality of conditions. He wanted to put movement within logic. Method very much is the ongoing process, and logic regards the cross-sections at any moment. So logic is within method."

When asked about his growing interest in *meaning* since he wrote *Insight* Fr. Lonergan remarked:

"Well, it was being sent to Rome and having to deal with students from northern Italy and France and Germany and Belgium who were totally immersed in continental philosophy— I had to talk meaningfully to them, and it involved getting a hold of the whole movement of the *Geisteswissenchaften*, from Friedrich Wolf on, to be able to communicate with my students. And it's, of course, something that stretches one. And I've learnt a lot since. It's still a moving viewpoint—after *Insight*. It kept on moving."

On the contrast between Dewey's view of knowing as within experience and his own of experience as within knowing, Father Lonergan commented:

"There are two different ways you can take the word 'experience.' The 'man of experience,' say, is the man of common sense, with a lot, a terrific development, of intelligence. Albright received a consignment of jars from Qumran and one of them was broken. He took the dust between his fingers and said: 'Now this was done in such and such a century.' A man of experience! That's experience in one sense. Or, you consult the man of experience: 'What can I do about this?' That's a sense of the word 'experience' which includes everything that is in the person's development. Then there's experience in a technical sense of the data—what I call experiential objectivity—the givenness that constitutes the data, which is the presupposition of the act of understanding."

Regarding Symbols and Ricoeur on Symbolism:

"Well, I can't match Ricoeur on symbolism. The symbol for me is the 'affect-laden image.' It's evoked by an affect, or the image evokes the affect. They're linked. It's the means of internal communication between psyche and mind and heart. Where mind is experience, understanding, judgment; and heart is what's beyond this on the level of feeling and 'is this worthwhile?'—

judgment of value, decision. Without feelings this experience, understanding, judgment is paper-thin. The whole mass and momentum of living is in feeling.

"Feelings: there's a whole series of categories on them—to go into them would take too long. You get them in Scheler, and then von Hildebrand, in his *Christian Ethics*, distinguishing different kinds—different meanings of the word 'feeling,' different types. But there are feelings that are apprehensions of value in a strict sense. There are vital values. Then social values— the vital values of the group. Then cultural values—'not in bread alone does man live.' There's the personal realization, incorporation of values, religious values, the personal appropriation of values, the development of one's feelings, the education of feeling. This is all on the level of the apprehension of values.

"Beyond that there's the transcendental notion of values, in the question for deliberation—'Is this worthwhile? or are we wasting our time?' It stops you—and in the judgment of value in answer to that question. This demands not only these feelings—if you just have these feelings, well, you have a moral idealism that usually does more harm than good—you have to have also an apprehension of human reality, and possibility, and what probably will happen from different courses of action.

"For your judgment of values, for the objectivity of a judgment of value, the criterion is the good conscience of the virtuous man. You're not sure of your moral judgments unless you're sure you're a virtuous man! It's very Aristotelian, incidentally. Aristotle made ethics empirical by postulating the existence of virtuous men."

Affectivity

On the movement after *Insight* to an increasing interest in affectivity and feeling, Fr. Lonergan commented:
"There is in *Insight* a footnote to the effect that we're not

attempting to solve anything about such a thing as personal relations. I was dealing in *Insight* fundamentally with the intellectual side—a study of human understanding—in which I did my study of human understanding and got human intelligence in there, not just a sausage machine turning out abstract concepts. That was my fundamental thrust.

"Once I did that, well, you had to go out and go on to a theory of judgment—because you had obviously separated yourself from any possible intuitive basis of knowledge. And I had to have a *true* judgment, one true judgment at least, so I had to have chapter XI, 'I am a knower.'

"Then 'What do you know?' so I had another chapter on being.

" 'How do you know you know it?' I had to have another chapter on objectivity.

"When I had that much done, I could see people all around saying, 'Well, if you have this sort of position you can't have a metaphysics.' So I thought I'd be safer to put in four more chapters on metaphysics.

" 'Well, you can't have an ethics,' so I put in a chapter on that.

"And, 'You can't prove the existence of God,' so I put a chapter on that.

"Then, 'What has this to do with your being a priest?' So I put a little bit on religion in chapter XX—a moving viewpoint!

"The viewpoint kept moving. In the summer of 1959 (when you're teaching in Rome you also have to get a bus fare to escape the hospitality of the continent) I gave an institute at Xavier in Cincinnati, on the philosophy of education. In preparing that I read a lot of Piaget, also Susanne Langer, *Feeling and Form*, things like that, and that was the beginning of entry into these things. Then von Hildebrand, and Frings' book on Scheler were a big help. I was also meeting questions of my own. One also has feelings oneself too, you know.

"There is a spreading out, moving on, including more. Like

recently what I've got a hold of is the fact that I've dropped faculty psychology and I'm doing intentionality analysis. And what I did in *Insight* mainly was intentionality analysis of experiencing, understanding, judging. Add on to that on this side, the different types of feeling:

"Feelings that are just states or tendencies—You feel hungry, but you don't yet know that what you need is something to eat—

"Then there are feelings that respond to objects—pleasure and pain and so on. But of themselves they do not discriminate between what is truly good and what is only apparently good.

"There are feelings that are intentional responses and that do involve such a discrimination and put themselves in a hierarchy—and you have your vital values, social values, cultural values, religious values.

"Then, dominating all this, according to Scheler and von Hildebrand, and what really reveals values and lets you really see them, is being in love.

"Now you get the synthesis of this feeling side and the cognitional side on the level of the question, 'Is this worthwhile?' the judgment of value, the decision, the action. So, when you bring in the fourth, you move into a philosophy of action. You're up with Blondel."

On the Place of Imagination and Affectivity:

"Imagination, first of all, is a big part of understanding. To have an insight, you have to have an image. The sensible data are so complex, so multiform, that you simplify in imagination. You get a schematic image, and you get hold of something and you compare your schematic image with your data. And you see, well, your schematic image has to become more complex; and you get an insight into that. And you keep on building up. So there's this development of imagination in connection with understanding itself, even a very technical type of understanding.

"There's imagination as art, which is the subject, doing—in a global fashion—what the philosopher and the religious person and so on do in a more special fashion. It's moving into the known unknown in a very concrete, felt, way. I think Susanne Langer has a wonderful analysis of artistic creation. I wouldn't want to attempt to repeat it now. But the significance of art is a liberation from all the mechanizations of sensibility. The red and green lights are signals that let you take your foot off the brake and put it on the accelerator. There's the routinization of sensibility—the ready-made man and the ready-made world, with set reactions responding to stimuli—and art liberates sensitivity, allows it to flow in its own channel and with its own resonance; and it reveals to man his openness to more than the world he already is functioning properly in."

Does one not seem to move away from imagination as one moves from experience and understanding to judgment?

"It's not moving away but adding to it."

And in what sense does return to imagination constitute an opening for the experiencing, understanding, judgment, deciding?

" 'The return to' is always the wheel, circular. And different people develop differently. There are literary people, there are artistic people, there are different potentialities, opportunities of life, and so on. But even though you write a book like *Insight*, you can enjoy Beethoven."

There was a question about chapter XIX of *Insight*. Would this chapter at most say to someone coming to it from outside the Christian tradition that the religious self-transcendence, which occurs in Christian conversion, is not contradictory to the cognitive self-transcendence which was studied in the first sixteen chapters or to the moral conversion of the chapter on ethics?

"I think chapter XIX was mainly the product of an entirely different type of thinking than was being built up. I'd be quite ready to say: let's drop chapter XIX out of *Insight* and put it inside of theology. I say that much pretty well in my article in the

Proceedings of the American Catholic Theological Society in 1968.[3] In this paper on natural knowledge of God, I say about the proof of God's existence, while there exists a valid proof, and while the apprehension of that proof is not a supernatural act *quoad substantiam* in the technical sense, still people who do prove the existence of God have had God's grace. What was defined in Vatican I is not that anyone ever proved, or ever will prove, the existence of God. It's a question of possibility. What they were thinking of was not any concrete subject but 'right and reason.' It's an issue that goes back to Christian Wolff.

"And today when that question is put it is entirely in terms of the concrete person in a concrete context who is becoming religious or is finally discovering that he has become religious and wants to know whether he's crazy or not. It's an entirely different context; chapter XIX is prior to my concern with the existentialists and so on—*Insight* was finished before I went to Rome."

Myth

On the category of *myth* in *Insight* Fr. Lonergan's comment was:
"In *Insight* I use two categories, mystery and myth. Both mean the same thing. You could include both under the word 'symbol.' But myth is also used in the sense of a narrative that embodies symbols, like Northrop Frye's *Fables of Identity*. There is terminological difficulty with the usage in *Insight*; but I believe in the permanent necessity of the symbol for human living. You can't talk to your body without symbols, and you have to live with it."

And myth in the sense of symbol, therefore, Lonergan would conceive to be a permanent structure?

"Yes, but there is such a thing as people who have fantastic notions of what the world is. Cassirer talks about the tribe that—

[3] Reprinted above, pp. 117 ff.

while they've never seen the villages that the tigers have, and the elephants have—they were quite certain that such superior beings would have enough sense to live in villages too. This construction of reality is something that goes on, that man spends millennia developing."

On the idea that mythic consciousness is a definitively past period in human history:

"You can get right back to it very easily. All you have to do is to have a breakdown. It's not an irreversible process. The process of education is maintaining the gains we've already made. And you have mythic consciousness—a whole different series of it—you have the mythic consciousness of the primitive, the mythic consciousness in the ancient high civilizations, in which the King was the god and the source of order in the universe, and so on—they're all identified—religious, political, and natural order—the cosmological order. And that broke when the ancient high civilizations broke down, when you had the development of the individual. You got much more individual responsibility.

"Then, with Plato and Aristotle you have the distinction between the world of theory and the world of common sense. Plato's *phainomena* and *noumena* and Aristotle's *priora quoad se* and *priora quoad nos*. But humanism immediately stepped in and obliterated that difference. Isocrates said: 'What differentiates man from the animals is speech.' And the rhetoricians are the people who know how to speak. Subsequent philosophy in general—with rare exceptions—has been the work of people in the humanist tradition who did *not* want to have any distinction between the world of common sense and the world of theory. It is modern science—with Eddington's two tables—that has forced that distinction on us again."

Interiority

On being asked, in the context of Jaspers' discussion of axial periods, whether the shift, or the possibility of a communal shift, to interiority, was axial, Fr. Lonergan replied:

"Yes. Of course, with Jaspers, his axial age is the emergence of individualism more than anything. My distinctions are first of all: realms of meaning. There's the realm of meaning of common sense—and the Greek development was a differentiation—the world of common sense and the world of theory. And that is what remained. Like Thomas; he's in the two. Augustine is just in the world of common sense, a beautiful rhetorician; Newman too. They're not technical people. They did tremendous work, but are not technical in the way that Thomas was and Aristotle was. In the present situation there are the world of common sense and the world of science. And to relate one to the other you have to go into interiority—to understand why you have different cognitional procedures in one and in the other and you're knowing quite different worlds.

"The scientist has a language of his own and his own society —he can love his wife but he can't talk to her about his science. There are terrific relationships between it and the world of common sense—with communications and feedback into industry, technology and so forth. But they're two different sets of fundamental concepts, modes of procedure, etc. You have to go into interiority to understand why there should be these differences and to relate them and you have to do it too, if you want to have good *human* science. As Professor O'Dea said yesterday, cognitional theory reveals to the sociologist what he's doing and it reveals something—not everything—about the object he's dealing with.

"And beyond the three, the most common differentiation of consciousness is not common sense and theory but common sense and transcendence. As you have it in the Asian peoples, and you have it in the Christian tradition of spiritual men and women —the lives of the saints."

On the danger of the neglect of *Insight* and its complex methods, due to more immediate interest in *Method in Theology*,[4] Fr. Lonergan remarked:

"Well, they're there, people will have them. When you have a structure of eight ongoing and interdependent processes you can't hide the genetic element; and when they're conflicting with one another, when one of the processes is dialectic, you can't hide the dialectical element. But this is much more complex. *Insight* is the way *into* them, and the function of the method is simply to set up limits and define tasks, and so on."

To the question whether the horizon set up in us by God's gift of love, discussed in Fr. Lonergan's article "Faith and Beliefs,' which grounds religious conversion, transcends the horizon of being, the reply was:

"I wouldn't say so. The good is beyond the intelligible, the true and the real. It's more comprehensive. Moral conversion takes you beyond intellectual conversion; and religious conversion takes you beyond both. But it's not beyond being, if this being in love, total commitment, if that is the full actuation, the ultimate actuation of the movement towards the intelligible, towards the true, towards the real, towards the good. This is the ultimate step in it. It's what your *a priori*, what your authentic subjectivity, is open to. It occurs, insofar as it does, through God's grace. My doctoral thesis was on operative grace in St. Thomas. It's a notion thought up by Augustine, when he was dealing with the monks of Hadrumetum who said, 'Well, if it all depends on God's grace, why do superiors correct us?' But the fundamental text with regard

---

[4] *Method in Theology* pivots on the key chapter, "Functional Specialities," already published in *Gregorianum*, 1969. That chapter is preceded by a series of chapters on such topics as "Method," "Meaning," "The Good" which provide its concrete context, and it is followed by chapters which consider the specialties in detail. Insofar as these eight specialties gradually become operative, through an extension of the self-appropriation of *Insight*, in the community of theologians, they will provide a means of transforming the theological enterprise in the radical manner required by the present axial shift mentioned in the text above.

to this operative grace is Ezekiel: God plucking out the heart of stone which has no desire whatever to be a heart of flesh and putting in the heart of flesh, totally beyond the deserts, ambitions even, of the heart of stone.

"Now that operative grace, as sanctifying grace and not merely as actual grace, is the thing in that article. It is this 'being in love,' and I think it ties in with Friedrich Heiler's chapter in *The History of Religions*, on 'The History of Religions as a Preparation for the Cooperation of Religions.' A person who has a different set-up from mine might well interpret it in the way you put it, but within my context, my opposition between reality as the unproblematic and reality as, too, the goal of the questioning subject—the authentic subject—it's on that side for me."

Lonergan, unlike Rahner, lays emphasis in his writings on clarity rather than mystery.

"But mystery remains. When you talk, you're not aiming at communicating a mystery. Buy you don't dispel it either. Rahner emphasizes mystery a lot. I have a few clear things to say."

Should one not critically ground religion?

"I put the question the other night. A person was demanding that I critically ground this religion and he was talking to Professor So and So and I went up to him and, said 'Would you require Professor So and So to critically ground the love he has for his wife and children?' Being in love is a fact, and it's what you are, it's existential. And your living flows from it. It's the first principle, as long as it lasts. It has its causes and its occasions and its conditions and all the rest of it. But while it's there it's the first principle and it's the source of all one's desires and fears, all the good one can see, and so on. And critically grounding knowledge isn't finding the ground for knowledge. It's already there. Being critical means eliminating the ordinary nonsense, the systematically misleading images and so on; the mythical account.

"Every scientific or philosophic breakthrough is the elimination

229

of some myth in the pejorative sense; the flat earth, right on. But if you are in love it doesn't need any justification. It's the justification beyond anything else. Just as you don't explain God, God is the ultimate explanation."

Might one not then be deceived?

"One can be deceiving himself. If one is deceiving oneself one is not in love. One is mistaking something for love. Love is something that proves itself. 'By their fruits you shall know them,' and 'in fear and trembling work out your salvation' and all the rest of it. Love isn't cocksure, either.

"I want to thank the organizers, the people who thought up and financed and organized all this; the people who organized the meetings; the people who came, the people who wrote papers, the people who sat around this morning and listened, and are taking part in this thing—very, very sincerely, as you all can understand."

REVOLUTION IN CATHOLIC THEOLOGY[1]

I may assume, no doubt, that everyone is aware of the profound changes that have occurred in the thought of Catholic theologians during the present century. But to enumerate in detail just what changes have occurred in the thought of individual theologians seemed to me to be just a long litany that presupposed a great deal of not very illuminating research. So I have been led to think it more profitable to inquire into the causes of such change and to estimate which changes have come to stay.

Now it is in the area of scholarship—of the linguist, the exegete, the historian—that the most startling changes have occurred in Catholic theology. More rapidly in the fields of patristic and medieval studies, more slowly in the field of Scripture, there gradually have been accepted and put into practice new techniques in investigating the course of history, new procedures in interpreting texts, new and more exacting requirements in the study of languages. The result of these innovations has been to eliminate the old style dogmatic theologian. For the old style dogmatic theologian was expected: (1) to qualify his theses by appealing to papal and conciliar documents from any period in church history and (2) to prove his thesis by arguing from the Old Testament and the New, from the Greek, Latin, and Syriac Fathers, from the

[1] Reprinted from *The Catholic Theological Society of America, Proceedings* 27 (1972), 18–23. © 1972 by Bernard J. F. Lonergan.

Byzantine and medieval Scholastics, and from all the subsequent generations of theologians. But the new techniques in history, the new procedures in interpretation, the new requirements in the study of languages reveal the performance of the old style dogmatic theologian to be simply out of date. For the new techniques, procedures, requirements demand specialization. They demand that opinions be based on full knowledge. They consider it self-evident that one man cannot know all there is to be known either on the Old Testament or the New, either on the Greek or on the Latin or on the Syriac Fathers; and, as the same holds for the Byzantine and the medieval Scholastics and for their later successors, the old style dogmatic theologian has simply become obsolete.

There are further and far more general consequences. Culture used to be conceived normatively. It was something that ought to be, and accordingly, *de iure* if not *de facto*, there was just one culture for all mankind. It was the fruit of being brought up in a good home, of studying Latin and Greek at school, of admiring the immortal works of literature and art of the classical period, of adhering to the perennial philosophy, and of finding in one's laws and institutions the deposit of the prudence and the wisdom of mankind. But exploration, anthropology, the proper inter-pretation of texts, and the composition of critical histories have given currency to an empirical notion of culture. A culture is simply the set of meanings and values that inform the way of life of a community. Cultures can decline rapidly, but they develop only slowly, for development is a matter of coming to understand new meanings and coming to accept higher values. Moreover, any notable culture has a long history: it has borrowed from other cultures; it has adapted what it borrowed into its new context; it has effected the development of its own patrimony. Cultures are many and varied; they all have their good points and their deficiencies; and the ideal culture is far far rarer than the ideal man.

To grasp the empirical notion of culture leads to a grasp of what is meant by a person's historicity. What counts in a person's life is what he does and says and thinks. But all human doing, saying, thinking occurs within the context of a culture and consists in the main in using the culture. But cultures change; they wax and wane; meanings become refined or blunted; value-judgments improve or deteriorate. In brief, cultures have histories. It is the culture as it is historically available that provides the matrix within which persons develop and that supplies the meanings and values that inform their lives. People cannot help being people of their age, and that mark of time upon them is their historicity.

What I have been saying has considerable importance in the Church's task of preaching the Gospel to all nations. A classicist could feel that he conferred a double benefit on those to whom he preached if he not only taught them the Gospel but also let them partake in the riches of the one and only culture. But the empirical notion of culture puts an entirely different light on the matter. The preacher's task now becomes one of inserting the Gospel within a culture in which it has not been known. To make it known there, there must be found in the local language the potentialities for expressing the Gospel message, and it is by developing these potentialities and not by imposing an alien culture that the mission will succeed.

There are further implications to the shift from a normative to an empirical apprehension of culture. For the normative apprehension projects upon laws and institutions a permanence and rigidity that the study of history finds to be illusory. From the normative viewpoint one will think of the Church as a *societas perfecta*, a perfect society endowed with all the powers necessary for its autonomy. From the empirical viewpoint one will conceive the Church, as in the *Handbuch der Pastoraltheologie*,[2] as a

---

[2] F. X. Arnold, F. Klostermann, K. Rahner, V. Schutt, and L. Weber, eds, Freiburg-Basel-Wien, 1964, 1966, 1968, 1969, 4 vols.

Selbstvollzug, an ongoing process of self-realization, as an ongoing process in which the constitutive, the effective, and the cognitive meaning of Christianity is continuously realized in ever changing situations.

There are not a few writers who assert that the normative view of culture and the universal uniformity it implies derive from Greek thought and, specifically, from Greek philosophy. And while I believe it is true that the Greek philosophers did not know about the techniques developed by more recent exegetes and historians, it remains that a more exact understanding of the normative approach is to be had by turning from the Greek philosophers to the humanists, the orators, the schoolteachers, to the men who simplified and watered down philosophic thought and then peddled it to give the slow-witted an exaggerated opinion of their wisdom and knowledge. After all, from a contemporary viewpoint it seems an incredible conceit to suppose that one's culture is the one and only uniform and universal culture.

However that may be, we must go on to further sources of change in the thought of Catholic theologians. Not only is it true that the Greek philosophers did not foresee the implications of contemporary hermeneutics and history. It also is true that they did not grasp contemporary notions of science and of philosophy. Only in the nineteenth century was it recognized that Euclid's *Elements* was not the one and only geometry, but just one out of many possible geometries. Only more recently did mathematicians deduce their conclusions not from necessary truths but from suitable postulates. For years physicists proclaimed the necessary laws of nature, but less than fifty years ago they began to speak of the statistical probabilities of quantum theory. Even economists spoke of the iron laws of economics, only eventually to renounce them and turn their hand to advising bureaucrats on the probable results of this or that course of action. There has emerged a new notion of what a science is, and it in no way corresponds to the knowledge of the cause, knowledge that it is the cause, and knowledge that the effect cannot be other than it is, that is set forth in Aristotle's *Posterior Analytics*.

The content of modern scientific doctrine is not an intelligibility that is necessary but an intelligibility that is: (1) possible and (2) probably verified. Moreover, to give an account of a modern science one cannot be content to list logical operations, that is, operations with respect to terms, propositions, and inferences. The modern scientist does perform logical operations: he formulates, defines, infers. But he also observes, discovers, experiments. Moreover, the two sets of operations are interdependent. Discoveries are expressed in definitions and formulations. Inferences from formulations are checked by observations and experiments. Checking by observation and experiment can give rise to new discoveries, and the new discoveries in turn generate new definitions and formulations to make science not an unchanging system but an ever ongoing process.

There is a further departure from Aristotle in modern science. Aristotle wanted the sciences to derive their basic terms from metaphysics. Potency and act, matter and form, substance and accident were key concepts. Such sciences as physics or psychology obtained further key concepts proper to their respective fields by adding appropriate further determinations to the metaphysical basic terms. In contrast, modern science sets up its own basic terms; it does so by deriving them from empirically established laws; and such are the concepts of mass, temperature, the electromagnetic field, the elements of the periodic table, the branching of the evolutionary tree.

Now when the modern procedure is adopted in cognitional psychology, then one's basic terms will refer to conscious operations and one's basic relations will refer to conscious relations between operations. Through such basic terms and relations one can tell just what one is doing when one is coming to know. From such cognitional theory one can go on to explaining why doing that is knowing, and so arrive at an epistemology. From cognitional theory and epistemology one can go on to setting up a metaphysics, that is, to state in general what one knows when one does come to know. On this showing metaphysics ceases to be the first science on which all others depend. But ceasing to be the first science has its advantages, for now a metaphysics can be critically established; every statement it makes about reality can be validated by a corresponding cognitional operation that is verifiable.

We have been observing both in science and philosophy a shift from the intelligibility that is a necessity to the intelligibility that is a possibility and, as well, probably verified. Now this shift means the dethronement of speculative intellect or of pure reason. Neither the scientist nor the philosopher has at his disposal a set of necessary and self-evident truths. He has to observe external nature. He has to attend to his own internal operations and their relations to one another. Neither the observing nor the attending reveals necessity. They merely provide the data in which insight may discern possible relationships, and which further experience may confirm as *de facto* valid.

The dethronement of speculative intellect has been a general trend in modern philosophy. Empirical science led to empiricist philosophy. Empiricist philosophy awoke Kant from his dogmatic slumbers. The German absolute idealists, Fichte, Schelling, Hegel, attempted to restore speculative reason to her throne, but their success was limited. Kierkegaard took his stand on faith, Schopenhauer wrote on the world as will and representation, Newman toasted conscience, Dilthey wanted a *Lebensphilosophie*, Blondel wanted a philosophy of action, Ricoeur is busy with a philosophy of will, and in the same direction tend the pragmatists, the personalists, the existentialists.

I am far from thinking that this tendency is to be deplored. What once was named speculative reason today is simply the operations of the first three levels of consciousness—the operations of experiencing and inquiring, understanding and formulation, checking and judging. There operations occur under the rule and guidance of the fourth level, the level of deliberating, evaluating, deciding. Philosophers and scientists recognize this fact when they deliberate about the proper method to be followed in their work.

I have said that contemporary hermeneutics and history have made the old style dogmatic theologian obsolete. I have gone on to argue that the contemporary notion of science and its consequences in forming the notion of philosophy are quite different from the notions entertained up to the eighteenth and nineteenth centuries. It is not only the old style dogmatic theologian that is obsolete. It is also true that the old style dogmatic theologian cannot be replaced on the basis of old style notions of science and of philosophy.

What the new style is to be, I cannot prophesy. But perhaps I should mention what I tend to think. First, then, there is going to be a lot less metaphysics. It has ceased to be the basic and universal science, the *Grund- und Gesamt-wissenschaft*. General theological terms will find their roots in cognitional theory. Specific theological terms will find their roots in religious experience. There will be far less talk about proofs, and there will be far more about conversion, intellectual conversion, moral conversion, religious conversion. The emphasis will shift from the levels of experiencing, understanding, and judging, to the level of deliberating, evaluating, deciding, loving.

In the present century, then, theology is undergoing a profound change. It is comparable in magnitude to the change that occurred in the Middle Ages, that began with Anselm's speculative thrust, Abaelard's hard-headed *Sic et Non*, the Lombard's *Sentences*, the technique of the *Quaestio*, and the fusion of these elements in the ongoing process of commentaries on the *Sentences*, *Quaestiones disputatae*, and the various *Summae*. Then, without any explicit advertence to the fact, theology operated on the basis of a method. For over a century it brought forth precious fruits. To theology as governed by method and as an ongoing process the present situation points. If that pointing is accurate and effective, then the contemporary revolution in theology also will have the character of a restoration.

THE ORIGINS OF CHRISTIAN REALISM[1]

My approach to the question of the origins of Christian realism is determined by three topics. Elsewhere I have treated these topics separately. But it is my hope that you will be interested in having them brought together in a single focus.

The first topic is the notion of critical realism, i.e., the attempt to get beyond the empiricism of Hume, the critical idealism of Kant, the absolute idealism of Fichte, Schelling, and Hegel, and the subsequent varieties of subjectivism. The second topic is how did it happen that the Christian Church became involved in such issues. To this the common answer since the pronouncements of Harnack has been the influence of Hellenistic thought. Such an answer, as I have argued in the first volume of my *De Deo Trino*,[2] is quite inadequate. The third topic has to do with contemporary Roman Catholic Christology. Some years ago, Fathers Hulsbosch, Schillebeeckx, and Schoonenberg discussed or proposed revisions of Christological doctrine.[3] Father Piet Schoonenberg in 1969 published a book on the topic; a German translation was published in the same year; and in 1971 there appeared an English translation under the title, *The Christ*.[4]

[1] The Seventeenth Annual Robert Cardinal Bellarmine Lecture, delivered at Saint Louis University School of Divinity, September 27, 1972. Reprinted in *Theology Digest*, 20 (1972), 292-305. © 1972 by Theology Digest, Inc.

[2] Rome, 1964.

[3] *Tijdschrift voor Theologie*, 6 (1966), 249-306.

[4] New York, 1971.

Apparently contrary to Father Schoonenberg's views, the Congregation for the Doctrine of the Faith on February 21, 1972 reaffirmed the doctrines of the Councils of Nicea and Chalcedon. The materials then of this third topic come from Dutch and Roman theology. But the question I propose to treat is the relation of this Dutch-Roman conflict to the views I set forth in my Père Marquette lecture on *Doctrinal Pluralism*.[5]

I. *The Ambiguity of Realism*

Many no doubt will feel it quite ridiculous for a theologian to confront head-on a philosophic issue. While at the back of their minds there may linger some old and mistaken notions of sciences defined by their formal objects and consequently completely disparate, more probably in the foreground will be the conviction that philosophic issues are tremendously profound and difficult.

Let me begin then by assuring you that in proposing to speak of the ambiguity of realism I have not the slightest intention of touching on anything either profound or difficult. For in my opinion the ambiguity of realism arises from the very simple and evident fact that infants do not speak while most adults do speak. From this simple and evident fact it follows that infants, because they do not speak, do not live in a world mediated by language. Their world is a world of immediacy, of sights and sounds, of tastes and smells, of touching and feeling, of joys and sorrows. But as infants learn to speak, they gradually move into a far larger world. It includes the past and the future as well as the present, the possible and the probable as well as the actual, rights and duties as well as facts. It is a world enriched by travellers' tales, by stories and legends, by literature, philosophy, science, by religion, theology, history.

Now the criteria of reality in the infant's world of immediacy

5 Milwaukee, 1971.

240

are given in immediate experience. They are simply the occurrence of seeing or hearing, tasting or smelling, touching or feeling, enjoying or suffering. But the criteria of reality in the world mediated by meaning are far more complex. They include immediate experience but they also go beyond it. To the criteria of immediate experience they add the criteria of relevant understanding, of accurate formulation of correct judgment or prudent belief.

For the world mediated by meaning is not just given. Over and above what is given there is the universe that is intended by questions, that is organized by intelligence, that is described by language, that is enriched by tradition. It is an enormous world far beyond the comprehension of the nursery. But it also is an insecure world, for besides fact there is fiction, besides truth there is error, besides science there is myth, besides honesty there is deceit.

Now such ambiguity and insecurity do not bother the average man but they do trouble philosophers. For philosophers ask strange questions. What am I doing when I am knowing? Why is doing that knowing? What do I know when I do it? Having put to themselves the questions of cognitional theory, of epistemology, and of metaphysics, they are apt to go into a deep huddle with themselves, to overlook the number of years they spent learning to speak, to disregard the differences between the infant's world of immediacy and the adult's world mediated by meaning, to reach back to their infancy, and to come up with the infantile solution that the real is what is given in immediate experience. Knowing, they will claim, is a matter of taking a good look; objectivity is a matter of seeing what is there to be seen; reality is whatever is given in immediate experience.

Such is naive realism. Its offspring is empiricism. For the empiricist takes naive realism seriously and so proceeds to empty the world mediated by meaning of everything that is not given to immediate experience. In turn empiricism begets critical idealism.

It awakens Kant from his dogmatic slumbers by revealing to him that the one and only immediate apprehension we have of objects is by sensible intuition. It follows that the categories of understanding of themselves are empty, that they can refer to objects only insofar as they are applied to the data of sense. It further follows that the ideals of reason are doubly mediated, for they can be referred to objects only insofar as they guide the use of the categories of understanding when the categories themselves are applied to the data of sense.

There results Kant's critical idealism. Because we have access only to objects sensibly presented, we are confined to a merely phenomenal world. "Things themselves" become a merely limiting concept, a *Grenzbegriff*, by which we designate what we cannot know. Knowledge of the soul, of morality, of God, arises only as conclusions from the postulates of practical reason.

In reaction to Kant's critical idealism, there were propounded the absolute idealisms of Fichte, Schelling, and Hegel. It was their aim to restore speculative reason to its ancient eminence though in a new idealist context. But while they enriched philosophy enormously, their basic project has not prospered. In a variety of ways the primacy of practical reason has been reaffirmed. Schopenhauer wrote on *Die Welt als Wille und Vorstellung*. Kierkegaard took his stand on faith. Newman toasted conscience. Nietzsche praised the will to power. Dilthey wanted a *Lebensphilosophie*. Blondel insisted on a philosophy of action. Laberthonnière criticized Plato and Aristotle for reducing life to the contemplation of abstractions. Paul Ricoeur has not yet finished his three-volume philosophy of the will. And in similar directions move pragmatists, personalists, and many existentialists.

I too hold for the primacy of conscience, for the primacy of the questions that lead to deliberation, evaluation, decision. Still, responsible answers to those questions presuppose sound judgments of fact, of possibility, and of probability. But such sound judgments, in turn, presuppose that we have escaped the clutches of naive realism, empiricism, critical and absolute idealism, that we have succeeded in formulating a critical realism. The key to such a formulation is basically simple. It is the distinction already drawn between the infant's world of immediacy and the adult's world mediated by meaning. In the infant's world of immediacy the only objects to which we are related immediately are the objects of sensible intuition. But in the adult's world mediated by meaning the objects to which we are related immediately are the objects intended by our questioning and known by correct answering. In more traditional language, the objects intended are beings: what is to be known by intending *Quid sit* and *An sit* and by finding correct answers.

I have been stressing a contrast between a world of immediacy and a world mediated by meaning. But I now must add certain further features that will round out the picture and, perhaps, forestall objections. The recurrent difficulty in cognitional theory and in psychology generally arises from a failure to distinguish between our actual performance and our abbreviated objectification of that performance. Both the world of immediacy and the world mediated by meaning are abbreviated objectifications. They are not full accounts of what actually occurs. But they are fair approximations to the accounts that people are prone to give of their own performance. Inasmuch as they are fair approximations to what people think they do, they also are fair approximations to the confusions in which cognitional theory becomes involved.

Infancy, as studied and described by Jean Piaget, is a time of enormous operational development. It is a time in which we learn to use our limbs and senses and to coordinate different uses in all their possible combinations. It is the time in which we discover what is other than ourselves and learn to respond with appropriate affects. It is the time in which we learn to speak and so learn to move beyond the immediate to the world mediated by meaning. All this is true, but it would be untrue to suppose that the infant is a strict empiricist. His activity may be predominantly on the sensitive level but there is no reason to suppose that intelligent activity is to be excluded.

Again, the entry into the world mediated by meaning does not exclude immediate consciousness of the operations by which that entry is effected. On the contrary, it is only by the objectification of such conscious operations, of our acts of understanding and formulating, of reflecting, weighing the evidence, and judging, of deliberating, evaluating, deciding, that we can reach any real apprehension of the mediation that meaning effects, of the broad and the fine structures of the world that meaning mediates.

II. *Realism and Christianity*

Insofar as Christianity is a reality, it is involved in the problems of realism. But this involvement is twofold. There is a remote involvement in which the problems of realism have not yet appeared. There is a proximate involvement in which the problems of realism gradually manifest themselves and meet with an implicit solution. Finally, there is the explicit involvement which arises when people discuss whether or not there is a Christian philosophy. Let us consider in turn the first two of these.

First, then, there is the remote involvement inasmuch as Christianity is mediated by meaning. It is mediated by meaning in its communicative function inasmuch as it is preached. It is mediated by meaning in its cognitive function inasmuch as it is believed. It is mediated by meaning in its constitutive function inasmuch as it is a way of life that is lived. It is mediated by meaning in its effective function inasmuch as its precepts are put into practice.

However, the ambiguity of realism is not absent from Christianity. For the Christian world is not exclusively a world mediated by meaning. It includes as well a world of immediacy. For there is the new man in Christ Jesus, and the new man is primarily, not the product of the preacher, not the fruit of one's own free choice, but the effect of God's grace. Moreover, though the matter has been disputed in various ways, in my opinion at least God's gift of his grace occurs not unconsciously but consciously. It is not confined to some metaphysical realm so that experiencing it would be impossible. It can come as a thunderclap as when, in the prophet Ezekiel's words, God plucks out man's heart of stone and replaces it with a heart of flesh. But more commonly it comes so quietly and gently that it is conscious indeed but not adverted to, not inquired into, not understood, not identified and named, not verified and affirmed. For, as you know, consciousness is one thing and knowledge is another.

So much for the remote involvement of Christianity in the problems of realism. This involvement arises inasmuch as Christianity is a reality. It arises in two manners because, in part, Christianity is a reality in the world of immediacy, and in part, it is a reality in the world mediated by meaning.

The proximate involvement of Christianity in the problems of realism arose in the developments effected in Christological thought in the third, fourth, and fifth centuries. We shall take these samples of Christian thought and find them to represent three views on the nature of reality. Tertullian we shall find to represent the influence of Stoic materialism; Origen to represent a variant of Platonist idealism; Athanasius to represent the thrust to realism implicit in the fact that, in part, Christianity is in the world mediated by meaning.

Tertullian was concerned to refute an otherwise unknown Praxeas who maintained that God the Father was identical with God the Son and consequently that it was God the Father who was crucified on Calvary. Against this view Tertullian recites a creed very similar to our Apostles' Creed. He insists that God the Son is both real and really distinct from God the Father. Inevitably such a contention has its philosophic underpinnings, for it presupposes some notion of reality and some notion of what is really distinct. And so while Tertullian's intention is apologetic, while his main concern is to defend the faith, while his arguments are from Scripture, while his thinking is largely a matter of simile and metaphor, nonetheless there is to his expression an undertow of Stoic materialism.

Ernest Evans, in his invaluable introduction, edition, translation, and commentary on *Tertullian's Treatise against Praxeas*,[6] remarks that it was a Stoic fancy that all reality was corporeal. Cicero maintains that Zeno held every cause and every effect to be a body. Other authorities concluded that truth, knowledge, understanding, and mind were bodies because they produced effects. So it is that Tertullian approved the Stoic view that the arts were corporeal and, since the soul was nourished by the arts, the soul too must be corporeal (*De Anima*, 6). He would grant that corporeal and incorporeal constituted a logical disjunction (*Adv. Hermog.*, 35), but he would also claim that what is incorporeal also is non-existent (*De Carne Christi*, 11; *De Res. Carnis*, 11, 53; *De Anima*, 7).[7] If one were to urge that invisible spirits are real and exist, he would answer that spirits are invisible to us but nonetheless they have their own bodies and shapes by which they are visible to God alone (*Adv. Prax.*, 7).

It is within this horizon that the peculiarities of Tertullian's Christology have to be understood. He was aware that the Greek word *logos* meant both the rational principle within man and, as well, the language that man speaks. He maintained that God the Father always had within himself his rational principle, his wisdom. But when the Father at the moment of creation uttered his wisdom with the command, "Let there be light," then his wisdom by being uttered became a Son. Tertullian considered the objection that an utterance is just voice and sound and smitten air intelligible in the hearing, and for the rest an empty something

[6] London, 1948.
[7] For the foregoing and further erudition, see Evans, *op. cit.*, pp. 234 ff. Also M. Spanneut, *Le Stoicisme des Pères de l'Eglise*, Paris, 1957.

void and incorporeal. But Tertullian denied that anything void and empty could come forth from God, least of all the Word through whom were made all things, since nothing can be made through something void and empty (*Adv. Prax.*, 7).

Further, Tertullian was careful to distinguish his position from that of the Gnostics, such as Valentine, who spoke of emissions from the *pleroma*. The Valentinian emission, he claimed, was separated from its source. In contrast, the Word is always in the Father, as he says "I am in the Father" (Jn 14: 11); and always with God, as it is written, "And the Word was with God" (Jn 1: 1); and never separate from the Father or other than the Father, because "I and the Father are one" (Jn 10: 30). To the comment that, if there are Father and Son, then there is not just one but two, Tertullian's reply is to distinguish root and shoot, spring and stream, the sun and its beam. He points out that root and shoot are two things but conjoined, and the spring and the river are two manifestations but undivided, that the sun and its beam are two aspects, but they cohere. Whatever proceeds from something must be another beside that from which it proceeds, but is it not for that reason separate from it (*Adv. Prax.*, 8).

While he insisted that the Son was distinct from the Father and that the Holy Spirit was distinct from both Father and Son, Tertullian also insisted that there was only one God, only one substance. His justification was that there are three not in quality but in sequence, not in substance but in aspect, not in power but in manifestation, yet of one substance and one quality and one power (*Adv. Prax.*, 2).

Although Tertullian found very happy formulae for expressing Christian beliefs, still he did not draw one conclusion that later was drawn. If the Father is God and the Son is God, then all that is true of the Father must also be true of the Son, except that the Son is not the Father. For Tertullian there were things true of the Father but not of the Son. He could write, "There was a time when there was neither sin to make God a judge nor a Son to make God a Father" (*Adv. Hermog*, 31). Again, he wrote, "The Father is the whole substance, while the Son is an outflow and assignment of the whole, as he Himself professes, 'Because my Father is greater than I' " (*Adv. Prax.*, 9; Jn. 1:428). Again, he distinguished the Father as giving the order to create and the Son executing it (*Adv. Prax.*, 12). In a later theology such expressions were regarded as subordinating the Son to the Father; for, if the Son is God, he has all the divine attributes and, if he has not all the divine attributes, then he is not God.

While Origen also was later regarded as subordinationist, his thought unfolds in an entirely different climate of opinion. Where Tertullian considered the incorporeal to be nonexistent, Origen strongly and insistently affirmed the strict immateriality of both the Father and the Son.[8] While Tertullian could admit the divine wisdom to be eternal, he held that the Son came into existence only at the creation of the world. In contrast, Origen held the Son to be no less eternal than the Father.[9] Tertullian thought of the generation of the Son as of a bodily substance proceeding from the bodily substance of the Father but in no way separated from it. Origen rejected any account of the Son's generation that appealed to the analogy of human or animal generation or to some mythic extrusion from the godhead.[10] For Origen the Son is the image of the Father; he proceeds from the Father spiritually as a choice from the mind: again, whatever the Father does, he also does (John 5: 19).[11]

But the basic contrast lies in differing notions of reality. For Tertullian the real had to be bodily; it was what elsewhere I have named the already-out-there-now of extroverted animal consciousness. But for Origen the real was idea, as in middle

[8] *On John*, 13, 21–25; Preuschen 244–250; *De Princ.*, 1, 1, 1–9; Koetschau 16–27.
[9] *De Princ.*, 1, 2, 204; Koetschau 29–33.
[10] *De Princ.*, 1, 2, 4 and 6; Koetschau 32, 35.
[11] *De Princ.*, 1, 2, 6; Koetschau 34 f.

Platonism. Moreover, because the Father and the Son were distinct, theirs had to be the reality of distinct ideas. The Father was divinity itself, but the Son was divine only by participation.[12] The Father was goodness itself, but the Son was good only by participation.[13] On the other hand, the Son was light itself, wisdom itself, truth itself, life itself, and justice itself, but the Father was the source of all of these and in himself something far better, far more profound, far more mysterious.[14]

The distinction between Father and Son is sharp and subordinationist. Their unity is what today would be called moral. We worship, he wrote, the Father of truth and the Son that is truth. They are two realities in respect of hypostasis, but a single one by consent, concord, and identity of will. So he who sees the Son, who is the effulgence of God's splendor and the stamp of God's very being, also will see the Father in him who is the image of God.[15] It is an image in which participation reaches its supreme perfection for it consists in the Son's eternal contemplation of the Father and his constant acceptance of the Father's will.[16]

Let us now briefly revert to our discussion of the ambiguity of realism. There we distinguished two different meanings of the immediate object of our knowledge. There was the object in the world of immediacy and the object in the world mediated by meaning. The first is immediately experienced in the data of sense or of consciousness. The second is immediately intended in the questions we raise but mediately known in the correct answers we reach. We now must add that the questions we raise are of different kinds. There are questions for intelligence that ask, What? Why? How? There are questions for reflection that ask

---

[12] *De Princ.*, 1, 2, 6; Koetschau 34, 21 ff. *On John* 2, 2; Preuschen 54, 23 ff.
[13] *De Princ.*, 1, 2, 13; Koetschau 47, 3 ff.
[14] *On John*, 2, 23; 13, 3; 6, 6 (3); 13, 25; Preuschen 80, 12–15; 229, 9 f.; 114, 22; 115, 1; 249, 14 ff. *De Princ.*, 1, 2, 13; Koetschau 47, 3 ff.
[15] *C. Celsum* 7, 12; Koetschau 229, 31 ff.
[16] *On John*, 2, 2; 13, 36; Preuschen 55, 4 ff.; 261, 24 ff.

whether or not this or that really is so. There are questions for deliberation that ask whether or not this or that course of action is truly good.

Now it would seem that Tertullian's Christology and, specifically, his identification of the incorporeal with the non-existent, are connected with an apprehension of reality in terms of the world of immediacy. Again, it would seem that Origen's Christology pertains to the world mediated by meaning, where the meanings in question are ideas, that is, answers to questions for intelligence. But there is a third possibility, in which one's apprehension of reality is in the world mediated by meaning, where the meanings in question are affirmations and negations, that is, answers to questions for reflection. It is this third view that finds expression in the Scholastic tag, *ens per verum innotescit*, reality becomes known through knowing what is true. It is this third view that we find in Christian preaching and teaching and more generally, in Christianity as a reality mediated by meaning. Finally, it is this third view that is implicit in conciliar pronouncements and particularly in the canons to the effect, If anyone says so and so, then let him be anathema. What is said is all-important to a group whose reality, in part, is mediated by meaning.

The origins, then, of Christian realism are twofold. Their root lies in Christian preaching and teaching and in local, regional, and ecumenical gatherings that sought to control preaching and teaching. But that root remained implicit for a long time. Tertullian wrote against Praxeas because he considered Praxeas' teaching to be mistaken and pernicious. Origen rejected Stoic materialism and opted for Platonism because that enabled him to treat of things of the spirit. But it was the Council of Nicea and the ensuing controversies that provoked from Athanasius, along with his other clarifications, the fundamental little rule that all that is said of the Father also is to be said of the Son except that the Son is Son and not Father.[17]

---

[17] *Orat.* 3 c. *Arianos*, 4; MG 26, 330 B.

III. Nicea and Chalcedon: What Was Meant

From Athanasius' rule one may proceed in either of two directions. One may make it more concrete, and this was the course taken by the Latin liturgy in its preface for Trinity Sunday: *Quod enim de tua gloria revelante te credimus, hoc de Filio tuo, hoc de Spiritu sancto sine differentia discretionis sentimus*—"What from your revelation we believe about your glory, that without difference or distinction we hold about your Son and about the Holy Spirit." This statement is more concrete: first, because it occurs in a prayer addressed to God the Father; secondly, because it refers to what has been revealed by God about his glory; and thirdly, because it is a profession of belief in that revelation.

But as one can move to what is more concrete, so too one can move to what is more general. From the context of Athanasius' statement it would seem that his indefinite "whatever" really means "Whatever Scripture says of the Father, it also says about the Son." Accordingly, one moves to a far more general meaning when one takes the rule as a proposition about propositions. Then it becomes: "Whatever propositions are true of the Father also are true of the Son, except that the Father is Father and not Son and that the Son is Son and not Father."

Moreover, this transition to a proposition about propositions, technically, to a proposition of the second degree, is not without precedent. For the Christological rules for the *communicatio idiomatum*, the interchange of properties, are quite openly propositions about propositions. They are the traditional rule-of-thumb device for the correct interpretation of the Council of Chalcedon.

Finally, in interpreting the councils, it is desirable not to assume that the participants possessed, or the conciliar decree intended, some precise technical meaning. Augustine was a thinker of considerable acumen. The Western Church was long familiar with the Trinity, Yet Augustine employed a purely heuristic device to say what was meant by "person." What, he asked, are there three of in the Trinity? Father, Son, and Spirit are three. But there are not three Gods, nor three Fathers, nor three Sons. What, then, are there three of? It is to have an answer to this question that one says there are three persons.[18]

Such a notion of person is, of course, merely heuristic. It puts a question but does not supply a determinate answer. But there was an earlier experience of this state of affairs when Socrates asked for definitions, *omni et soli*, of fortitude, temperance, justice, and truth. While no Athenian could afford to admit that he did not know what the words meant, it also was true that none, not even Socrates, could produce the desired definitions. Indeed, definitions of the virtues and the vices were not forthcoming until Aristotle wrote his *Nicomachean Ethics* and that writing involved the enormous shift from the commonsense Socratic viewpoint to the elaborate systematic viewpoint of the Aristotelian corpus. The same fact has been experienced in recent times; for the linguistic analysts claim, rightly I believe, that one clarifies the meaning of a word, not by some universal definition, but by showing how the word is used appropriately.

Now if one follows the lead of Augustine and profits by the experience of Socrates and the analysts, then one will explain the meaning of "nature," "person," and "hypostasis" in the decree of Chalcedon by saying that "nature" means what there are two of in Christ while "person" or "hypostasis" means what there is one of in Christ. Nor is there doubt about what is the one and what are the two. For in the prior paragraph the subject is the one and the same Son, our Lord, Jesus Christ. Of this one and the same there is the fourfold predication of opposed attributes.

> He is perfect in divinity and the same perfect in humanity, truly God and truly man with a rational soul and a body, consubstantial with the Father in his divinity and the same consubstantial with us in his humanity, . . . before all ages

[18] See *De Trin.*, V. ix, 10 and VII, iv, 7; PL 42, 918 and 939 f.; *In Ioannis Evang.*, 39, 4; PL 35, 1683.

begotten of the Father in his divinity and the same in these last days for our sakes and for our salvation born of the Virgin Mary, mother of God, in his humanity.[19]

But there is a further clarification to be added. For a nominalist the subject of the statement, namely, "the Son, our Lord Jesus Christ" is just a proper name and two or perhaps three titles, while "truly God" and "truly man" involve the addition of further titles. But if one acknowledges the reality of the world mediated by meaning, then the subject of the statement is not just a proper name with certain titles but primarily a reality and, indeed, a reality begotten of the Father before all ages.

In similar fashion one will say that *ousia* means the reality mediated by meaning when one speaks of God the Father. Again, one will say that realities are consubstantial when what is true of one also is true of the other, except that one is not the other.

Such a mode of exposition is, of course, minimal. It is not intended to prevent the work of the historical theologian from investigating the use of terms in previous, contemporary, or subsequent writers. It is not intended to replace the work of the systematic theologian who compares the various interpretations and theories that have been propounded and determines where his own preferences lie. But, I believe, a minimal interpretation, however tautologous, nonetheless has a real utility. It is easily grasped and easily accepted. It accords with the canonical and no less theological principle that what has not been evidently defined has not been defined at all.[20] It provides a guideline in one's estimate of the dogmatic significance of subsequent definitions of the person and metaphysical, psychological, phenomenological, existential, and personalist theories of the person.

IV. *The One Person*

The Third Council of Constantinople (681 A.D.) added to

---

[19] DS 301.
[20] *Codex iuris canonici* 1323, § 3.

Chalcedon's affirmation of two natures in Christ the further affirmation of two wills and two operations. Naturally enough, it placed before its own decree a repetition, with variants, of the decree of Chalcedon. One of the variants that has been thought significant is as follows. Where at Chalcedon the subject of the statement is "the Son, our Lord Jesus Christ," at Constantinople III the subject is "our Lord Jesus Christ, our true God, one of the holy, consubstantial, life-giving Trinity."[21]

The significance of this variant is that it makes very explicit that the one person in Christ is a divine person. It follows that there is not a human person in Christ. This conclusion was acceptable enough as long as theologians confined their thought on the person to metaphysical definitions and theories. But today thought about the person runs in psychological, phenomeno-logical, existential, and personalist channels. In such a context to deny that Jesus was a human person seems tantamount to denying that he was a man. Such, it seems to me, was the basic contention of the Dutch theologians already mentioned and, in particular, of Piet Schoonenberg in his book, *The Christ*.

On this topic I must confine myself exclusively to two brief points. The first is historical. When did there begin explicit recognition of the person of Christ as divine? The second pertains to systematic theology. What precisely is it that is one in Christ?

On the first question Father Schoonenberg has been translated as writing as follows:

> But it was not only with Chalcedon that the pattern of classical Christology was born. Chalcedon names the one person of Christ first in a concrete way by indicating by Jesus' name and titles and by the seven times repeated "the same," afterwards more technically as the "prosopon" and "hyposta-sis," in which the divine and the human natures come together (DS 301 f.). The latter expression, used also in Pope Leo's letter

[21] DS 554.

to Flavian, suggests just as much (or just as little) concerning a pre-existence of the human in Christ as a pre-existence of the divine. The actual personal pre-existence of the Logos or the Son entered the Chalcedonian pattern through later theological expositions, especially that under Alexandrian influence.[22]

This I think is true enough in the sense that speech about one divine person with two natures is later than Chalcedon. But there was a good deal of Alexandrian influence exercised at Ephesus, and Ephesus is the background to Chalcedon. The proceedings there under the presidency of Cyril of Alexandria on June 22, 431, were in their main lines as follows.[23]

After procedural discussions, there was read the Nicene Creed (2, 12). Next was read Cyril's second letter to Nestorius and, when it had been read, Cyril asked whether it were in conformity with the Nicene Creed (2, 13). One hundred and twenty-five Fathers singly and then the rest together pronounced in Cyril's favor (2, 13–31). The second letter of Nestorius to Cyril was then read and again Cyril asked the Fathers if it were in agreement with Nicea (2, 31). Thirty-five Fathers spoke in turn against Nestorius and then the rest together pronounced against him (3, 31–35). Other documents were read (3, 36–52), but no vote was taken. Finally, Nestorious was excommunicated (2, 54), and one hundred and ninety-seven bishops signed the document (2, 55–64).

We have now to ask what in Nestorius' second letter to Cyril grounded his condemnation. And since the synod agreed with Cyril, we have only to select passages in which Nestorius disagrees with Cyril. Early in his letter he quotes Cyril's statement to the effect that "The holy and great synod said that the very only begotten Son, generated according to nature from God the Father, the true God from true God, the light from light, the one

---

[22] *The Christ*, p. 57.

[23] Parentheses refer to E. Schwartz, *Acta Concili rum Oecumenicorum*, Tom. I, Vol. I, Parts 1 & 2. The first number indicates the part; the second, the page; and if there is a third, it refers to the line or lines.

through whom the Father made all things, came down, took flesh, became a man, suffered, rose again" (1, 29, 12–14). To this Nestorius strenuously objects. Cyril thinks the Fathers at Nicea taught that the Word, coeternal with the Father, was passible (1, 29, 20f.) He should pay closer attention to their words and then he will discover that that divine chorus did not say the consubstantial divinity was passible, or that the one coeternal with the Father was recently born, or that the dissolved temple that rose from the dead did the raising (1, 29, 21–24).

Nestorius goes on to beg Cyril to observe how Nicea began from names common to both the divine and the human, from "Lord," "Jesus," "Christ," "only begotten," and "Son." On the basis of common signs referring to both natures, it was possible for the Council to speak of both the divine and the human without either separating filiation and lordship or risking a confusion of the two natures (1, 29, 28–1, 30, 4).

He praises Cyril for his distinction between the two natures and their union in a single person, for his assertion that God the Word had no need for a second birth from a woman, for his confession that the divine nature was impassible. But he feels that Cyril nullifies all this when he goes on to assert that the one said to be impassible and incapable of a second generation turns out to be passible and produced for a second time. It is as though what naturally pertains to the Word was abolished by his conjunction with his temple (1, 30, 18–28). After all, our Lord did not say, "Dissolve the divinity and in three days it will rise again." He said, "Dissolve this temple" (1, 30, 29–31).

Wherever the divine Scriptures refer to the economy of the Lord they ascribe his birth and death not to the divine but to the human nature. For that reason, if we weigh matters properly, the Blessed Virgin is to be named not the Mother of God but the Mother of Christ (1, 30, 33–1, 31, 3). In defense of this view Nestorius went on to cite Scripture at some length.

Later he added that it is right and in agreement with Gospel

THE ORIGINS OF CHRISTIAN REALISM

tradition to acknowledge that the son of David's body is the temple of the divinity of the Son and that that body is linked to the divinity by so sublime and divine and admirable a connection that we can say that the divine nature makes its own what otherwise pertains to the body. But on the basis of this appropriation to ascribe to the divine Word birth and suffering and death and the other properties of the flesh, that, dear brother, is either a Hellenist aberration of mind, or the sickness of Apollinarius and Arius and the other heretics, or even some graver malady (1, 31, 25–31).

We have been paraphrasing Nestorius' second letter to Cyril. What Nestorius rejected was Cyril's view that, according to the decree of Nicea, it was the eternal Son of the Father who took flesh and became man, was born of the Virgin, suffered, died, and rose again. For Nestorius there were two quite distinct natures that were so marvellously joined together that common names existed to denote the resulting union. Of this union there could be predicated both the attributes of divinity and the attributes of humanity. But it was madness to assign attributes of the divinity to the humanity or attributes of the humanity to the divinity.

If Nestorius did not get Cyril's point, still Cyril made it. His second letter to Nestorius provides an excellent introduction particularly to the first paragraph of the definition promulgated at Chalcedon. Its repeated "one and the same" has a prelude in Cyril's contention that we worship, not a man along with the Word, but one and the same. Similarly, he rejected the notion that there were two sons in Christ, and added that unless one acknowledges the union to be hypostatic, one is compelled to acknowledge two sons (1, 28, lines 3–5, 7 f., 10 f.).

To return, then, to Fr. Schoonenberg, it is true that Chalcedon does not speak of the actual personal pre-existence of the Logos or the Son. But it also is true that it speaks of the Son, our Lord Jesus Christ, perfect in divinity and the same perfect in humanity, before all ages begotten from the Father in his divinity, and in these last days the same for our sakes and our salvation born of the Virgin Mary, the Mother of God, according to his humanity.

There remains the systematic issue. Just what was meant by "person or hypotasis" in the context of Chalcedon? To put the question equivalently but differently, How are we to understand these terms as they occur in the Chalcedonian decree without intruding into them the many and varied associations they have since acquired? As long as Scholastic theology was alive, answers were available. But today in many parts of the world Scholasticism has withered and vanished. Can anything be done to meet the current needs for clarification?

A first step in this direction I have already suggested. It is to overcome the ambiguity of realism. As long as the world of immediacy and the world mediated by meaning are not clearly distinguished, as long as the criteria to be used with respect to these two worlds are not clearly distinguished, confusion will be endless and attempts at clarification will largely be unsuccessful.

A second step would be to distinguish three meanings of the word, "one." The first of these meanings is associated with experiential activity; it is "one more"; it is the numerical "one" in the sense that one is more than zero, two is more than one, three is more than two, and so on indefinitely. The second meaning of "one" is associated with understanding. Understanding grasps the functional unity of the parts of a machine, the functional and organic unity of a living thing, the developmental unity of a person's life. The third meaning of "one" is associated with judgment: it is "one" in the sense of identity. To affirm implies negations. Jones is all that Jones is, but he is not somebody else or all that somebody else is. He is himself and just himself.

A third step would be to state the conditions of the possibility of the Incarnation. A first condition would be that the Father, Son, and Spirit be identities in the positive sense: each is himself. A second condition would be that they be identities in the restrictive sense with regard to one another: The Father is not the Son; the

Father not the Spirit; the Son is not the Spirit. A third condition would be that the Son need not be an identity in the restrictive sense with regard to some rational creature: the Son can become a man. A fourth condition is that a man may have his identity not in himself but in another. To affirm the possibility of the Incarnation is to affirm that these conditions can have been fulfilled. To affirm the Incarnation as a fact is to say that these conditions have been fulfilled. To say what the Incarnation means is to explain the conditions of its possibility.

The foregoing statement is a statement of the meaning of the repeated "one and the same" in Cyril's second letter to Nestorius and in the decree of Chalcedon. There is in Christ, God and man, only one identity; that one identity is the identity of the Word; the man, Jesus, has an identity but not in himself but in the Word. Finally, the person or hypostasis of the second paragraph of the Chalcedonian decree refers back to the "one and the same" of the first paragraph. The distinction between persons and nature is added to state what is one and the same and what are not one and the same. The person is one and the same; the natures are not one and the same. While later developments put persons and natures in many further contexts, the context of Chalcedon needs no more than heuristic concepts.[24] What is a person or hypostasis? It is in the Trinity what there are three of and in the Incarnation what there is one of. What is a nature? In the Trinity it is what there is one of and in the Incarnation it is what there are two of.

I have still to relate the foregoing to what I said both in the Père Marquette lecture on *Doctrinal Pluralism* and once more in my chapter on "Doctrines" in *Method in Theology*.[25] In both these writings I accepted the statement of the first Vatican council that what has been both revealed by God and defined by the Church is permanently valid in the sense determined by its own historical

[24] This, I feel, is borne out by Aloys Grillmeier's study of "The Eve of Chalcedon" in *Christ in Christian Tradition*, New York, 1964, pp. 456–477.
[25] London and New York, 1972.

259

context. But similarly, in both this and other writings, I contrasted classicist assumptions to the effect that there exists *de jure* one fixed and immutable culture for the whole of mankind with the empirical fact that there have existed and exist several human cultures all of which are subject to development and decay. When classicist assumptions are pushed to the point of denying matters of fact, I feel I must disagree. The meaning of the term "person" at Chalcedon is not what commonly is understood by the term today, and theologians at least have to take that fact into account.[26]

V. *Conclusion*

It is time to conclude. We have been discussing the origins of Christian realism. We began from an account of the ambiguity of realism with one meaning relevant to the world of immediacy and the other relevant to the world mediated by meaning. Between these extremes we intercalated the confusions of naive realists, empiricists, critical idealists, absolute idealists, and subsequent philosophies of pessimism, faith, conscience, power, life, action, will.

Turning to Christianity we noted that both the world of immediacy and the world mediated by meaning were vital to it: the world of immediacy because of religious experience, because of God's love flooding our hearts through the Holy Spirit given to us (Rom. 5: 5); the world mediated by meaning because divine revelation is God's own entry into man's world mediated by meaning.

It remains, however, that the ambiguity of realism was not among the revealed truths. Christians had to find out for themselves that it was a mistake to assume with Tertullian that the criteria for the world of immediacy also held for the world

---

[26] This is not the occasion for a discussion of Fr. Schoonenberg's process theology, much less the very numerous issues he settles in summary fashion.

mediated by meaning and so to conclude that what was incorporeal also was nonexistent. They had to find out for themselves that it was a mistake to assume with Origen that the meanings relevant to the world mediated by meaning were ideas, the contents of acts of understanding, and so to arrive at the conclusion that the Father was goodness itself and divinity itself while the Son was good and divine only by participation. At Nicea and in the numerous subsequent synods and decrees that kept multiplying as long as Constantius was emperor, there did emerge in some implicit fashion that the reality of the world mediated by meaning was known not by experience alone, not by ideas alone or in conjunction with experience, but by true judgments and beliefs. For that became the presupposition not only of their preaching and teaching but also of their deliberations, their decrees, and their anathemas. They wrote, explained, defended, impugned; they invented distinctions and used technical terms; they laid the foundations for the medieval endeavor in systematic thinking. In brief, they employed the criteria relevant to the world mediated by meaning, but they did not thematize the fact they were doing so.

Such, I conceive, were the origins of Christian realism. Implicit from the beginning in preaching and teaching, through mistakes and the correction of mistakes the implication gradually took shape in modes of procedure ever more elaborate and ever more refined in a long series of crises, debates, deliberations, decisions.

INSIGHT *REVISITED*[1]

It will perhaps be of interest if I narrate briefly how *Insight* came to be written. I studied philosophy at Heythrop[2] from 1926 to 1929. At the same time I was to prepare for a degree as an external student at the University of London. Many of my fellow students had a similar lot, and classes on the Latin and Greek authors were regularly held by Fr. Harry Irwin and on mathematics by Fr. Charles O'Hara.

Philosophy, accordingly, had no monopoly on our time or attention. The textbooks were German in origin and Suarezian in conviction. The professors were competent and extremely honest in their presentation of their wares. I was quite interested in philosophy, but also extremely critical of the key position accorded universal concepts. I thought of myself as a nominalist, made a detailed study of H.B.W. Joseph's *Introduction to Logic*, and read several times the more theoretical passages in Newman's *A Grammar of Assent*. Newman's remark that ten thousand difficulties do not made a doubt has served me in good stead. It encouraged me to look difficulties squarely in the eye, while not letting them interfere with my vocation or my faith. His illative sense later became my reflective act of understanding.

It was on leaving Heythrop that I was encouraged to think I

[1] Paper for discussion at the thirty-fifth annual convention of the Jesuit Philosophical Association, April 3, 1973, held at Collège Jean-de-Brébeuf, Montréal. © 1972 by Bernard J. F. Lonergan.
[2] Heythrop College, Oxfordshire, for Jesuit seminarians.

might work in philosophy. I was bidding Fr. Joseph Bolland[3] farewell, listed for him the subjects I was doing at London, and asked him which was the one I should concentrate on. He replied that I should keep in mind that superiors might want me to teach philosophy or theology. I answered that there was no question of that since I was a nominalist. He in turn said, "Oh! No one remains a nominalist very long." It was, in current parlance, a quite "cool" reply from a high member of the establishment at a time when anti-modernist regulations were still in full force.

In the summer of 1930 I was assigned to teach at Loyola College, Montreal, and despite the variety of my duties was able to do some reading. Christopher Dawson's *The Age of the Gods* introduced me to the anthropological notion of culture and so began the correction of my hitherto normative or classicist notion. As Fr. Bolland had predicted, my nominalism vanished when I read J. A. Stewart's *Plato's Doctrine of Ideas*. In writing this paper I recalled that I had been greatly influenced by a book on Plato's ideas by some Oxford don. I had forgotten his name and the exact title of the book, so I went down to the library, patiently worked through the cards listing books on Plato and, finally, when I got to "S" found my man. I got the book out of the stacks, took it to my room, and found it fascinating reading. It contained much that later I was to work out for myself in a somewhat different context, but at that time it was a great release. My nominalism had been an opposition, not to intelligence or understanding, but to the central role ascribed to universal concepts. From Stewart I learnt that Plato was a methodologist, that his ideas were what the scientist seeks to discover, that the scientific or philosophic process towards discovery was one of question and answer. My apprehension, at that time, was not that precise. It was something

---

[3] Fr. Bolland held many positions of authority in the Society of Jesus: he was then a consultor of the English province of Jesuits, later its provincial superior, its tertian instructor, English assistant in Rome, and the "visitor" sent to evaluate the Jesuit seminaries in the United States.

vaguer that made me devote my free time to reading Plato's early dialogues (Stewart followed Lutoslawski's order) and then moving on to Augustine's early dialogues written at Cassiciacum near Milan. Augustine was so concerned with understanding, so unmindful of universal concepts, that I began a long period of trying to write an intelligible account of my convictions.

I was sent to Rome for theology, and there I was subject to two important influences. One was from an Athenian, Stefanos Stefanu, who had entered the Jesuit Sicilian province and had been sent to Louvain to study philosophy at a time when Maréchal taught psychology to the Jesuit students and the other professors at the scholasticate taught Maréchal. Stefanu and I used to prepare our exams together. Our aim was clarity and rigor—an aim all the more easily obtained, the less the theses really meant. It was through Stefanu by some process of osmosis, rather than through struggling with the five great *Cahiers*, that I learnt to speak of human knowledge as not intuitive but discursive with the decisive component in judgment. This view was confirmed by my familiarity with Augustine's key notion, *veritas*, and the whole was rounded out by Bernard Leeming's course on the Incarnate Word, which convinced me that there could not be a hypostatic union without a real distinction between essence and existence. This, of course, was all the more acceptable, since Aquinas' *esse* corresponded to Augustine's *veritas* and both harmonized with Maréchal's view of judgment.

I did my tertianship in France at Amiens, but the moment memorable for the present account occurred after Easter when we were sent to Paris to the *Ecole sociale populaire* at Vanves to listen for a week to four leaders a day of the *mouvements spécialisés* of Catholic Action then in full swing. The founder of the school and still its Rector, Père Desbuquoix, had built the school in the teeth of great opposition, and had obtained the money to pay the workmen in the same last-minute style as that narrated by Teresa of Avila in her account of her foundations. He was a man

I felt I must consult, for I had little hope of explaining to superiors what I wished to do and of persuading them to allow me to do it. So I obtained an appointment, and when the time came, I asked him how one reconciled obedience and initiative in the Society. He looked me over and said: "Go ahead and do it. If superiors do not stop you, that is obedience. If they do stop you, stop and that is obedience." The advice is hardly very exciting today but at the time it was for me a great relief.

Meanwhile in Rome the Jesuit General Fr. Ledochowski was holding a special general congregation. An item of interest to me was his exhortation to the assembled provincials to donate men to the Gregorian University. The Upper Canadian provincial at the time was a relief pitcher from England and he donated me. I was informed of this at the end of tertianship and told to do a biennium in philosophy. The following September, however, I had a letter from Fr. Vincent McCormick informing me that most of the English-speaking students at the Gregorian were in theology and that I, accordingly, was to do a biennium in theology. During the course of the same year I was informed that I was to begin teaching theology, not at the Gregorian, but at L'Immaculée Conception in Montreal.

There I went in 1940 and for six years I had considerable opportunities to add research and writing to my duties as a professor. *Theological Studies* had just been founded and a friend who knew the editor let me know that copy would be welcome. So I rewrote my dissertation and the result was accepted.[4] In 1933 I had been much struck by an article of Peter Hoenen's in *Gregorianum* arguing that intellect abstracted from phantasm not only terms but also the nexus between them. He held that that certainly was the view of Cajetan and probably of Aquinas. Later

---

[4] "St. Thomas' Thought on *Gratia Operans*," *Theological Studies*, 2 (1941), 289–324; 3 (1942), 69–88, 375–402, 533–578. The work has been recently issued in book form with updated references by J. Patout Burns with the title *Grace and Freedom*, London and New York, 1971.

he returned to the topic, arguing first that Scholastic philosophy was in need of a theory of geometrical knowledge, and secondly producing various geometrical illustrations such as the Moebius strip that fitted in very well with his view that not only terms but also nexus were abstracted from phantasm.[5] So about 1943 I began collecting materials for an account of Aquinas' views on understanding and the inner word. The result was a series of articles that appeared in *Theological Studies* from 1946 to 1949. They took into account the psychological, metaphysical, and trinitarian aspects of Thomist thought on the subject. Their basic point was that Aquinas attributed the key role in cognitional theory not to inner words, concepts, but to acts of understanding. Hoenen's point that intellect abstracted both terms and nexus from phantasm was regarded as Scotist language, both terms and nexus belong to the conceptual order; what Aristotle and Aquinas held was that intellect abstracted from phantasm a preconceptual form or species of *quod quid erat esse*, whence both terms and nexus were inwardly spoken.[6]

As soon as I finished the *Verbum* articles I began writing *Insight*. But before speaking of it I must add a few further items in its prehistory. When I began teaching at L'Immaculée Conception, Fr. Eric O'Connor returned from Harvard with his Ph.D. in mathematics and began teaching at Loyola College in Montreal. Later in a conversation it transpired that he was having difficulty in his efforts to teach; I asked him whether he was using the highly formalized methods then in vogue. He said that he was and

[5] Petrus Hoenen, "De origine primorum principiorum scientiae," "De philosophia scholastica cognitionis geometricae," and "De problemate necessitatis geometricae," *Gregorianum*, 14 (1933), 153–184; 19 (1938), 498–514; 20 (1939), 19–54.

[6] "The Concept of *Verbum* in the Writings of St. Thomas Aquinas," *Theological Studies*, 7 (1946), 349–92; 8 (1947), 35–79; 404–44; 10 (1949), 3–40; 359–93. The articles appeared in book form under the editorship of David Burrell with the title *Verbum: Word and Idea in Aquinas*, Notre Dame, 1967, and London, 1968.

I suggested that he concentrate on communicating to his students the relevant insights and that on this basis the students would be able to figure out the formalizations for themselves. My suggestion worked. The result was that I had an expert mathematician who also knew his physics (during the Second World War he helped out at McGill University and taught quantum theory there) whom I could consult when writing the earlier chapters of *Insight*.

Another factor was that a group of Montrealers, including Fr. O'Connor, founded the Thomas More Institute for Adult Education after the end of the war in 1945. I gave a course there on *Thought and Reality*. In September there were about forty-five students coming; at Easter there were still forty-one. It seemed clear that I had a marketable product not only because of the notable perseverance of the class but also from the interest that lit up their faces and from such more palpable incidents as a girl marching in at the beginning of class, giving my desk a resounding whack with her hand, and saying, "I've got it." Those that have struggled with *Insight* will know what she meant.

I worked at *Insight* from 1949 to 1953. During the first three years my intention was an exploration of methods generally in preparation for a study of the method of theology. But in 1952 it became clear that I was due to start teaching at the Gregorian University in Rome in 1953, so I changed my plan and decided to round off what I had done and publish it under the title, *Insight, A Study of Human Understanding*.

The problem tackled in the book was complex indeed. At its root was a question of psychological fact. Human intellect does not intuit essences. It grasps in simplifying images intelligible possibilities that may prove relevant to an understanding of the data. However, naive realists cannot remain naive realists and at the same time acknowledge the psychological facts. For them knowing is a matter of taking a good look; objectivity is a matter of seeing just what is there to be seen. For them my account of human understanding would appear to present intelligence as merely subjective and so imply an empiricism and, if they managed to get beyond empiricism, they would find themselves mere idealists. Accordingly, besides convincing people of the precise manner in which human understanding operates and develops, I also had to persuade them to drop intuitionist assumptions and come to understand the discursive character of human knowledge. Besides the world of immediacy alone known to the infant, there is also the world mediated by meaning into which the infant gradually moves. The former is Kant's world in which our only intuitions are sensitive. The latter is the world of a critical realism in which the objects are intended when we ask questions and are known when the questions are answered correctly.

The first eight chapters of *Insight* are a series of five-finger exercises inviting the reader to discover in himself and for himself just what happens when he understands. My aim is to help people experience themselves understanding, advert to the experience, distinguish it from other experiences, name and identify it, and recognize it when it recurs. My aim, I surmise, is parallel to Carl Rogers' aim of inducing his clients to advert to the feelings that they experience but do not advert to, distinguish, name, identify, recognize.

The first chapter draws on instances of insight in mathematics. I began there because it is in mathematics that the content and context of an insight are more clearly and precisely defined. Again, it is in mathematics that one has the clearest proof of the existence of preconceptual operations on the intellectual level. Apart from its mistaken assumption of uniqueness, Euclidean geometry is not mistaken. But this does not mean that it is rigorous. Euclidean proofs frequently rest on valid but unacknowledged insights.[7] Contemporary mathematicians employ highly formalized methods to avoid the use of insights that are not explicitly

[7] See my *Method in Theology*, London and New York, 1972, p. 213, note 63.

formulated, for what is not explicitly formulated is not subject to control.

Chapters two to five draw on physics for their illustrations. Here insights are well enough defined, but they are much more in a context of ongoing process. Again, while mathematical formulations rest on insights, and while the insights rest on diagrams and other symbols, still this process can remain implicit, with explicit attention concentrated on rigorously logical formulation and proof. In contrast, in the natural sciences, besides the logical operations of description, the formulation of hypotheses, the deduction of assumptions and implications, there also occur such nonlogical operations as observation, discovery, the planning and execution of experiments, the presence or absence of verification and, in the latter case, the modification of the hypothesis or the substitution of another hypothesis. So the second chapter is devoted to ongoing structures of discovery, the third to the canons of empirical method, the fourth to the complementarity of classical and statistical heuristic structures, and the fifth to a clarification of the meaning of special relativity.

Chapters six and seven are concerned with the operations of common-sense intelligence. While this is the universal manifestation of intelligence, it also is the most difficult to objectify clearly and distinctly. Common sense is more at home in doing than in speaking, and its speaking is apt to be terse and elliptical, or else metaphorical if not fanciful. It is a development of intelligence that is prior to that achieved in system, science, logic, and so it is prior to the systematic mode of differentiated consciousness. Common sense does not argue from principles but attends to proverbs, i.e., to brief bits of advice that are worth attending to when the occasion arises. It does not define terms but, along with the analysts, knows when terms are used appropriately. It is a specialization of intelligence in the realm of the particular and the concrete and, while it always remains a necessary specialization, still it is open to as many revisions and qualifications as there develop other specializations which take over areas that common sense once assigned to its own omnicompetence.

Chapter six touches on the bias of the dynamic unconscious; here I wish to take advantage of the present opportunity to draw attention to two works that I found very enlightening and, in some measure, to confirm the surmises I expressed in *Insight*. Herbert Fingarette in *The Self in Transformation*[8] conceived neurosis as cumulatively misinterpreted experience. Both the experience and the misinterpretation are conscious though not adverted to, identified, named, distinguished from other experience and interpretations. What is properly unconscious and, as well, the goal of the psyche's profound striving is the correct interpretation of the misinterpreted experience. Eugene Gendlin in "A Theory of Personality Change"[9] set himself the task of saying just what was meant by personality change and just how psychotherapy brings it about. I found it a most helpful study.

It was about 1937-38 that I became interested in a theoretical analysis of history. I worked out an analysis on the model of a threefold approximation. Newton's planetary theory had a first approximation in the first law of motion: bodies move in a straight line with constant velocity unless some force intervenes. There was a second approximation when the addition of the law of gravity between the sun and the planet yielded an elliptical orbit for the planet. A third approximation was reached when the influence of the gravity of the planets on one another is taken into account to reveal the perturbed ellipses in which the planets actually move. The point to this model is, of course, that in the intellectual construction of reality it is not any of the earlier stages

[8] Herbert Fingarette, *The Self in Transformation*: *Psychoanalysis, Philosophy and the Life of the Spirit*, New York, 1963 and 1965.

[9] A chapter in *Personality Change* edited by Philip Worchel and Donn Byrne, New York, 1964.

of the construction but only the final product that actually exists. Planets do not move in straight lines nor in properly elliptical orbits; but these conceptions are needed to arrive at the perturbed ellipses in which they actually do move.

In my rather theological analysis of human history, my first approximation was the assumption that men always do what is intelligent and reasonable, and its implication was an ever increasing progress. The second approximation was the radical inverse insight that men can be biased, and so unintelligent and unreasonable in their choices and decisions. The third approximation was the redemptive process resulting from God's gift of his grace to individuals and from the manifestation of his love in Christ Jesus. The whole idea was presented in chapter twenty of *Insight*. The sundry forms of bias were presented in chapters six and seven on common sense. The notion of moral impotence, which I had studied in some detail when working on Aquinas' notion of *gratia operans* in my dissertation, was worked out in chapter eighteen on the possibility of ethics.

The first seven chapters of *Insight* deal with human intelligence insofar as it unifies data by setting up intelligible correlations. The eighth chapter moves on to a quite different type of insight, in which one grasps a concrete unity-identity-whole. This I referred to as a "thing," and I contrasted it with the already-out-there-now-real of extroverted animality, which I referred to as "body." Both of these, of course, are to be contrasted with Aristotle's substance, which is the first of a series of predicaments and arises, not from a study of human intelligence, but from an analysis that basically is grammatical. It arises, I mean, not in an account of the genesis of the mediation of a world through meaning, but in a study of the meanings so generated. Finally, when Aristotle's notion of substance is taken over by a naive realist, it acquires the meaning of what is underneath the already-out-there-now-real.[10]

[10] See index to *Insight*, s. v. "real."

Chapters nine, ten, and eleven have to do with judgment. Chapter nine endeavors to say what we mean by judgment. Chapter ten investigates the immediate ground of judgment and finds it in a grasp of the virtually unconditioned, a view that was preceded in my thinking by some acquaintance with Newman's illative sense. It differs from the naive realist and empiricist opinion, which thinks of verification simply as a matter of attending to data and not as a matter of finding data that fit in with a hypothesis. It further differs, of course, from the old notion that judging can be a matter of comparing concepts and discovering that one entails another. Such entailment we considered to yield no more than analytic propositions. To reach analytic principles the compared concepts in their defined sense have to be verified in experience.

Chapter eleven asks whether any true judgments occur and it attempts to meet the issue by asking whether I am a knower. The "I" is the unity-identity-whole given in consciousness; a "knower" is one who performs the operations investigated in the previous ten chapters; the reader is asked to find out for himself and in himself whether it is virtually unconditioned that he is a knower. The alternative to an affirmative answer, as presented in *Method in Theology*, is the admission that one is a nonresponsible, nonreasonable, nonintelligent somnambulist.[11]

Not only are the "I" and its cognitional operations to be affirmed, but also the pattern in which they occur is acknowledged as invariant, not of course in the sense that further methodical developments are impossible, nor in the sense that fuller and more adequate knowledge of the pattern is unattainable, but in the sense that any attempt to revise the patterns as now known would involve the very operations that the pattern prescribes.

Chapter twelve attempts an account of the notion of being. It distinguishes notion, idea, concept, and knowledge of being. Knowledge of being occurs in true judgments. Concepts of being

---

[11] See *Method in Theology*, p. 17.

are objectifications of the notion of being. The idea of being is the content of the act of understanding that understands everything about everything. The notion of being is our ability and drive to ask questions for intelligence (What? Why? How? What for? How often?) and for reflection (Is that so? Are you certain?). That ability and drive is prior to all acts of understanding and also to all concepts and judgments. As there is no limit to the questions we can ask, the notion of being is unrestricted. Accordingly, it is not categorial but transcendental.

A point not made in *Insight* I have since learnt from Fr. Coreth. It regards spheres of being. Real being is known when the fulfilling conditions are data of sense or of consciousness. Restricted spheres of being are known when the fulfilling conditions are not data but some lesser requirement: the merely logical is what satisfies criteria of clarity, coherence, and rigor; the mathematical is any freely chosen set of suitable postulates with their conclusions rigorously drawn; the hypothetical is an instance of the logical that has some likelihood of being relevant to an understanding of the data of sense or of consciousness. Finally, there is transcendent being, and to this topic we return in chapter nineteen.

Chapter thirteen raises the key question of objectivity. It is a key question because insights are not intuitions. They are not of themselves knowledge of what really is so. Of themselves they merely grasp what may be relevant to what one is imagining and, if one's imagining is sufficiently accurate, to an understanding of what is so. Now if the intuitionist view of insight is mistaken, some other meaning has to be found for object, objective, objectivity. Hence, I distinguished a principal notion and three partial notions. The principal notion is that A and B are objects if it is true that (1) A is, (2) B is, and (3) A is not B. Further, if it is true that A is the subject and that B is not the subject, then there occurs an instance of the subject–object relation. The three partial notions of objectivity were referred to as the experiential, the normative, and the absolute. Absolute objectivity is reached with the grasp of a virtually unconditioned. Experiential objectivity is provided by the data as given. Normative objectivity arises when the exigences of one's intelligence and of one's reasonableness are met. If the virtually unconditioned is represented by the syllogism, If X, then Y; but X; therefore Y, then the major becomes known through normative objectivity, the minor becomes known through experiential objectivity, and the virtually unconditioned becomes known when the conclusion is drawn.

With chapter thirteen the book could end. The first eight chapters explore human understanding. The next five reveal how correct understanding can be discerned and incorrect rejected. However, I felt that if I went no further, my work would be regarded as just psychological theory incapable of grounding a metaphysics. Unfortunately that type of argument could be repeated. A metaphysics could be possible and yet an ethics impossible. An ethics could be possible and yet arguments for God's existence impossible. In that fashion seven more chapters and an epilogue came to be written. Some of the points made then I still like; others have been superseded in the light of further reading, conversing, reflecting.

I have not been moved to change my mind about the first three chapters on metaphysics, i.e., on chapters fourteen, fifteen, sixteen. But in chapter seventeen my usage of the word "myth" is out of line with current usage. My contrast of mystery and myth was between symbolic expressions of positions and of counter-positions. It was perhaps justifiable in the context of *Insight*, but it is not going to be understood outside of it, so another mode of expression is desirable. Further, the account of mystery has to be filled out with what chapter four of *Method in Theology* says about religious experience.

Similarly, the third section of chapter seventeen on truth of interpretation has been given a more concrete expression in chapters seven to eleven of *Method*. A systematic account of the problems of interpretation there yield place in the later work to an orderly set of directions on what is to be done towards moving to the attainment of universal viewpoint. In this connection I might mention a doctoral dissertation presented at Fordham by Terry J. Tekippe on *The Universal Viewpoint and the Relationship of Philosophy and Theology in the Works of Bernard Lonergan*. It illustrates very well an intermediate position between what I had worked out in *Insight* and, on the other hand, the views presented in *Method in Theology*.

A principal source of the difference between these two works is that I was transferred from Toronto to the Gregorian University in Rome in the summer of 1953. For the first ten years I was there I lectured in alternate years on the Incarnate Word and on the Trinity to both second and third year theologians. They were about six hundred and fifty strong and between them, not individually but distributively, they seemed to read everything. It was quite a challenge. I had learnt honesty from my teachers of philosophy at Heythrop College. I had had an introduction to modern science from Joseph's *Introduction to Logic* and from the mathematics tutor at Heythrop, Fr. Charles O'Hara. I had become something of an existentialist from my study of Newman's *A Grammar of Assent*. I had become a Thomist through the influence of Maréchal mediated to me by Stefanos Stefanu and through Bernard Leeming's lectures on the *unicum esse in Christo*. In a practical way I had become familiar with historical work both in my doctoral dissertation on *gratia operans* and in my later study of *verbum* in Aquinas. *Insight* was the fruit of all this. It enabled me to achieve in myself what since has been called *Die anthropologische Wende*.[12] Without the explicit formulations that later were possible, metaphysics had ceased for me to be what Fr. Coreth

---

[12] See the study of Karl Rahner by Peter Eicher, *Die anthropologische Wende, Karl Rahners philosophischer Weg vom Wesen das Menschen zur personalen Existenz*, Freiburg/Schweiz, 1970.

named the *Gesamt- und Grundwissenschaft.* The empirical sciences were allowed to work out their basic terms and relations apart from any consideration of metaphysics. The basic inquiry was cognitional theory and, while I still spoke in terms of a faculty psychology, in reality I had moved out of its influence and was conducting an intentionality analysis.

The new challenge came from the *Geisteswissenschaften,* from the problems of hermeneutics and critical history, from the need of integrating nineteenth-century achievement in this field with the teachings of Catholic religion and Catholic theology. It was a long struggle that can be documented from my Latin and English writing during this period and from the doctoral courses I conducted *De intellectu et methodo, De systemate et historia,* and eventually *De methodo theologiae.* The eventual outcome has been the book, *Method in Theology.*

In *Insight* the good was the intelligent and reasonable. In *Method* the good is a distinct notion. It is intended in questions for deliberation: Is this worthwhile? Is it truly or only apparently good? It is aspired to in the intentional response of feeling to values. It is known in judgments of value made by a virtuous or authentic person with a good conscience. It is brought about by deciding and living up to one's decisions. Just as intelligence sublates sense, just as reasonableness sublates intelligence, so deliberation sublates and thereby unifies knowing and feeling.

Again, in *Insight* the treatment of God's existence and nature, while developed along the lines of the book, nonetheless failed to provide the explicit context towards which the book was moving. In *Method* the question of God is considered more important than the precise manner in which an answer is formulated, and our basic awareness of God comes to us not through our arguments or choices but primarily through God's gift of his love. It is argued that natural and systematic theology should be fused in the manner of Aquinas' *Contra Gentiles* and *Summa theologiae.*

Finally, what is perhaps novel in *Insight,* is taken for granted in

Method. The starting point is not facts but data. Development is a gradual accumulation of insights that complement, qualify, correct one another. Formulation sets the development within its cultural context. Marshalling and weighing the evidence reveals judgment to be possible, probable, and at times certain.

INDEX OF NAMES

Abelard, P., 46, 237
Albright, W. F., 220
Altaner, B., 59
Anselm, St., 108, 237
Apollinaris, 257
Apostolic Fathers, 212
Arianism, 22, 24
Aristotelian, 3, 49, 51, 53, 56, 60, 72, 84, 95, 104, 112, 136, 139, 140, 196, 205, 221, 252
Aristotle, 3, 24, 26, 46, 47, 48, 53, 58, 62, 73, 82, 94, 103, 104, 106, 136, 137, 139, 140, 143, 183, 196, 197, 200, 201, 205, 221, 226, 235, 242, 252, 267, 272
Arius, 257
Arnold, F. X., 233
Athanasius, 23, 26, 212, 245, 250
Augustine, St., 25, 38, 73, 137, 146, 150, 153, 155, 199, 200, 205, 227, 228, 251, 252, 265
Augustinian, 29, 196
Augustinian–Aristotelian conflict, 90
Averroes, 53, 137
Avicenna, 137

Bañez, 71
Barth, K., 157
Becker, C., 218
Bernheim, E., 218
Billot, L., 71
Blondel, M., 14, 184, 223, 236, 242

Boeckh, A., 183, 195
Boethius, 25, 62, 200
Bolland, J., 264
Bonhoeffer, D., 157
Bratuscheck, E., 195
Brown, J., 70
Buber, M., 70
Buckley, J., 1
Bultmann, R., 205, 218
Burne, D., 271
Burns, J. P., viii
Burrell, D., 33, 40, 64, 267
Butterfield, H., 55, 56, 103

Caesar, 193
Cajetan, 196, 200, 266
Cano, M., 52, 57, 109, 197
Capreolus, 200
Carter, B., 157
Cartesian, 200
Cassirer, E., 194, 195, 205, 225
Celsus, 24
Chadwick, O., 59, 136
Chalcedon, 26, 205, 240, 251, 252, 254, 255, 257, 258, 259, 260
Churchill, W., 210
Clement of Alexandria, St., 109
Collingwood, R. G., 218
Collins, J., 209
Congar, Y., 55, 57
Constantinople II, 26
Constantinople III 253, 254

Constantius, 261
Copleston, F., 78, 122
Coreth, E., 78, 274, 276
Coriden, J., 1
Cox, H., 32
Crowe, F., vii
Cyril of Aleaxndria, St., 26, 255, 256, 257, 259

Dante, 62
Dawson, C., 264
de la Taille, M., 25
de Lugo, 71
Desbuquois, Père, 265
Descartes, 106
Deuteronomist, 7
Dewart, L., 11, 14, 15, 16, 17, 18, 19, 20, 21, 22, 24, 26, 27, 28, 31
Dewey, J., 218, 220
Dilthey, W., 104, 195, 263, 242
Droysen, J., 195, 218

Eddington, A., 214, 226
Eicher, P., 276
Einstein, A., 36
Eliade, M., 146, 149
Ephesus, 205
Euclid, 108, 234
Euclidean, 269
Evans, E., 246

Fichte, 122, 236, 239, 242
Fingarette, H., 271
Flanagan, J., 209
Flavian, 255
Franzelin, J., 118
Freud, S., 105, 106
Fries, H., 60
Frings, M., 120, 222
Frye, N., 225

Gadamer, H.-G., 194, 195
Galileo, 89, 125
Gay, P., 56
Gendling, E., 271
Gilbert of la Porrée, 46
Gilson, E., 78
Gnostic, 24, 205, 247
Gooch, G., 194, 195
Greek Fathers, 59, 212, 232
Grillmeier, A., 259

Hazard, P., 55, 57
Heelan, P., 106
Hegel, 70, 80, 122, 236, 239, 242
Hegelian, 80
Heidegger, M., 70, 205
Heiler, F., 146, 149, 151, 155, 156, 229
Hellenic, 12, 19, 20, 22, 23, 24, 29, 45
Hellenism, 19, 21, 24, 27, 32
Hoenen, P., 266, 267
Houtart, F., 215
Hübner, R., 195
Hulsbosch, A., 239
Hume, D., 239
Hünermann, P., 136, 195
Husserl, E., 122

Ignatius of Loyola, St., 115, 173
Incarnation, 22, 258, 259
Irwin, H., 263

Jaspers, K., 209, 226, 227
Jesuit, 101, 160, 165, 170, 182, 183, 186, 209, 265
Johann, R., 218
John XXIII, Pope, 11, 55, 116
Joseph, H. W. B., 38, 263, 276
Judaeo-Christian, 18

Kant, 31, 70, 78, 121, 122, 236, 239, 242, 269
Kantian, 78, 84, 123, 124, 127, 130, 181, 184, 207
Kierkegaard, 70, 122, 184, 236, 242
Kitagawa, J., 146, 149
Kleutgen, J., 118
Klostermann, F., 233
Kraus, D., 43

Laberthonnière, L., 242
Lamb, M., 209
Langer, S., 222, 224
Langlois, C., 218
Laotse, 150
Lateran I, 26
Latin Fathers, 59, 232
Ledochowski, W., 266
Leeming, B., 265, 276
Lehnert, F., 190
Lennerz, H., 71
Leo I, Pope, 254
Leo XIII, Pope, 184
Lonergan, B., works referred to:
Collection, vii, viii, xi, 76, 78, 122
De Deo Trino, 211, 213, 239
"Dimensions of Meaning," vii
Doctrinal Pluralism, x, 240, 259
"Existenz and Aggiornamento," vii
"Faith and Beliefs," 228
Grace and Freedom, viii, 131, 226, 276
Insight, viii, xi, 7, 8, 34, 37, 38, 39, 64, 70, 76, 95, 120, 126, 127, 213, 218, 220, 221, 222, 223, 224, 225, 227, 228, 263, 267, 268, 269, 271, 272, 274, 275, 276, 277
"Insight Revisited," xi
De Intellectu et Methodo, 277
Method in Theology, viii, ix, x, xi, 210, 228, 259, 269, 273, 275, 276, 277

De Methodo Theologiae, 277
The Subject, ix, xi, 121, 122
"Theology and Man's Future," 215
"Theology in Its New Context," ix
De Systemate et Historia, 277
"Thought and Reality," 268
De Verbo Incarnato, 7, 9, 211
Verbum, 38, 53, 64, 73, 267, 276
Lutoslawski, W., 265
Lyonnet, S., 211

McCormick, V., 266
McGrath, F., 142
McKeon, R., 82
McLuhan, M., 16
McShane, P., 209
Mansi, J., 118
Maréchal, J., 265, 276
Marrou, J., 218
Martin, J., 122
Marty, M., 184
Marxist, 7, 93, 115
Maslow, A., 106, 143
Matson, F., 57, 106, 143
Mead, G., 216
Mills, C. W., 190, 216, 217
Molière, 106
Mooney, C., 101
Moule, C. F. D., 156

Nash, P., 33
Neoplatonism, 137
neo-Thomist, 37
Nestorius, 26, 255, 256, 257, 259
Newman, J. H., 38, 97, 141, 142, 148, 185, 227, 236, 242, 263, 273, 276
Newton, 36, 57, 108, 271
Nicea, 22, 23, 24, 205, 212, 240, 250, 251, 256, 257, 261
Nicene creed, 26, 255

Nietzsche, ix, 70, 122, 184, 242
Novak, M., 33, 39, 40
Nuttin, J., 105

O'Connor, E., 267, 268
O'Dea, T., 227
O'Hara, C., 263, 276
Origen, 22, 137, 150, 204, 212, 245, 248, 250, 261
Ottaviani, Cardinal, 197
Otto, R., 173

Palmer, R., 194, 195
Parmenides, 19, 21, 27, 28
Parsons, T., 105, 143, 144, 190, 216, 217
Pascal, 118, 162
Peter Lombard, 46, 201, 237
Piaget, J., 24, 211, 222, 243
Plato, 24, 38, 205, 226, 242, 264
Platonic, 1, 212
Platonism, 137, 204, 212, 245, 249, 250
Pottmeyer, H., 117, 118
Praxeas, 245, 250
Prestige, G., 22
Pseudo-Dionysius, 62

Rahner, K., 6, 29, 60, 114, 147, 148, 161, 174, 210, 229, 233, 276
Reck, A., 33
Richard of St. Victor, 25, 200
Ricoeur, P., 105, 220, 236, 242
Rock, C., 269
Ross, W. D., 82, 201
Rothacker, E., 102
Runyon, D., 212

Sabellianism, 26
Sabellius, 26
Sarason, I., 105

Scheler, M., 119, 120, 122, 131, 132, 221, 222, 223
Schelling, 122, 236, 239, 242
Schillebeeckx, E., 239
Schleiermacher, F., 183, 194, 195
Scholastic, 19
Schoonenberg, P., 239, 249, 254, 257, 260
Schopenhauer, 122, 184, 236, 242
Schutt, V., 233
Schutz, A., 190
Schwartz, E., 255
Scotist, 84, 184, 267
Scotus, 25, 200
Seignobos, C., 218
Shils, E., 105, 143
Shook, L., 55
Simmel, G., 159
Snell, B., 205
Socrates, 72, 252
Spanneut, M., 246
Spiegelberg, H., 142
Stefanu, S., 265, 276
Stewart, J. A., 264, 265
Stoic, 24, 205, 212, 245, 246, 250
Stoicism, 173, 204
Sturzo, L., 157
Suarez, 71, 200
Suarezian, 184, 263

Teilhard de Chardin, P., 7, 93, 112
Tekippe, T., 276
Teresa of Avila, St., 265
Tertullian, 22, 137, 204, 212, 245, 246, 247, 248, 250, 260
Thomas Aquinas, St., 17, 25, 38, 40, 43, 44, 45, 46, 47, 48, 49, 52, 53, 62, 64, 73, 99, 108, 110, 137, 138, 193, 196, 200, 201, 205, 227, 228, 266, 267, 272, 277
Thomism, 38, 43, 47, 48, 49, 50, 53, 110

Context, contextual, 56, 97, 142, 162, 170, 194, 198, 199, 201, 206, 218, 277; c. and horizon, 56, 142, 162; c. as horizon, 56; c. of modern science, 56; c. related to one another, 208; theological c., 97, 198–99, 207

Continuity of human operations, 128; c. in truth, 18

Control, 168; c. and results, 104; c. in theology, 148; c. of beliefs, 88–90; c. of common-sense, 89; c. of intending, 41; c. over nature, 113–14

Convenientia, 201; *see also Rationes convenientiae*

Convergent probabilities, 45

Conversion, ix, 65–67, 79, 217, 237; c. and community, 66; c. as historical, 66; c. as ontic, 66; *see also* Intellectual, Moral, Religious c.

Corporeal, 246

Correlation, 51, 94, 104

Correspondence view of truth, 15–16

Crises, 183, 186, 206, 209

Criterion, criteria, 70, 218–19, 221; c. of reality, 70, 258; c. of reality in world mediated by meaning, 218, 241, 261, c. of value, 221

Critical, 229; c. grounding of knowledge, 229; c. grounding of religion, 229; c. history, 218,; c. idealism 219, 239, 242; c. realism, 30, 239, 243

Critique of biblical statements, 109

Cultural, 91–93, 102; c. change, 91, 112, 161, 233; c. crisis, 209; c. permanence, 233; c. superstructure, 21, 91–92, 97, 103, 104, 112; *see also* Empirical, Normative, Social and c. Classicist

Culture(s), 183–84, 232; c. and history, 233; c. and meaning, 102,

183, 232; c. and value, 102, 183, 232; anthropological notion of c., 264; c. as man-made, 92, 115, 141, 184; c. as meanings and values, 183, 232; stability of c., 90, 92; c. subject to change, 184; universality of c., 193

D

Data, 74, 95, 107; d. and interpretation in theology, 58–59; d. as including meaning, 104–105; d. as just given, 104; c. of consciousness, 37, 74, 76, 127; d. of sense, 37, 76, 126

Deacons, 181

Death, 8; d. of Christ, 8–9

Deceiving oneself, 230

Decline, 7–8; *see also* Progress and decline

Deductive logic, 201; d. theology, 45, 58, 63, 161, 211

Definition, 34, 252; *see also* Heuristic

Dehellenization of dogma, 11–32

Demythologization, 12, 143; d. of Scriptures, 109

Development, developing, 15, 199; d. of concepts, 74, d. of dogma, 15–16, 22, 59; theological d., 199

Dialectic, 165–66, 205, 217

Differentiated consciousness, 29, 102, 132, 227

Difficulties and doubt, 97, 263

Discourse, 122

Discovery, 235, 264, 270

Discursive knowledge, 269

Doctrines, 213

Dogma, 71, 111; d. as meaningful, 111

Dogmatic theologian, theology, 57, 110, 212, 231, 236

Doing, 79; d. theology, 138, 211

Doubt, 97, 263

Dream, dreaming, 166
Dutch theology, 240
Dynamic, 165; d. structure, 215; *see
also* Change, Ongoing, Static

E

Economics, iron laws of, 201, 234
Ecumenism, ecumenist, 62, 138, 162
Education, 226; *see also* Liberal e.
Educational psychology, 24; *see also*
Philosophy of education
Efficiency, 186
Egoism, 115
Elders, 179
Empirical human studies, 189–92; e.
intuition, 31; e. (notion of) cul-
ture, x, 92–93, 101, 141, 182, 232,
233; e. psychology (of religion),
216; e. religious studies, 189–92;
e. science, 120, 183, 189, 277; e.
sociology (of religion), 216; e.
theology, 58–59
Empiricism, empiricist, 82, 219,
239, 241, 269, 273; empiricist
philosophy, 236
Enlightenment, 56–57, 185
Ens per verum innotescit, 250
Entailment, 273
Epistemology, 37, 85, 86, 106, 138,
203, 236, 241
Eros for self-transcendence, 130; e.
of the mind, 35
Esse, 219, 265
Esse est percipi, 219
Essence(s), 92; e. and existence, 27,
30–32, 265; e. and properties, 104;
e. of the soul, 58
Eternal principles, 47; e. truth(s),
verities, 47, 109, 141, 193, 194, 198,
202, 206, 207–208
Ethics, 19–20, 189, 222, 275
Euclidean geometry, 269

Example, 83
Exist, existing, 28, 29
Existential, 79–84, 168; e. approach,
162; e. philosophy, 225, 276
Expansion of knowledge, 135
Experience, 35, 65; e. of mystery,
172; two senses of e., 220; e. vs.
knowledge, 172
Experiential objectivity; *see* Objec-
tivity
Experiment, 106, 235
Eye of faith, 129

F

Fact(s), 144
Faculty psychology, x, 79, 170, 223,
277
Faith, 17, 96, 119, 154; f. and reason,
119; f. and religious experience,
17; f. as ontic, 17; f. as eye of love,
154; f., hope and charity, 8; f.
without love, 154
Feeling(s), 220–21; types of f., 221, 223
Felt presence, 28
Financial powers, 114
First law of motion, 271
First principles, 38, 48, 65; f.p., vs.
transcendental method, 51–52
First-level propositions, 19
Flight from understanding, 7
Formal objects, 240
Formalized mathematics, 267–68
Formally unconditioned, 70; *see also*
God
Foundation(s), need of, 63; new f.,
64; f. of ethical decision, 39; f. of
hermeneutics, of history, 203; f.
of modern science, 64; f. of
theology, 63–67; old f., 63
Fourth level of consciousness, vii; *see
also* Levels of consciousness, Ques-
tions for deliberation, etc.

288

Free, freedom, 79, 83
Fulfillment of human authenticity, 147; f. of human spirit, 129, 153–54; f. of man's being, 145; f. of self-transcendence, 129, 147; f. through love of God, 147; f. thrust to (capacity for) self-transcendence, 156, 171–72
Functional specialization, 210–11, 217, 228
Further questions, 215
Future of Christianity, 149–63; f. of humanity, 115, 135–48; f. of man, 135–48; f. of Thomism, 43–53

G

Geisteswissenschaften, 104, 105, 183, 220, 277
Gesamt- und Grund-wissenschaft, 237, 277
Ghetto, 98
Gift of God's love, *see* God's gift
Gift of the Spirit, 146, 174, 175, 204
Gnostics, 24
God and everyday life, 111–116; G. and modern science, 45, 107–108; G. and undifferentiated consciousness, 132; G. as being, 27; G. as dead, 86; G. as highest good, 150, 156; G. as immanent, 150; 156; G. as immaterial, 248; G. as object, 119, 123, 127; G. as principle and end, 118; G. as subject, 123, 129; G. as three, 174, 199–200; G. as transcendent, 149–50; G. as ultimate and supreme, 150; G. as ultimate explanation, 230; G. as ultimate love, 150; (man's) knowledge of G., 95, 127; G. not a datum, 95, 107; G. of the philosophers, 57, 120, 121, 131–32; G. of religion, 120, 121, 131–32; G. wills all men to be saved, 174; G. within the horizon of man, 130
God's entry into life (world) of man, 62, 97, 130, 260; G. entry into man's making of man, 62; G. existence, 27, 31, 40, 85, 86, 222, 225, 275, 277; G. gift of love, 153, 155, 156, 158, 162, 172–73, 228, 245, 277; G. goodness, 85–86; G. presence, 19, 28, 116; G. self-communication, 18; G. self-disclosure 162, 163; G. self-manifestation, 162
Good, 6, 81–84, 85, 228, 277; g. beyond intelligible, 228; g. of order, 81, 84; g. of value, 81; particular g., 81
Good will and performance, 147
Gospel, 206
Grace, 146–47, 272; g. occurs consciously, 245; g. sufficient for salvation, 139, 146, 155, 174
Greco-Roman culture, 199
Greek achievement, 5; G. and Arabic: culture, 45, 47, 99, 138; science and philosophy, 44; thought, 45, 62. G. and Scholastic thought, 19, 21; G. miracle, 20; G. philosophy, 22, 44, 234; G. science, 44; G. thought 19, 21, 45, 62; *see also* Hellenic
Gregorian University, 213, 266, 276
Ground of judgement, 273
Grounding objective statements, 110–111; *see also* Critical grounding, Foundation(s)
Group, 99; *see also* Collaboration, Community

H

Harvest of the Spirit, 172
Heightening of consciousness, 214

Hellenic, Hellenism, Hellenist, Hellenistic, 19; h. achievement, 21, 24; h. concepts, 22, 23; h. culture, 212; h. limitations, 21, 24, 27; h. metaphysics, 20; h. past, 12; h. technique of second-level propositions, 23-24; h. thought, 22, 24, 239; h. world, 94; see also Dehellenization, Greek

Hermeneutics, 15-16, 105, 194, 195; see also Interpretation

Heroic charity, 116

Heuristic, 251; h. concept, 25, 259; h. meaning, 199; h. structure, 211, 214-15; h. structure as (un)developed, 25

Historical, 6; h. consciousness, viii, x; h. method, 136; h. mindedness, 1-7; h. process, 4, 109; h. theologian, theology, 205, 253

Historicity, 48, 52, 233

History, 96, 105, 195, 199, 271; analysis of h., 7-8, 272; h. of dogma, 16; h. of philosophy, 204; theories of h., 7

Holy Spirit, 107-73

Homoousios, 22, 23; see also Consubstantial

Horizon, 2, 41, 56, 69, 142, 154, 162, 172, 206, 213; h. and Insight, 213; h. and self-transcendence, 162; contemporary shift in h., 206; limited h. of subject, 69, 142; h. of being, 228; h. of being in love, 154, 172

Human, 165; h. behavior, 143; h. doing, 79; h. history, 3-7, 272; h. knowing, see Knowledge; h. living, 103, 143, 145; h. nature, 3-6, 47, 48, 60, 194; h. nature vs. h. history, 3-6, 51; h. sciences, 104-105, 142-44, 183-84, 186; h. studies, 144; see also Man

Humanism, 226, 234; h. as religious, 144

Humanities, 144

Hypostasis, 25, 26, 252, 258; see also Person

Hypothesis, hypothetical, 21, 274

I

"I", 273

"I" and "Thou", 85, 200

Idea, 248

Ideal of logic, see Logical ideal

Idealism, 30, 218, 236, 239, 242, 269

Ideals of reason, 219, 242

Identity, identities, 258-59

Illative sense, 263, 273

Image, 77, 220

Imagination, 167, 223-24

Immanence, 76-79

Immateriality of God, 248

Immature, 29

Immediacy, immediate, 78; i. experience, 166, 241; i. knowledge, 41, 78, 95, 118; i. object of knowledge, 249

Immobilism, 39, 50, 74-75; see also Change, Static

Incarnate subject, 61, 85

Incarnation, 265; conditions of possibility of I., 258-59

Incorporeal, 248, 250

Indirect verification, see Verification

Individualism, 227

Infancy, infant, 20, 240, 243; infancy and operational development, 243; infant's world, 20, 240-43; see also Childhood

Infinite understanding, 40

Inner word, 267

Inquiry, 33-42

Insight(s), 35-36, 74, 114, 126, 274; i. into concrete situation, 114; three functions of i., 74

Insight, how it came to be written, 38, 95, 213, 222, 263–78; *I*. ch. XIX, 40, 127, 244–45; three questions of *I*., 37, 86, 138, 203, 207, 241; *I*., way or theory? 34, 213
Institution, institutional, 175; institutionalized mediation, 175, 177
Integrated consciousness, integration of c., 21, 29
Integrism, 114
Intellect, x, 79, 84
Intellectual conversion, ix, 228, 237; i., moral, religious, as continuous, 127–130, 132
Intelligibility, complete, 40, 41–42; immanent i., 75; incomplete i., 41–42; necessary i., 236; i. of possible, 140, 202, 235, 236; i. of science, 201; probably verifiable i., 235
Intelligible, completely, 40, 41–42; i. correlations, 272; good beyond i., 228; i. possibilities, 268; i. unities, 107, 125
Intend, intending, 34, 75, 123–24, 126, 166, 243; intending as comprehensive, 124; i. as dynamic, 123; i. as meaning, 42; i. as unrestricted 41; i. subject, x, 166; i. vs. knowing, 40–41
Intention of being, 75; i. of good, 83–84
Intentional, 70; i. acts (operations), 3–4; i. responses, 223; i. responses of feeling to value, 277; i. self-transcendence, *see* Self-transcendence
Intentionality analysis, vii, x, 170, 204, 223, 277; i. as constitutive, 6
Intentionality of embodied consciousness, 190
Interdisciplinary, 135–48, 189, 215
Interiority, 226–27

Interpretation, interpreting, 275–76 interpreting the Councils, 251
Intersubjective matrix, 190; i. meaning, 91
Intuit, intuition, 78, 122, 242, 243, 268, 274; *see also* Empirical intuition
Invariant structures, xi, 39, 161, 215
Investigation, 33, 35
"is" and "is not," 28

J

Jesuit(s), 165, 181–87
Judgement(s), 14, 28, 36–37, 71, 77–78, 215, 218, 222, 265, 273; *see also* Question for reflection, Value-judgements

K

Kant's Copernican revolution, 70; K.'s world, 269
"Know thyself," 29
"Knower," 273
Knowing, 40, 76; k. and (vs.) believing, 87–89; k. and (vs.) thinking, 31–32
Knowing–objectivity–reality, 38
Knowledge (human) and action, 168; k. and love, 161–62; k. mediated by creation, 118; k. not intuitive but discursive, 265; k. of being, 83, 273–74; k. of God, 127, 174; k. of this world, 95; suppression of k., 142, 185

L

Language, 167, 240–43
Law(s), 6, 141, 160; divine l., 2; natural l., *see* Natural l.; l. of the cross, 7, 8–9, 113; positive Church l., 1–2

Leadership, 183
Learning, 34
Lebensphilosophie, 236
Lebenswelt, 191
Lectio, 196
Levels of consciousness, x, 73, 80–81,
84, 127–28, 152, 166–69, 173, 236;
see also Fourth level, Promotion
from level to level
Lex crucis, see Law of the cross
Liberal education, 92, 101, 160
Limitations of Hellenism, 21, 24, 27
Linguistic analysis, analysts, 252
Logic, logical, vii, 47, 49, 122, 165,
170, 197, 201, 206, 270, 274; logic
vs. method, 50; l. within method,
219; logical ideal (clarity, co-
herence, rigor), 50, 197–99, 202;
l. operations, 235, 270; l. positivism,
73, 122
Logos, 246; *l.* vs. myth, 20
Lonergan Congress, 209
"Lonerganian," 213
Lonergan's development, vii, *see*
Insight
Look, looking, 76–77, 124, 219, 241,
268; *see also* Super-look
Love, a dynamic state, 152; l. in
Christ Jesus, 156; l. of God, 151,
153, 171–74; l. of neighbor, 145,
151, 153, 154, 155, 158, 171, 174;
see also Being in Love, God's gift
of love

M

Magic, 20
Man as historical, 60; m. as such, 5,
161, 165; m. not static, 147, 165;
see also Human
Mankind as concrete aggregate, 5
Man's apprehension of man, 186;
m. capacity for God, 146; m.

development, 144; m. making of
man, 62; m. way to God, 150
Mathematical, mathematician, mathematics, 269, 274; *see also* Modern
m.
Maturity, 29
Meaning, vii, 14, 62, 85, 91, 102, 143,
220; m. and culture, 102, 183, 232;
m. and meant, 14–15, 16; m. and
value, x, 91, 143; m. and value in
the sciences, 143; m. as apprehended, 102; m. as cognitive, 234,
244; m. as communicated, 102,
244; m. as constitutive, 4, 6, 51,
61, 105, 234, 244; m. as effective,
234, 244; m. as function of a context, 142; m. for undifferentiated
consciousness, 102; m. in the
dream, 102; m. in the work of
art, 102; m. incarnate, 175; m.
linguistic, 175; m. of Christianity,
244, 250; m. of everyday speech,
102; m. of gesture, 190; m. of interpersonal relations, 102; m. of intersubjective, 102; m. of way of life,
102; m. of word(s), 252; m. subject
to change, 51
Meaningful statements, 111
Meant, 14–15, 16
Mediate, mediated, 78; mediated
knowledge, 78, 118
Mediation of mediator, 20; m. of
reality by meaning, 20; m. of
reality by propositions, 20; m.
of the word, 175–81
Medieval cultural synthesis, 44; m.
theology, 97, 136, 196
Metaphysical psychology, 48
Metaphysics, x, 37, 85, 86, 95, 106,
138, 203, 222, 235–36, 237, 241,
275, 276–77; m. as critically established, 236; m. as derivative, x,
37, 138, 203–204, 207, 241, 277;

m. as first (basic) science, 236, 277; m. as universal science, 276–77; m. of person, 200; m. of presence, 19, 20; m. of soul, 48, 72–73

Method(s), 50, 52, 64–65, 203, 212; m. generally, 268; m. of historical investigation, study, 135, 195; m. of (natural, human) science, 190; m. of science as foundations for science, 64; m. of (in) theology, 96, 144, 201–202, 207, 211, 268

Mind and heart, 220–21

Models, 205–206, 271

Modern, modernity, 5, 18, 98–99, 183–84, 186, 210; m. culture, 27, 44, 91, 103, 111–13, 115, 141, 160–61; m. humanism, 144; m. languages, 94, 183, 210; m. living 90–91; m. man, 4–5; m. mathematician, mathematics, 24, 234; m. (notion of) culture, 92; m. (notion of) philosophy, 109–110; 137, 236; m. (notion of) science, 21, 94–95, 103, 106, 112, 137, 139–40, 226, 235; m. (notion of) science and religious studies, 107; m. (notion of) science as empirical, 107; m. paganism, 56–57; m. theology, 97; see also Contemporary

Modernism, 94, 112

Moral agent, 79, 86; m. conversion, ix, 224, 228, 237; m. idealism, 221; m. impotence, 272; m. self-transcendence, 168

Motion, first law of, 271

Mysterium fascinans et tremendum, 173

Mystery, mysteries, 172, 174, 225, 229, 275; mysteries not demonstrable, 71; m. of faith, 71, 197

Mystical, 157–58

Myth, mythic, 20, 225–26, 275; mystic consciousness, 226

N

Naive idealism, 219; n. realism, 15, 30, 219, 241, 268, 272, 273

Naming, 34

Natura, 25

Natural and human sciences, 104; n. and supernatural, 46–47, 119, 131; n. and systematic theologies, 277; n. knowledge of God, 117–33, 225; n. knowledge of God and grace, 133–34, 225; n. law, 2, 3, 6; n. light of human reason, 118–19, 125; n. religion, 61; n. science, 142–43, 184, 186

Nature, 26, 34, 131, 252; n. and history, 61; n. (in patristic theology), 252

Necessary, necessity, 51, 103–104, 139, 140, 201; n. principles, 47, 112; n. truths, 201

Neurosis, 139, 271

New and Aggiornamento, 113; n. and conceptual apparatus of theology, 60–61; n. context of theology, 55–67; n. cultural context, 58; n. cultural context not new faith, 58; n. ideas and old doctrine, 56; n. methods in human studies, 194–95; methods in religious studies, 195–96; n. methods in theology, 198; n. methods not new revelation, 196; n. philosophies, 110–111, 137, 143; n. sense of power and responsibility, 114–15; n. thought-forms, 202–207; see also Contemporary, Modern

Nominalism, nominalist, 253, 263, 264

Nonlogical operations, 270

Normative (notion of) culture, x, 91–93, 101, 141, 210, 232; n. pattern (of operations), 50, 65; n. structure, 214–15

Notion of being, viii, 75, 77, 82–83, 126, 273–74; n. of value, viii, 82–83, 221

O

Obedience and initiative, 266
Object, 36, 76, 78, 121–24, 130, 242, 274; o. and subject, 214, 274; o. as experienced, 249; o. as intended in questions, 123–24, 243, 249; o. in Kantian sense, 121–22, 130; o. in the world mediated by meaning, 249; o. in the world of immediacy, 249
Objectification, objectify, 15, 65, 85, 103, 126, 273; o. as intentional, 14; o. of conscious operations, 244; o. of intersubjectivity, 131; o. of performance, 243; o. of self-appropriation, 214; o. of the self, 14, 131
Objective, 30, 274; o. statements, 111
Objectivism, 119
Objectivity, 38, 39, 70–71, 76–79, 214, 218–19, 221, 222, 274; absolute o., 76, 275; criteria of o., 38–39; normative o., 76, 275; principal notion of o., 274
Obscurantism, 41
Observation, 124, 235
One, 258–59; "one and the same," 259; three meanings of o., 258
Ongoing context, 173; conversion as o. process, 66; methods as o., 198; modern science as o. process, 235, 270; strategy as o., project, 187; structuralism as o. process, 211; theology as o. process, 201, 203
Ontic faith, 17
Ontological and moral judgements, 121

Open, openness, 182; open context, 170; o. structure(s), 23, 215; openness of method, 217; o. to questioning, 171
Operations as related, recurrent, 50; cognitional o., 35, 65; logical o., 235, 270; o. on propositions, 24; see also Levels of consciousness
Operative grace in St. Thomas, 228
Organizational vs. mystical, 157–58; see also Religious organization
Origins of modern science, 55–56
Other-worldly, 113, 129, 172; see also Being in love with God
Ought, 121; see also Questions for deliberation
Ousia, 253
"Out there," "Out there now," 39, 219, 248, 272

P

Particular, particularity, 3, 74–75, 161; p. culture, 101
Past, 115; rejecting the p., 43; studies of the p., 195
Pattern(s) of conscious operations, 29; p. of inquiry, 35; p. of related and recurrent operations, 50–51
People of God, 7–9
Per se subject, 110
Performance, 243
Permanence of dogma, 59, 259–60
Person, 24, 199, 251–53, 253, 258; p. and object, 119–20, 131; heuristic notion vs. definition of p., 199–200, 252; p. in patristic theology, 24–25, 251–53, 258; p. of Christ, 253–60
Persona, 25
Personal decision, 39; p. relations, viii, 222
Personality change, 271
Phainomena and noumena, 226

Phenomenonology, 105
Philologie, philology, 194, 195
Philosophical system(s), 37–38
Philosophy, 106; p. and religion, 131; p. and science, 106, 108; p. of action, 207, 223, 236; p. of culture, 206; p. of education, 222; p. of religion, 138, 191, 204, 216; p. of will, 236; perennial p., 93, 110, 141, 160, 232; social p. 191, 216
Philosophy's contribution to theology, 202–207
Physics, 270
Picture-thinking, 76–78
Platonic forms, 4; p. ideas, 264
Platonist idealism, 245
Pluralism, 114, 185
Policy of religious group, 191
Popularization, 112
Positions vs. counter-positions, 275
Positive studies, 213; p. theologians, and method, 212–13
Positivism, positivist, 184, 218
Possible being, 21
Postulates of practical reason, 242
Power(s), 115, 190; financial p., 114; p. to ask and answer questions, 125–26
Practical, practice, 168
Pragmatism, pragmatist, 73
Praise and blame, 83
Praktische Theologie, 192
Prayer, 150, 155
Preaching the Gospel (to all nations), 141, 206, 233
Preconceptual, 267, 269
Premisses vs. data, 58
Presbúteros, 180
Principle(s), and verification, 126; first p., 39, 48, 65; propositional p., 6–7, 39; verifiable p. 120,
Priora quoad and quoad se, 226
Privileged data, 37

Probability, probable, 51, 94, 104
Progress, 7, 113; p. and decline, 7–8
Promotion from level to level o consciousness, 81, 123, 127
Proof of thesis (in theology), 57, 196–97, 231
Proposition(s), 18, 28, 39; analytic p., 120, 273; p. about propositions, 251; p. of the second degree, 215; reflection on p., 23; second-level p., 19, 23
Propositional principles, 6–7, 39; p. truth, 13, 16, 19, 28–29
Psyche, 220, 271
Psychiatry, 172
Psychological subject, 200
Psychology, 243; metaphysical p., 48
Psychotherapy, 271
Public examination (of proposals), 15
Pure detached desire for value, viii, 228; p. reason, 72, 263

Q
Quaestio, quaestiones, 46, 47, 49, 57, 196, 200
Queen of the sciences, 62
Question(s), 75, 77, 198, 215, 243, 264; q. for deliberation, 144, 168, 221, 242, 250, 277; q. for intelligence (understanding), 125, 168, 249, 273; q. for reflection, 126, 168, 249–50, 273; q. of God, 95; q. of the day, 198–99; three (cogn. theory, epist., metaph.) q., 37, 86, 138, 203, 207, 241
Quid sit, 243

R
Rational objectivity, 29
Rationalism, rationalist, 72, 162, 185

Rationes convenientiae, 45; *see also* Convenientia

Real, 228; already-out-there-now-r., 39, 219, 248, 272; r. distinction, 30; r. self-transcendence, 128–29, 144, 152; r. world, 219

Realism, 218; ambiguity of r., 240–44, 249, 258; r. and Christianity, 244–50; childhood r., 30; *see also* World

Reality, 248; r. and being, 23, 24; r. as corporeal, 246

Realms of meaning, 227

Reason(s) and faith, 119; r. and objects, 78; r. of the heart, 129, 162; pure r., 72, 236

Redemption, 8

Reductionism, reductionist, 107, 143, 158, 218

Reflecting on propositions, 23

Reflection, questions for, 126, 168, 249–50, 273

Reflective act of understanding, 263

Reinterpretation of man in his world, 112–113

Relativism, 6, 207

Religion, 60, 67, 97, 107, 115, 129, 147, 158, 185, 187, 222; r. and culture, 97; r. and human living, 151–55; r. and humanism, humanities, 147–48; r. and reductionism, 158; r. and secularism, 185, 187; r. and theology, 67, 97; r. and traditionalism, 115; r. as complete self-transcendence, 129; r. as total commitment, 211; r. in *Insight*, 222; natural r., 61; organized r., 147; revealed r., 61; science of r., 107–108

Religionless Christianity, 157–59

Religions of mankind, *see* World religions

Religious community, 146; r. conversion, ix, 228, 237; r. experience,

ix, 17, 18, 127, 129, 150, 191, 216, 237, 260, 275; r. faith, 96; r. organization, 114, 175, 177; r. policy, 216; r. sciences, 107, 215; r. self-transcendence, *see* Self-t.; r. studies, 107, 109, 138, 191, 204, 216; r. tradition, 146; r. transformation of culture, of world, 43–44, 141

Renaissance, 165, 181–82

Renewal of theology, 55

Reordering of society, 114

Responsibility, 115, 211; r. for the world, 93

Responsible, 79, 93; r. society, 191

Revealed religion, 61–62

Revelation, divine, 18, 61–62, 71, 260

Revising cognitional theory, 37, 273

Revision (in science), 107

Rhetoric, rhetorician, 197, 226, 234

Rigor, 50, 198, 199, 201, 265; *see also* Logical ideal

Roman theology, 240

Royal Society, 106

S

Sacrifice, 150

Salva substantia, 2

Sanctifying grace, 229

Satisfaction(s), 144

Schematic image, 223

Schematism, 79

Scholarship, 231

Scholastic(s), 21, 99; s. categories, 161; s. theology, 57, 258; s. thought, 19, 21; s. transcendentals, 81

Science, 21; s. and data, 120; s. of religion, 107–108; s. of religion and natural science, 107; *see also* Empirical s., Human s., Natural s.

Scientific community, 51, 140; s. investigation, 33, 35; s. knowledge, 88–89; s. statement, 89
Scientist and philosophy, 106, 226, 227
Second differentiation of consciousness, 20, 21
Second-level propositions, 19, 23
Secular, secularism, secularist, 114, 115, 158, 184–85, 187
Selbstvollzug, 234
Self, 73, 190
Self-appropriation, 51, 79, 213–14, 228, 269
Self-control, 168
Self-correcting process of learning, 36, 126, 205
Self-destructive, self-destructiveness, 36, 185–86
Self-donation, 173–74
Selfishness, 168, 169
Self-justifying love, 229–30
Self-surrender, 173
Self-transcendence, 115, 128–30, 131, 152, 155, 159, 162, 166–69, 174; affective s., 223; s. and horizon, 162; cognitional s., 144, 152, 167, 224; complete, total, s., 129; intentional s., 70, 75, 128–29; moral s., 168; real s., 128–29, 144, 152; religious s., 224
Self-transcending realization, 166
Semper idem, 197
Sending, 175–81
Sensibility, 144, 224
Sensitive operations, 35
Seven, the, 177
Seven features common to religions, 146, 149–51, 155
Seventy-two, the, 177
Sin, 8, 83
Situation ethics, 6
Skepticism, skeptics, 53, 196

Social and (vs.) cultural, 102, 115; s. change, 90; s. ethic, 189–91, 216; s. philosophy, 191, 216; s. policy, 189–91, 216; s. science, 189–91, 216; s. structures, 190
Socio-cultural change, 135; s. studies, 205
Sociology, 189
Son's (divine) generation, 248
Soul, x, 72; essence of s., 48; metaphysics of s., 48, 72–73; s. vs. subject, 51
Special relativity, 270
Specialized, specialization, 29, 91, 108, 210, 232, 270; s. of consciousness, 29
Speculative intellect (reason), 236, 242; s. system(s), 37
Spheres of being, 274
Spirits, 246
Spirit, Holy, 170–73
Statement(s) and context, 194; s. and stating subject, 67; s. of common sense, 125; s. of science, 89
Static, 48, 50, 165, 170, 187; s. abstractions, 47; s. metaphysics, 50; s. periods in cultures, 2; s. view of man, 48, 165
Statistical probabilities, 234
Stoic materialism, 22, 245–46
Strategy in meeting crises, 186–87
Structural invariants, 52
Structuralism, 211
Structure, 211, 214–15; see also Heuristic
Subject, 48, 122–23; s. and soul, 73; s. as incarnate, 85; s. (neglected, truncated, immanentist, existential, alienated), 69–86
Subjective pole of objective field, 214
Subjectivism, 239
Subject–object relation, 214, 274
Subject-to-subject relation, 129, 131

Sublate, sublating, sublation, 80, 84, 169, 277
Substance, 272
Substantia, 25–26
Sufficient grace for salvation, 139, 146, 155, 174
Superlook, 15
Symbol(s), 220, 225
Symbolism, 220
Synthesis of feeling and cognition, 223; *see also* Value
System, systematic, systematics, 200, 213; systematic theologian, theology, 46–47, 212, 253; s. viewpoint, 252

T
Taken-for-granted, 90, 218–19
Teaching, 183
Technique, 186
Technological establishment, 186
Terms and relations, 34, 46; *see also* Basic t. and r.
Theism, Christian, 12
Theological anthropology, 147, 148; t. method, 111 (*see also* Method in t.); t. terms, general, 237; t. terms, specific, 237
Theology and communications, 140–41; t. and cultural change, 161; t. and cultural context, 58, 61–62; t. and culture, 184; t. and Enlightenment, 57–58; t. and history, 135–36; t. and human sciences, 139, 142–44; t. and humanities, 147; t. and man's future, 135–48; t. and method, 139, 237–28 (*see also* Method in t.); t. and other disciplines, 135–48; t. and philosophy, 108, 136–38, 143, 193–208, 276; t. and religion 67, 97; t. and religious studies, 189–92; t. and social sciences, 215–17; t. and transformation of cultures, 62; t.

and university, 142; t. anthropological, 161–62; t. as classicist, 109; t. as deductive, 45, 58, 63, 161, 211; t. as queen of sciences, 62; t. as reflection on religion, 67; t. as science, 139, 197; conceptual apparatus of t., 60; doing t., 211; t. of renewal, 55; older t., 197; popular t., 30; systematic t., 46–47, 212, 253; t. vs. method in theology, 211; *see also* Deductive t., Empirical t., New t.
Theory, 214; t. and practice, 140; *Insight* as t., 34, 213
Thesis, Scholastic, 57
Thing(s), 272; t. themselves, 242
Thomism, 38; classical T., 47–49; collapse of T., 110; contemporary T., 43; future of T., 43–53
Thomist, cognitional theory, 15; Lonergan as T., 38, 276; T. thought, 184
Three questions (of *Insight*), 37, 96, 138, 203, 207, 241
Time of confusion, 93, 160
Total commitment, 228; t. context, 154; t. mentality (horizon), 2; t. self-surrender (love), 145; t. view (horizon), 162
Totalitarian ambitions (and methods), 212–13
Tradition, 167, 185
Traditionalism, 115, 118
Transcendent being, 156, 274; *see also* God
Transcendental(s), 81, 128; t. intending, 81–83; Kantian t., 207; t. method, 6–7, 203, 205, 207; t. notion of being, viii, 274; t. notion of value, viii, 221; t. precepts, 170; t. questions and answers, 147; Scholastic t., 81, 207; t. turn, 190, 191

Transformation of control over nature, 113–14; t. of order of society, 113–14

Transition from classicist to modern (views on) culture, 98, 112; t. from normative to empirical (views on) culture, 233; t. from classicist world-view to historical-mindedness, 1–10

Transposition from Hellenic to Christian context, 45–46; t. from 13th to 20th century, 49–52

Trinitarian doctrine, processions, 22–27, 200, 212, 245–53, 276; see also God as three

Tritheism, 26

True, truth, 30, 47, 70, 94, 140, 228; t. as *adaequatio rei et intellectus*, 13–16; t. in faith, 140; t. in science, 140; see also Eternal

Twelve, the 177

Two natures in Christ, 254–57; 259

U

Ultimate concern, 116, 173

Unbelief, 185

Unconscious, 271

Understanding, 36, 77, 222, 223, 265, 267

Undifferentiated consciousness, 21, 102–103, 131–32

Unicum esse in Christ, 38, 276

Union of object and subject, 15

Unity-identity-whole, 272, 273

Unity of human spirit, 128; u. of levels of consciousness, 81, 169

Universal(s), 3, 74–75, 92–93, 104, 161; u. concepts, 39, 263, 264; u. viewpoint, 276

Universality of culture, 93; u. of dogma, 59

Unknown, 34, 75, 77, 199, 224

Unverifiable principle, 120, 124

Uomo universale, 92, 182, 210

V

Value(s), viii, 81–82, 84, 91, 102, 143–44, 168, 189, 223; cultural v., 168, 221; feelings and v., 223; notion of v., viii, 82–83, 221; v. of way of life, 102; personal v., 169, 221; religious v., 221; social v., 168, 221; vital v., 168, 221

Value-free science, 144

Value-judgements, viii, 144, 189, 221, 277

Variables of Christianity, 181

Verifiable knowledge, 95; v. possibility, 51, 104, 140; v. principle, 120

Verification, 21, 31, 89, 96, 107, 124, 126, 273; direct v., 89, 124; indirect v., 89, 125; need of v., 125–26, 140

Veritas (Augustine), 38, 265

Verum est medium in quo ens cognoscitur, 17; see also True, Truth

Vetera novis augere et perficere, xi

Via purgativa, 150

Virtually unconditioned, 70, 273, 275

Virtue, 82

W

Waking state, 73, 80, 151

"We," 85

Wendung zur Idee, 159

Will, x, 79, 84

Withdrawal from world of immediacy, 20

Wonder (intellectual), 33, 144

Wonder workers, 176

Word as vehicle of meaning, 62; w. of God, 96, 173–75; see also Language

World(s), 69, 85, 86, 190, 241, 269; w. mediated by language, 240–43; w. mediated by meaning, 20, 167, 218–19, 241, 243, 245, 249, 253, 258, 269; w. of common sense, 226, 227; w. of critical realism, 269; w. of immediacy, 20, 167, 240–43, 249, 258, 269; w. of the take-for-granted, 218; w. of theory, 226, 227; w. of religions, 174; w. view, 196

BIOGRAPHICAL NOTE

Bernard J. F. Lonergan was born December 17, 1904, in Buckingham, Quebec, Canada, to Gerald Joseph Lonergan and Josephine Helen (Wood) Lonergan. He attended Loyola High School and Loyola College in Montreal. In 1922 he entered the Society of Jesus and spent four years at the Jesuit Novitiate at Guelph, Ontario.

He studied philosophy at Heythrop College in Chipping Norton, Oxfordshire, England, from 1926 to 1929 and took an external B.A. degree at the University of London in 1930. After teaching three years at Loyola College in Montreal, he began studies at the Gregorian University in Rome. There he earned his licentiate in theology in 1937 and finished his work for a doctorate in theology in 1940.

Beginning that year, Lonergan taught for thirteen years in Jesuit seminaries in Montreal and Toronto and in 1953 returned to the Gregorian University in Rome, where he was a professor for twelve years. He returned to Canada in 1965 to become Research Professor at Regis College, Willowdale (Toronto), Ontario. He has served as a member of the International Theological Commission and Consultor to the Secretariat for Non-Believers in Rome. Dr. Lonergan was in 1971–72 Stillman Professor at the Divinity School, Harvard University. He has been awarded many honors, including the Aquinas Medal of the American Philosophical Association, Companion of the Order of Canada, and the John Courtney Murray Award of the Catholic Theological Society of America. He has received honorary doctorates from twelve American and Canadian universities.

Books by Bernard J. F. Lonergan

In English:

Insight: A Study of Human Understanding. London: Longmans, Green and Co; New York, Philosophical Library, 1957.

Verbum: Word and Idea in Aquinas. Edited by David B. Burrell, C.S.C. University of Notre Dame Press, Notre Dame, 1967.

Collection. Papers by Bernard Lonergan, S.J. Edited by F. E. Crowe, S.J. New York: Herder and Herder, 1967.

The Subject. The Aquinas Lecture, 1968. Marquette University Press, Milwaukee, 1968.

Grace and Freedom. Operative Grace in the Thought of St. Thomas Aquinas. Edited by J. Patout Burns, S.J. London: Darton, Longman & Todd (New York: Herder and Herder), 1971.

Doctrinal Pluralism. The 1971 Pere Marquette Lecture. Marquette University Press, Milwaukee, 1971.

Method in Theology. London: Darton, Longman & Todd; New York: Herder and Herder, 1972.

Introducing the Thought of Bernard Lonergan. Three Papers from 'Collection' with an Introduction by Philip McShane. London: Darton, Longman & Todd, 1973.

Philosophy of God, and Theology. St. Michael's Lectures, Gonzaga University, Spokane. The inaugural lectures, 1972, with a foreword by Patrick B. O'Leary, S.J. London: Darton, Longman & Todd; Philadelphia: The Westminster Press, 1974.

A Second Collection. Papers by Bernard J. F. Lonergan, S.J. Edited by William F. J. Ryan, S.J., and Bernard J. Tyrrell, S.J. London: Darton, Longman & Todd; Philadelphia: The Westminster Press, 1975.

In Latin—Volumes published by the Gregorian University Press, Rome:

De Constitutione Christi Ontologica et Psychologica, 1956;

De Verbo Incarnato, 1964;

De Deo Trino (2 vols.), 1964.